D0903895

"THE TERRIBLE SIREN"

VICTORIA CLAFLIN WOODHULL

"THE TERRIBLE SIREN"

VICTORIA WOODHULL

(1838 - 1927)

By EMANIE SACHS

Author of "RED DAMASK" *and* "TALK"

"The terrible syren has defeated you
and charmed your cohorts and
battalions to silence and inaction."

—Credited by Victoria Woodhull Martin to
WILLIAM CULLEN BRYANT,
New York Evening Post, January 9, 1873

HARPER & BROTHERS PUBLISHERS
NEW YORK
1928

PRINTED IN THE U. S. A.

M-C

▼

To Katherine Angell

Who first told me about the Claflins

CONTENTS

CHAPTER		PAGE
I.	Bitter-Sweet	1
II.	Alloys	16
III.	Demosthenes and the Golden Goose	30
IV.	"Tomato Soup for Three"	47
V.	Humpty-Dumpty	65
VI.	"Because I Am a Woman"	96
VII.	Social Freedom	112
VIII.	"The Woodhull"	139
IX.	Cell II, Ludlow Street Jail	163
X.	Woodhull Witchery	188
XI.	"The Scare-crows of Sexual Freedom"	213
XII.	Mr. Benjamin R. Tucker's Story	236
XIII.	Apostasy	267
XIV.	The Cuckoo	287
XV.	The Siege of London	312
XVI.	The Leopard's Spots	333
XVII.	Whiter Than Snow	360
XVIII.	Apotheosis	387
	Bibliography	416

ILLUSTRATIONS

Victoria Claflin Woodhull .... *Frontispiece*
Label on the "Elixir" bottles .... *Page* 31
One of the old handbills .... " 40
Colonel James H. Blood .... *Facing p.* 42
Tennie C. Claflin in the semi-masculine costume she and Victoria sometimes wore " 48
The lady brokers driving the bulls and bears of Wall Street.................. *Page* 53
The bewitching brokers according to Matthew Hale Smith in "Bulls and Bears of New York"................... *Facing p.* 54
Stephen Pearl Andrews .... " 56
"Tomato soup for three"................ *Page* 64
"Woodhull & Claflin's Weekly"........ " 72
General Benjamin F. Butler .... *Facing p.* 74
Her campaign button .... " 74
Victoria Woodhull presenting her memorial before the Judicial Committee of the House of Representatives in Washington .... " 76
Commodore Vanderbilt .... " 82
Henry Ward Beecher .... " 82
Theodore Tilton .... " 98
Victoria C. Woodhull at the polls, November, 1871, asserting her Constitutional right to vote .... " 118
The memorial procession of the International Workingmen's Association in honor of Rossel and his companions.... " 146
"Get thee behind me (Mrs.) Satan!".... " 150
Victoria C. Woodhull nominated for the Presidency of the United States....... " 158

ILLUSTRATIONS

"The Woodhull" .... *Facing p.* 166
The arrest of the Claflin sisters, November 2, 1872 .... *Page* 179
Victoria C. Woodhull .... *Facing p.* 202
"The Thunderbolt" .... *Page* 204
Benjamin R. Tucker when twenty-three years old .... *Facing p.* 238
Facsimile of manuscript in which Mr. Benjamin R. Tucker tells his story of Victoria Woodhull .... *Page* 240
Spiritualist camp meeting in 1873 at Silver Lake Grove, Plympton, Mass. .... *Facing p.* 254
Roxanna Hummel Claflin photographed in San Francisco, California, in 1874, when Victoria was speaking there ..... " 276
"Victoria C. Woodhull, candidate for the Presidency of the United States" ...... " 292
Mrs. John Biddulph Martin of No. 17, Hyde Park Gate .... " 318
Rubin Buckman Claflin in his later years .... " 320
Sir Francis Cook .... " 330
Lady Cook .... " 330
One of the proof sheets that were sent to all the important newspapers in England and America .... *Page* 334
Mr. and Mrs. John Biddulph Martin .... *Facing p.* 338
Victoria Woodhull Martin .... " 384
Getting older .... " 384
Norton Park, the Manor House, and the old tithe barn .... " 388
Old age: Victoria Woodhull Martin in the side car in front of the Manor House .... " 408
Victoria with the Earl of Coventry ..... " 408

Foreword

VICTORIA WOODHULL was the firebrand of her time, and her story is as strange as her personality.

It is a story of violent action and romantic contrasts, dominated by the courage and vitality of a woman who was brilliant and ignorant and beautiful; who emerged from a background which explains much that seems inexplicable, since few ever have emerged into public notice from such a sordid beginning. Deeds that bewildered those with any standards of behavior were only natural to a hungry creature with none. She did anything she wanted to do, and then denied that she had done so, and died at eighty-nine in the odor of sanctity.

Throughout, like a tiger, she had purred when she was stroked, and torn when she was lashed. And like a tiger, she could see in the dark; she was a spiritualist. But she had an itch for greatness and an urge for reform, which brought her out of the jungle.

She was the first suffragist to have an official hearing in Washington. She memorialized Congress to claim votes for women under the Fourteenth Amendment. But she fought the folkways that oppressed her sex more than she fought for the franchise. She defied prudery in her life and in the press and on the platform. She was a great orator, and people flocked to hear her lecture on constitutional equality, and spiritualism, the social revolution, and the principles of finance, as well as free love. She was a priestess of publicity. And she figured in every history of Socialism in America, as well as in every history of Wall Street.

In 1870, she and her sister, Tennessee Claflin, were the famous Lady Brokers of Wall Street, or the Bewitching Brokers, according to some. They made a fortune, and lost most of it, through publishing *Woodhull & Claflin's Weekly,* which had "PROGRESS! FREE THOUGHT! UNTRAMMELED LIVES! Breaking the Way for Future Generations," on the cover. Anthony Comstock suppressed it for printing a scandal about the Rev. Henry Ward Beecher, and sent Victoria and Tennessee to Ludlow Street jail, though Victoria was a candidate for the Presidency of the United States. She was nominated by the Equal Rights Party, and her running mate for Vice-President was Frederick Douglass, the negro reformer.

Born in Homer, Ohio, in 1838, she was bred in poverty and chicanery. She died in 1927, the widow of a wealthy English banker, a lady bountiful in an English village, esteemed by the estimable. She had a varied life.

In the 'seventies, her heyday, newspapers called her "The Queen of the Prostitutes," but some said in representing suffrage, an unpopular cause, she paid the pioneer's penalty of misrepresentation, though none of the other suffragists paid it. One man called her a dual personality, half saint, half sinner, but altogether fascinating.

She fascinated me. My purpose, however, is neither to vindicate her nor to attack her, but to tell the story I found, after nearly two years' research. I went to Homer, Ohio, her birthplace, and saw old settlers there who remembered her and her family. I followed her trail to Mt. Gilead, Ohio, and to Columbus. It led to court records in Ottawa, Illinois, in Chicago, New York, and Brooklyn, to folk-lore in Pennsylvania, and old letters from everywhere. Newspaper files have been searched from Maine to California, and Mr. Daniel R. Maué of Columbia University went to England for material. The story of Mr. Benjamin R. Tucker's experience with Victoria Woodhull is printed from his own handwriting. Several published memoirs of her contemporaries mentioned her, and she was the subject of many biographical pamphlets, which are colorful, dramatic, and contradictory. Moreover, she had an engaging habit of public confessional in print and on the platform.

Hundreds who knew her, or whose parents knew her, have told me her legends. They are hearsay evidence, but inasmuch as they came from disconnected sources, without any reason for animus, they are consistent enough to be believable. And surely, when anyone has been interesting enough to inspire legends, they are valuable as an index of human behavior. Both the false and the true are significant, because both show what people thought and felt about Victoria Woodhull, what she meant in their minds and their emotions. Maybe she was merely a symbol of feminine activity in an age of male bluster when feminine activity was dreaded and feared. Maybe she personified men's erotic dreams, too, and women's audacious impulses, and like Johnny Appleseed and Paul Bunyan and other Gargantuan American figures, she and her remarkable family were only half real.

But it is undeniable that in Victoria Woodhull's heyday she wanted to live in the white glare of publicity. She sought it. Because she went into public life, she belongs to history, and because she was vivid and conspicuous there, her story cannot fade into the mists of oblivion with which decency covers the dead who had wanted privacy.

I shall try to tell what seems true to me, to revive the personality of Victoria Woodhull, a woman who dared to do anything she wanted to do. Those who lack her strength or her ruthlessness; those whose training or circumstances, or deepest desires, prevent them from obeying piratical impulses, may release them vicariously in her adventures without doing any harm to anyone. And those who haven't any piratical impulses will find Americana.

EMANIE SACHS

July 23, 1928

"THE TERRIBLE SIREN"

"THE TERRIBLE SIREN"

Chapter One

BITTER-SWEET

IN HOMER, OHIO, in the eighteen-forties, children ran off to play at the Claflin house, and were whipped when they got home.

Back of it was an orchard, with low-branched apple trees to climb and pick green apples from. Beside it flowed the mill-race which ran Buck Claflin's grist mill, a mill-race that went dry at every drought. Ready to wade in at the first rain, it was a boon to the children, if a bother to him. They liked to run across the Claflin porch and hear the loose boards rattle. The steps were hooded by a vine; bitter-sweet, poisonous it was, scarlet-berried all winter, dripping purple flowers in the summer time, never tended, growing out of sheer exuberance like the Claflin young, and quite as sweet and dangerous.

Self-respecting Homerites kept away from such a shiftless lot who lived just anyhow. The father, Buck Claflin, had a bad reputation. They said he came back from one of his trips with counterfeit money, and when the sheriff tried to arrest him he pulled a hundred-dollar bill out of his pocket, tore it up, and swallowed it, before the sheriff and a deputy. But he was a pettifogger. He read enough law to keep out of trouble. In fact, he cluttered the courts with litigation, always evoking the law before it caught him. He was queer and so were his family.

The woman they got milk from said they brought a green flask instead of a bucket. It made her nervous to pour milk into a green flask. And any of them would come for it at any time. The children had no regular chores. They ran wild, except at meal time, when they hung around the neighbors' kitchens, waiting for snacks. They didn't get much at home.

"Did you ever hear of such names?" said a neighbor's wife. "Maldon, and Hebern, and Tennessee, and Victoria. That little Victoria is going to be a beauty, though. When I saw her in church last Sunday, I thought to myself, what a pity it is that she's a Claflin."

Often Victoria sat on the porch steps under the bitter-sweet, her firm little chin digging into grubby hands, her elbows on knees covered with a red calico dress which had a large brown flowered pattern and wasn't very clean. Her thick brown hair hung loose, uncombed, and her fair skin was smudged. But her small teeth were shining white, and her blue eyes were clear and shining, too, though she sat there in a revery.

She had enough to think about, enough hurts and slurs to make so many wounds. And healthily she thought about them, and then escaped in such dreams as form scar tissue on the psychic wounds of the resilient young, creating a future irritant to fling them into the land of their dreams if they have the qualities for flight. Victoria Woodhull's later plans, and some of her accomplishments, must have been conceived in early childhood, because they were naïvely grand and cosmic and miraculous, in terms of supernatural endowments, and world reforms and presidential campaigns.

Some of her hurts and slurs came from the town. The Claflins were gutter folk in Homer, and Homer was merely an insignificant dot on the Middle Western frontier, its best people striving against every hardship. None were gutter folk without good reason. Victoria's mother, Roxanna Claflin, was a squalid, ignorant nuisance; Buck Claflin was considered a bad citizen. And yet Victoria saw him called on when a farm had to be surveyed; when anyone got into trouble, he was called on, usually on the sly. Somehow he was appointed postmaster. And yet he was supposed to have done everything the preacher said not to do, which was confusing. He could do anything; nothing daunted him or softened his cruelty. Victoria said he kept braided green withes made of walnut twigs in a barrel of rain water to make them sting when he whipped his children. When he came home after they were in bed at night, if Roxanna told him about some prank that annoyed him, he might waken the culprit and whip her for hours. That wasn't very gay when it happened to Victoria, and she could do nothing but seethe and suffer. No wonder she was vindictive when she had the chance. Then there were ten Claflins, and she was the seventh, neither baby nor boss. While her older sisters had beaux and the younger children had affection from Roxanna in her fondling moods, Victoria got no attention, and she needed quantities, for that was her nature.

She took it in dreams of power, and never played unless she could dominate.

Often a nice little girl next door who wasn't allowed to play with the Claflins watched them through the picket fence.

One day Victoria said, "Lemme alone," until the others started for the orchard without her. Then she shouted after them: "Wait, I'll tell you what. Let's go up to the Mount of Olive, and I'll preach."

Eating green apples in the Claflin orchard was worth a whipping afterward, but "Aw naw, we don't wanna hear you preach!" said one of the youngsters.

"You just will!" shrieked Victoria, in a fury, stamping her feet until the porch rattled. "You've got to, or I'll tell teacher on you!" she yelled. "I'll tell teacher!" Buck Claflin went to law; his child went to teacher or threatened to. Threats often worked because few dared to face them.

They worked now. The children followed Victoria across the town to the high Indian altar-mound she called "Mount of Olive." With measured step she walked up the rounded heap of earth; dramatically she paused a moment, and then prayed for forgiveness for their "terrible sins," in a tone to chill the warm orange sunlight of that mild June day.

Victoria had been saved, and couldn't sin, which was fortunate, hell being what the preacher said it was. To keep from fearing it, she preached about it, her preaching a marvelous safety valve for emotions that boiled fears and bewildered conflicts with ravaged vanity. Many fires blazed in her slim body, but it was a healthy body, fed with energy.

A soft breeze clapped calico skirts against her bare legs and played with tangled hair, but her deep-set eyes blazed, earnest and agonized, as if she braced herself against a tempest, a wild young priestess on an altar built to savage gods who must have been more merciful than hers.

Spellbound, the children listened for a time. But they were used to hell, and they soon moved restlessly. Whereupon Victoria thrilled them with a tale about three Indians scalping some settlers. At eleven she could feel the temper of an audience, and then, as always, she had to have one.

Victoria's father, Reuben Buckman Claflin, was born in 1796, in Sandisfield, Massachusetts, but his family moved to East Troy, Pennsylvania, in 1801, before Buck absorbed any Puritan traits.

When Michael Quigley bought the "Wiggins Tract" in the Susquehanna Valley in 1812, he built a grist mill and a house which started the village of Beech Creek. A few years later he rented a room to Buck Claflin to use as a store, but Buck didn't use it very long.

Buck had lost an eye in his childhood playing Indian with bow and arrows; and afterward, wherever he went, somebody would say that he could see more than any two-eyed man, and somebody would say it with apprehension. He travelled extensively, for it was his custom, wisely to leave the scene of his activities. He became a horse trader with a preference for the river towns, and about 1825, he turned up in Harrisburg.

In those days the Susquehanna River was the principal highway through the states it touched, and most of the men on its banks were boatmen or raftsmen. They were jolly dare-devils, fond of their whiskey-jugs, sure to gamble their money away as soon as they got it. And in the river towns, conveniently, gamblers and horse traders swarmed. They were a hardy breed with a simple code. Fools and suckers were born to be swindled by their betters; it's a pleasure to win stolen money, a duty to win hard-earned cash and teach a man to stick to his line, giving him experience while you get the cash.

None of these adventurers could flip a jack in a game of old sledge more deftly than Buck Claflin, none had more winning ways. His manner was rather high-toned and his quick, spluttery talk was pithy. He looked like a malevolent Lincoln, with a big bony nose and a fighter's jaw; and his strength inspired confidence, in spite of a baleful glint in his eye. Often he won a man and his money at the same time.

When he appeared at Selinsgrove with all his gifts and a string of black horses, John Snyder took him home as stableman for his private racing stable. Around Selinsgrove they said he fathered John's children, for a consideration. That was a common custom in those free and easy times for men who wanted a lazy living, and descendants of the Snyders insisted that Victoria had all the Snyder features. But Victoria was the seventh Claflin. In fact chronology as well as geography argued against this theory, which throws more light on old customs and the giants there were in those days than on Victoria's paternity.

In Pennsylvania, they declared that chronology and geography would have been trifling considerations for John Snyder. He was the fastest young blood in the county when young bloods were Gargantuan. He was best man at the Hall-Hammond wedding, and after the ceremony, when the bride peeped through the keyhole at the men having their toddies, she decided that John Snyder was the man for her. It was customary for the guests to start the happy pair on their wedding journey, and John took Miss Hammond in his gig. He took her on to Utica, and several months afterward he drew up in front of her husband's home and called out, "Here's your wife!" But Mr. Hall didn't see it that way. He had the marriage annulled; and the lady became a part of the Snyder household, along with several colleagues. Her daughter was named Utica.

Roxanna Hummel, who was Victoria's mother, was a maid at the Snyder's. She wasn't pretty, but she was fiery. And some said her mother was a Hummel, and that her father was Governor Snyder, John's father, a three-term governor of Pennsylvania. Others insisted the Governor "wasn't that kind of a man." Roxanna does not appear in the Hummel genealogy, and her children had some Snyder ways, but that doesn't prove anything.

No doubt she was the daughter of Captain Jake Hummel, a German who kept "The Rising Sun," the tavern at Hummel's Wharf. The Captain was a local politician and "no mean artist with the ladies," himself.

According to Pennsylvania folk-lore, the Hummels were descended from a German Jew named Hammel, one of a colony of German Jews that settled in Berks County about 1702. They found the Susquehannock Indians, who were so unlike other Indians that many ethnologists think they were the progeny of early Norsemen. But the Jews thought they were the lost tribe of Israel and tried to proselyte them, in vain. Instead they traded with them and married the women. Then their children married the children of German settlers, as well as the English, the Scotch, the Irish and the French Huguenots.

If true, this would give Victoria an interesting lineage.

It is a fact, however, that Buckman Claflin married Roxanna Hummel about 1825.

He had thrived with John Snyder; he put on a plug hat, a diamond stud and gold glasses.

But Captain Jake growled at the courtship and grumbled at the match. "Dese Yankee gamblers comin' down here, und marryin' our girls ought to be put a schtop to," he said. "Dat Buck now, he's married to Roxy. Dat's a fine ting. Well, as she her board make, so must her bed set up to her. I got nix more to say."

And nix more did he say. He never spoke to Roxanna again, though Buck and his fervid little frau lived in Selinsgrove for several years. Then Buck's luck must have turned. As if pursuing it, they moved to Troy, to Sinnahoning, back to Beech Creek, and to Glen Union, where their house was destroyed in the blizzard of 1837.

Buck joined his brother, who was a raftsman on the Susquehanna, but the work was hard and the pay was small.

So he went back to "The King of the Manor," as John Snyder was called. Snyder had dissipated his own inheritance, and it was said that he went through most of the Selin money too. He was the executor for Anthony Selin's estate, and Anthony Selin, the founder of Selinsgrove, had acquired some land grants at Marietta, Ohio, for his revolutionary services.

It was said that John Snyder sent Buck Claflin to

Marietta to "see about" that land. Inasmuch as it came intact to the Selin heirs, Buck couldn't have accomplished very much. But he stayed in Ohio and ran a tavern in Streetsboro, which was some distance from Marietta.

A few years later he settled in Homer, Ohio, for no apparent reason. It was a tiny hamlet, supported by a few farmers. In the northern end of Licking County, off the main highways without industries or sports, it was a strange choice for such an enterprising man, unless he wanted obscurity at the time, which was possible.

Buck's brother joined him there, and the two families lived together in an unpainted shack on a hill. Some slept in the parlor, some in the cellar. In each room were several beds, never made and rarely changed. Meals were eaten anyhow, at any time. Roxy was no housewife, and her sister-in-law couldn't do everything. They lived in squalor and turmoil, with the ague that haunted that pioneer region, a region in which conditions at best were horribly primitive. At the Claflin's, childbirth was the only regular occurrence. Roxy had ten children.

It was a rackety household, busy with wrangling, and praying, and scheming and fortune-telling. They were Spiritualists before the word was invented. They took their magic from the past and the future, naturally attuned to the miraculous.

Roxy was a mystic. She doctored her children with Mesmerism, and three died young; the others were durable. Years before spirit manifestations were announced formally, the Claflins had gone into trances with marvellous tales of things seen, while "out of the body." There was no trickery about their trances then; they began in religious frenzy.

At the annual Methodist revivals, Roxanna Claflin would rise from her seat as the general fervor mounted, and with clasped hands and upturned face, she would clap her hands together softly. Then, swaying her body to and fro for a moment, she would slide from her place, and, spinning round and round like a top, up one aisle and down another, her bonnet held in place only by its strings around her neck, she would shout "Glory!" and "Hallelujah!" with every breath until she sank down in front of the altar exhausted, in what she and her family called a trance.

Afterwards Victoria said her own spiritual visions began when she was three, on the day her nurse died in Homer. Picked up by the departing spirit—she was borne off into the spirit-world, a tiny St. Catherine, winged away by the angels. Roxanna swore the child lay as if dead for three hours.

But this was only the beginning of Victoria's adventures in the spirit-world. For years she talked to two sisters who had died in infancy, as most children talk to dolls, preferring their invisible society. At ten, she was sitting by a cradle, rocking a sick child to sleep, when two angels came and pushed her away. With strange white hands, they fanned the child until its face grew fresh and rosy. Roxy came into the room to find the little nurse in a trance on the floor, her face toward the ceiling, her charge in the bloom of health. Then there was a stately visitant, clad in a Greek tunic, who promised that Victoria would emerge from poverty and live in a mansion, that she would win great wealth in a city crowded with ships, and that she would become the ruler of her country! This prophet withheld his identity for some time, but he must have been a comfort. And one evening the family were gathered around the kettle in the fireplace; and, while Roxanna was praying for them, Victoria saw the door open to admit a tall man with a red silk handkerchief over his face. He had a cloven hoof. Of course some of this may have been the ague. The town scorched and shook with it regularly. The child wasn't properly fed; some may have come from plain hunger. But once there, what an escape those visions were from intolerable conditions! And visitations from angels and prophets in tunics, from the Devil himself, gave Victoria the importance which she had to have.

The family were suitably impressed with Victoria's experiences, though her mother and sisters had similar adventures in the otherwhere. Homer admitted that the Claflins were uncanny, but it didn't get excited about them because they were troublesome.

Every evening at sundown, Roxanna went to the orchard on a hill, facing the western horizon, and prayed loudly. She chanted her neighbors' sins that she was sure of and the ones she imagined. She begged the Lord to forgive them, reciting every detail in case He might have over-looked anything.

"My prayers come out as crooked as a ram's horn, but they go up as straight as a shinted shingle," said she.

Then she complained that her children didn't get enough attention at Sunday School. She kept them away for three weeks as a protest, but nothing happened. So she took them to the superintendent on a Sunday, interrupting him in the midst of a lesson.

"De other children yust push them avay. Like rams, pushing little lambs, pushing, pushing," she roared. (Rams must have fascinated Mrs. Claflin.)

A patient man, Superintendent Wheeler stopped and listened to the excited little creature. Ugly, dried up, hatchet-faced she was, surrounded by her lovely progeny like some witch with an enchanted retinue, in the aisle of that log church, a retinue as lamblike as a pile of rattle snakes.

She got abusive.

Superintendent Wheeler began to shoo the Claflins backward down the aisle, going on with the Sunday School lesson at the same time. The lady cursed him in German. Understanding some of it, Superintendent Wheeler, flushed but undaunted, went on with the lesson and on with the shooing until he closed the door on the lot.

As inconsiderate of one another as of outsiders, they were brutally disloyal and violently quarrelsome. But no matter what they had done, Roxy made them break bread together afterward, and then all was forgiven. This ritual was drilled into them, until it made up for anything, however awful. Instead of an "amen," it was Roxanna's custom to open the door, rush out on the porch, roll back her sleeves, wave her arms and shout, "Remember you have a holy mudder in Israel!"

The boy Maldon was ugly, and Roxy couldn't love him because she couldn't be proud of him. He ran away and worked on the railroad when he was very young.

Roxy's pride in her beautiful children was fierce and irrational anyhow. The miracle of their happening to her and her homelier spouse was enough to upset a hardier equilibrium. Through them, she planned to attain every illusion of grandeur.

She sent them to the little log schoolhouse, where they didn't stay long enough to get an education; but she wouldn't let them stop when the teacher put wire clothespins on their noses to punish them, in spite of their protests that they were different. For Roxy told them they were different from other people, which wasn't a bad salve for social ostracism, though it was ignorantly applied. It made them different. They never tried to conform. Roxy even tried to dress them differently, instead of trying to keep up with Homer, a pitiful effort when she scarcely had the wherewithal to clothe them anyhow.

Buck's opportunities were limited in Homer, but he wasn't generous with his family when he could have been.

He was not a loving father. And the boy Hebern dreamed that his mother and father gave their hearts to the Lord. When the Lord looked at his mother's heart, it was as white as snow. His father's heart was as black as his hat.

Proud of her white heart, Roxanna repeated this filial slander to all who would listen. She was a "holy mudder in Israel," a holiness which relieved her of any moral effort. She lied like a Judas and scolded like a drab, too holy to sin, because she was one of the elected. Every year, during the revival season, a new Eve was born in her, perfect in the spirit, called by the Lamb. Risen to a sphere of gospel liberty and light, she no longer dwelt on earth, subject to its laws. A new earth and a new heaven had been created, in which she lived and towards which she moved with her children. They, too, had been saved and could not sin. Whatever they did was right, because they did it.

Insurance was rare in those parts in the 'forties, and when Buck Claflin insured his grist mill for a large sum, it was talked about.

Shortly afterward, on a Sunday, Buck told several people that business called him to Mt. Vernon, ten miles away. He said he was going to spend the night there. Early in the morning he started walking, but when he got there, he didn't stay. He went back towards Homer; and in the late afternoon, he stopped at the village of Brandon, which was only four miles from home. He told the landlord at the Brandon tavern that he was too tired to go farther. He took a room for the night, insisting on a south window. Due south of Brandon was Homer.

He went to bed early; but at eleven, he arose, dressed, and called the landlord to lodge a bitter complaint. He couldn't sleep because he had a presentiment that something was happening at home. Anxiously he gazed southward until suddenly he exclaimed over an ominous light in the sky, a swiftly deepening red glow.

"You know," said he, "I have a presentiment that that's my grist mill on fire."

He borrowed a horse and hurried home too late to save the grist mill, a wooden building on a windy night. Homer had scant fire-fighting facilities, and none would take risks for Buck Claflin.

Everybody watched the mill burn though; it was a good fire to watch. And few ever forgot the wild antics of the boy Hebern, who left his bed clad only in a short shirt and his excitement. He made such an anatomical display that one of the neighbors took off her apron and firmly tied it around his waist.

The next morning people began to wonder about that fire, for the mill had been unused and empty since the previous Saturday. Some claimed Mrs. Claflin had lighted a torch; others said the hand was Victoria's. All believed it a plain case of arson. Of course talk never bothered Buck Claflin, and he took steps to collect his insurance. Then the talk turned to threats of tar and feathers. This was the climax of years of bad repute, and a committee of leading citizens advised a quick, quiet departure.

Buck went back to Pennsylvania.

And in the attic at the Homer postoffice, his successor found an old hair trunk filled with opened letters stating, "Enclosed find," with a careless confidence the writers should have been cured of, for the letters were empty.

But Homer, the first world Victoria lived in, provided for her and hers in their emergency; in the future she always expected other worlds to do likewise. (And they did.) Buck had left Homer too hurriedly to provide for his family. So its broader minded citizens gave a Claflin benefit to get them out of town.

Chapter Two

ALLOYS

IT IS impossible to fix the Claflins accurately in time or space after they left Homer in the late 'forties. Like gypsies, they wandered for awhile, trackless in their obscurity, until a legend locates one of them.

The child Tennessee stayed with relatives near Williamsport, Pennsylvania, and astonished the neighborhood with her "Satanic" powers. The children were afraid of her; they said she could read their thoughts; and, when she went sledding with them, they ran away from her as soon as it was dark. Didn't she tell Sallie Hepburn's Uncle Thomas what shed he could find his lost calf in and exactly how it was tied? And Mrs. McDowell offered her some pears and plums one day, and she asked where the best fruit was. "What fruit?" asked Mrs. McDowell. "The fruit you put away," said Tennessee, which embarrassed Mrs. McDowell because she had put the best of it away before Tennessee came. Then the child foretold the fire in the cupola of the Dickinson Seminary at Williamsport so literally that she was accused of starting it until an investigation absolved her from blame.

She was a pretty, fair-haired youngster, but her blue eyes saw all there was to see. She was shrewd, and she had the sharpness that children learn from parents who live by their wits. She must have had what might be called telepathic gifts too. When Buckman heard about them, he appeared in Williamsport, and on the outskirts of the town he put up a sign, "Have your past read, and future foretold. T. Claflin." The first fee was one dollar.

A few years later Tennessee and Victoria were lifting tables and making spirit music at Mrs. Webb's boarding house in Mt. Gilead, Ohio—until the other boarders got so nervous Mrs. Webb had to ask Victoria and Tennessee to leave.

At that time the revival spirit, and the free love movement, as well as spiritualism, were raging through Ohio, and the Claflins were likely tinder for all three.

Annually, from stumps, or wagons, on hillsides and in meadows, preachers tormented thousands into ecstatic anguish over guilts called forth, shaking them with fears. "The burning lake of Hell, to see its fiery billows rolling, to hear the yells and groans of the damned ghosts . . . roaring under the burning wrath of an angry God." . . . People fell, groaning for mercy. . . . A seven year old girl preached from a man's shoulder, "Oh, you little sinner, come to Christ!" A small boy dropped a handkerchief, "So shall sinners fall in Hell." Hundreds trembled in unison. . . . Some made hideous contortions; bosoms heaved until long hair cracked like a wagoner's whip. Back muscles twitched and men floundered like fish on dry land, beating the ground or bounced ball-fashion; or like dogs, they went on all-fours, barking, around a tree.

The inevitable fruit of such excitement was an increase in the illegitimate birth rate, but the ingenuity of man averted the wrath of a God who insisted on marriage certificates.

In Germany at Königsberg among the Pietists, in England among the Princeites at Spaxton, and in America at Oneida Creek, New York, and Kirtland, Ohio, appeared the doctrine called "Spiritual Wives," almost in concert but without any connection, except that everywhere it followed ecstatic revivals, and always, it was associated with the second coming of Christ. With the Kingdom of Heaven at hand, what had those who were saved and ready for it to do with earthly bonds? Since there was no marriage in Heaven, it was sinful for the elect, and churches sinned in solemnizing it. All should mingle and love as brothers and sisters, their only solace the holy kiss. Then the Reverend Erasmus Stone, one of the saints of the Perfect Church at Salina, New York, had a vision.

Stone saw a host of men and women in the sky, flying hither and thither with an eager want on every face. He said this was a foresight of the Day of Judgment when men and women, ill-paired in marriage on earth, had become too discerning to return to their false mates and were in painful want of true affinities. Whereupon, the Reverend Hiram Sheldon declared that these affinities should be found by delicate tests in this world to avoid the terrible search in the Beyond.

Meanwhile the Reverend John Humphrey Noyes of New Haven recovered from religious melancholy. "In a holy community there is no more reason why sexual intercourse should be restrained by law than why eating and drinking should be," said he. And he founded the Oneida Community which held that the more the human heart loved, the more it could love. Swedenborgians claimed that those who had been happily joined here melted into one angel in the hereafter, which was supposed to be very desirable; Goethe wrote about natural mates; but Dale Owen, (the son of Robert Owen), with his companion Frances Wright, boldly attacked the Bible and the old order, advocating free love and free divorce.

In the 'forties and 'fifties any theory got followers in America. The transformation of society didn't seem complicated to a people who rather recently had turned a wilderness into a state; and most of these theories glorified eroticism, which was comforting to those whose religion at once aroused and condemned it.

Somehow Spiritualism mixed into religion and reform; nearly all the free lovers were Spiritualists. But in Victoria Woodhull at her zenith, religious ecstasy, free love and Spiritualism met and merged. In her beauty and power they flowered and smothered her odor of quackery with the fragrance of sincerity.

The Fox sisters had started modern Spiritualism in 1847, near Rochester, New York, when they learned to crackle their toe-joints surreptitiously, making strange vibrant sounds. Katie Fox called the imaginary person who was supposed to make them, Mr. Splitfoot; and when she said, "Do as I do, Mr. Splitfoot," and clapped her hands, Mr. Splitfoot rapped likewise. Mrs. Fox tested him by asking the children's ages; and when they were rapped, successively, Mrs. Fox couldn't find an earthly explanation and looked for one in the spirit world. Public exhibitions were held; and finally the Rochester Rappings became famous, and the Fox sisters, the first mediums, got rich.

The Claflins produced spiritualistic phenomena almost coincidentally, and without guile; but the Fox family were in such good standing that nobody suspected their children of fraud, while few took the Claflins seriously.

Ohioans rushed to Dover Village to hear Jonathan Koons' controls, the Kings, who had lived on earth before Adam. There were six journals devoted to Spiritualism all over the country then, but none mentioned the Claflins.

Still they gathered slights instead of fame.

In Mt. Gilead, young Rhodes sent Victoria an invitation to a ball, and brother Hebern was enraged at the postscript, "Vehicles will be provided for the ladies' carcasses." Since ladies didn't have carcasses in 1853, Hebern challenged Rhodes to fight a duel.

When Rhodes' second called on Hebern, Hebern's handsome face turned brick-red, "I . . . I just had a talk with Vicky," he mumbled, "I . . . he . . . Oh, if I'd known Rhodes knew her so well, I wouldn't have raised a row about his language. You tell Rhodes it's all right. Damn it! The fight's off."

This story is significant only to the evil-minded, or to anyone who has studied the adolescence of gutter-folk in early Ohio. They were absolute pagans sexually, because their rough parents didn't care, or in connection with religious hysteria; and some got a mystic freedom from Spiritualism. Then, too, John B. Foot was tarred and feathered throughout the state for preaching about spirit brides, which brought him and his doctrine much renown. Later Francis Barry founded a free love colony with Spiritualistic overtones at Berlin Heights, Ohio, near Oberlin; whereupon there was enough agitation to spread that doctrine to all the youngsters in the state, and to teach Victoria that her naturalness was righteous, which would have given it a firm foundation.

Moreover, her older sisters were divorced in the 'fifties, when divorce was rare. The new idea that a painful marriage was not a life sentence must have impressed the young Victoria.

Margaret Ann and Polly Claflin had married sons of gentle-folk, and they might have enjoyed small-town placidity; but the Claflin impact against life meant melodrama as surely as pepper in the nose means a sneeze. That was their nature.

When Margaret Ann married Enos Miles of Hewitt, and Miles' drugstore in Mt. Gilead, he was the reputable son of a prominent family. Margaret Ann had babies with flattering regularity, but Roxy, Vicky, Tennie, Hebern and little Utica lived with him most of the time and their brawls never stopped. Enos wasn't used to a tempestuous life and it upset him. A few years after he bought the American House, (a hotel then new and the pride of the town) he rapped at a neighbor's house before dawn, with a butcher knife in his hand. "I'm looking for Mag," he said hoarsely. Of course he never harmed her, but such an outraged Puritan had to make a gesture. He went blind later, and the Miles moved to Mansfield where they were divorced. Both remarried, and drama left Enos with Margaret Ann. He is remembered as the beloved, blind book man who sold Bibles and encyclopedias in Morrow County. But he willed half his property to Victoria and Tennessee, which was a remarkable attention from a divorced and remarried brother-in-law!

Polly Claflin's first husband was Ross Burns, an able lawyer, eventually Lieutenant-Governor of Kansas. But in Mt. Gilead they told how Polly sent notes to her admirers by little boys around the town, little boys with eyes, and memories and tongues; and how Ross Burns divorced her. They told how he begged a teacher there to keep his child Rosa from her mother; but Polly took her by stealth. Polly claimed that Ross deserted her while one of her children was dying and that she pursued him for two days with the dead child in her arms. Whether true or untrue, what a macabre mind that pursuit sprang from!

And it, too, was a part of Victoria's background.

In 1853, before Victoria was sixteen years old, she was married to Dr. Canning Woodhull. They were divorced eleven years later.

According to "Mr. Tilton's Account of Mrs. Woodhull," which appeared in 1871, Canning Woodhull was a monster; but we have more reliable evidence that he was a martyr. That fantastic biography was Theodore Tilton's love-chant, and if we read it as a prose lyric instead of a frenzied melodrama, it is fascinating as well as faintly illuminating. For Victoria gave Tilton the material, and it probably throws a dim light on some of her activities during this period. There always were shreds of fact in her yards of fancy. She said Canning Woodhull's father was an eminent judge of Rochester, New York, and none of the numerous histories of Monroe County mentioned any Judge Woodhull; but she said Canning Woodhull's uncle was mayor of New York City, and there was a Mayor Caleb Woodhull in 1849, though he was a remote connection of Canning Woodhull's, not his uncle.

Mr. Tilton began with a description of Victoria's

childhood that must have surprised Homer. She was a slave to household tasks, he claimed. And ". . . From the endurable cruelty of her parents, she fled to the unendurable cruelty of her husband. . . . Dr. Canning Woodhull, a gay rake, but whose habits were kept hid from her, under the general respectability of his family connections . . .

"One day he stopped her in the street and said, 'My little chick, I want you to go with me to the picnic,' referring to a projected Fourth of July excursion. . . .

"The promise of a little pleasure acted like a charm on the house-worn and sorrow-stricken child. She obtained her mother's assent to her going, but her father coupled it with the condition that she should first earn money enough to buy herself a pair of shoes. So the little fourteen year old drudge became for the nonce an apple-merchant, and with characteristic business energy sold her apples and bought her shoes. . . . On coming home from the festival, the brilliant fop, who, tired of the demi-monde ladies whom he could purchase for his pleasure, and inspired with a sudden and romantic interest in this artless maid, said to her, 'My little puss, tell your father and mother that I want you for a wife.' The startled girl quivered with anger at this announcement.

". . . . But her parents . . . . thought it a grand match. They helped the young man's suit and augmented their persecutions of the child. Ignorant, innocent and simple, the girl's chief thought of the proffered marriage was an escape from the parental yoke. . . . Her captor, once possessed of his treasure, ceased to value it. On the third night after taking his child-wife to his lodgings, he broke her heart by remaining away all night at a house of ill-repute. Then for the first time, she learned to her dismay that he was habitually unchaste, and given to long fits of intoxication."

Dr. Woodhull was given to intoxication, though his friends said Victoria drove him to drink.

But fifteen months after Victoria's marriage, ". . . . while living in a little low frame-house in Chicago, in the dead of winter, with icicles clinging to her bed-post, and attended only by her half-drunken husband, she brought forth in almost mortal agony her first-born child. . . ."

Apparently the weather was a part of Fate's conspiracy against our heroine, for it is a ruthless icicle that can get to a bedpost. And "Once after a month's desertion by him, until she had no money and little to eat, she learned that he was keeping a mistress at a fashionable boarding-house, under the title of wife. The true wife, still wrestling with God for the renegade, sallied forth into the wintry street, clad in a calico dress without undergarments, and shod only with india-rubbers without shoes or stockings, entered the house, confronted the household as they sat at table, told her story to the confusion of the paramour and his mistress, and drew tears from all the company, till, by a common movement, the listeners compelled the harlot to pack her trunk and flee the city, and shamed the husband into creeping like a spaniel back into the kennel which his wife still cherished as her home."

Mr. Tilton told how Victoria took her husband to California to begin a new life. There she became a cigar girl, but when the proprietor noticed how she blushed at the customers' rude remarks he knew she was "too fine," and he returned her to her husband, whom he discovered to be a brother free-mason. He "gave his fair clerk of a day a twenty dollar gold piece, and dismissed her with his blessing. . . ."

Whereupon Victoria turned to her needle for support, and when she chanced to sew for Anna Cogswell, the actress, Miss Cogswell told her she should go on the stage. So Victoria became "a lesser light to the Cogswell star."

But "One night while on the boards, clad in a pink silk dress and slippers, acting in the ball-room scene in the Corsican Brothers, suddenly a spirit-voice addressed her, saying, 'Victoria, come home.' Thrown instantly into clairvoyant condition, she saw a vision of her young sister Tennie, then a mere child—standing by her mother, and both calling the absent one to return. . . . Victoria, thrilled and chilled by the vision and the voice, burst away at a bound behind the scenes, and without waiting to change her dress, ran, clad with all her dramatic adornments through a foggy rain to her hotel, and packing up her few things that night, betook herself with her husband and child next morning to the steamer bound for New York. On the voyage she was thrown into such vivid spiritual states that she produced a profound excitement among the passengers. On reaching her mother's home. . . ." she was told that at the time . . . the message "was uttered, her mother had said to Tennie, 'My dear, send the spirits after Victoria to bring her home.'

". . . She was now directed by the spirits to repair

to Indianapolis, there to announce herself as a medium and to treat patients for the cure of disease. . . ."

She "reaped a golden harvest," as well as "golden opinions," but "the dismal fact of her son's half-idiocy" "preyed upon her mind. . . ." Apparently Mr. Tilton thought the child was born so, though he was normal until he fell from a second story window when he was two years old. Maybe Victoria got some comfort from blaming it on alcohol and squalor. Accidents are incredible to the portentous. Mr. Tilton says she "prayed to God for another child—a daughter to be born with a fair body and a sound mind. Her prayer was granted, but not without many accompaniments of inhumanity . . . that first awoke her mind to the question, 'Why should I any longer live with this man?' Hitherto she had entertained an almost superstitious idea of the devotion with which a wife should cling to her husband. She had always been so faithful to him that, in his cups, he would mock and jeer at her fidelity. . . . At length . . . after eleven years . . . she applied in Chicago for a divorce and obtained it. . . ."

In fact, Canning Woodhull was a gentle, genial young man, so fond of children that when he left his home in Rochester, New York, after some medical education, and went out to Ohio to build up a small-town practise, he wanted to marry and settle down and have a large family. Then he met a savage goddess, a latter-day Helen, who played at magic and wanted the moon.

Victoria was a lovely child. Her blue eyes blazed

in skin like a flower-petal. Her features were as daintily cut as any cameo, and she carried her curly brown hair high. She had a quaint, quick, precise way of speaking, an unaccountable precision which emphasized her innate, her obvious superiority to her family. And she always had witchery.

After they were married, his little income, which had sounded like wealth to Victoria, wasn't enough. Domesticity bored her; and household tasks were done, when they were done, with fingers that took hold delicately as if they didn't want to touch anything.

She preferred to sit and dream about her destiny, her mind on cosmic plans instead of the usual girlish frivolities.

It is possible that, if Canning Woodhull had been the vigorous monster Tilton portrayed, she might have forgotten the cosmos.

And then, when she went to visit her husband's family in Rochester, it was a journey from frontier to gentility.

Gerritt Smith and the Tappans were talking abolition in New York State in the 'fifties; the Oneida Community was practising communism; a Woman's Rights Convention met at Albany; and Amelia Bloomer, Mrs. Stanton, Lucy Stone and Miss Anthony wore knickerbockers; but the mob said:

"Gibbery, gibbery gab,
The women had a confab,
And demanded the rights,
To wear the tights,
Gibbery, gibbery gab."

The mob echoed the average beliefs of the East, where radicals destined for posterity were distant criers to men between the pioneering and the industrial stage. Men whose energies needed more outlet than protecting and exchanging property assumed property rights over their women and children, an old custom, into which their spare fervor spilled.

To insure it, fictions that were hypocrisies in England and the socially sophisticated South, that the pioneering West and Middle West had no time for, that were neglected in metaphysical New England, were shouted so religiously down East that human beings actually were created in their image. Women were raised with limbs instead of legs; some neither thought nor saw nor felt anything unpleasant except sorrow or suffering, which they endured with resignation. Unpleasantness was morbid and forbidden, as was joy, if unrestrained. No "true woman" had interests outside her parents' home before she married. Then she endured her husband's animal instincts until she tamed them and inspired him to higher things.

It is likely that the Woodhull women were "true women." They left no records; true women would leave none. Knowing nothing of their characters, we cannot imagine what happened when Victoria arrived with her healthy animalism, her spirit-visitors, her beauty and her Methodism.

We can guess at a humiliation that added fuel to old grudges and started new ones. Much of her femininism could have been generated in such an encounter with "true women" and their careful, critical proprietors. They would have been outraged by her ignorance, and violence and vulgarities, and they would not have hidden their scorn, a scorn to which her beauty added, for it was enviable. When she fought conventions afterward, she might have been fighting Woodhulls, whom she did not conquer, those cruel Woodhulls whose scorn blurred her dreams.

But this is groping in one of Victoria's dark interludes, lit by few flashes of fact, by few glows of memory. There are several years when we have only an occasional twinkle from some law suit, until we come to the era when her private life blazed in the courts, the newspapers, her own paper, and on the platform.

Chapter Three

DEMOSTHENES AND THE GOLDEN GOOSE

SISTER TENNESSEE went ahead to fame. In 1859 Ohio papers advertised:

"A WONDERFUL CHILD!

"Miss Tennessee Claflin
"Who is only fourteen years of age!!

"This young lady has been traveling since she was eleven years old, and who has been endowed from her birth with a super-natural gift to such an astonishing degree that she convinces the most skeptical of her wonderful powers.

"She gives information of absent friends, whether living or dead, together with all the past, present and future events of life; also of lost money or property, identifying the person or persons concerned with so much certainty as scarcely to leave a doubt of their guilt.

" . . . She can see and point out the medicine to cure the most obstinate diseases—even those that for years baffled our best physicians, and can direct salves and liniment to be made and used that will cure old sores, fever sores, cancers, sprains, weakness in the back and limbs, and other complaints. . . .

"She will point out to ladies and gentlemen their former, present, and future partners, telling exactly those that are dead and living, their treatment, disposition and character in life; and when required will go into an unconscious state and travel to any part of the world, hunt up absent friends, whether dead or alive, and through her they will tell the inquiring friend their situation and whereabouts, with all the events of life since they last met. . . .

"She may be consulted at her room, United States Hotel,

MISS TENNESSEE'S
MAGNETIO
LIFE ELIXIR
— FOR —
BEAUTIFYING THE COMPLEXION,
And Cleansing the Blood.
Warranted to be perfectly harmless and purely vegetable.
DIRECTIONS.
A teaspoonful three times a day one half hour before each meal. Persons taking the Elixir should be careful in their Diet.
PRICE $2.00 PER BOTTLE.

LABEL ON THE "ELIXIR" BOTTLES

High Street, Columbus, from the hours of eight o'clock A.M. to nine o'clock P.M. Price of consultation, $1.00."

The Claflins left Mt. Gilead as a cure-all outfit, featuring Tennessee and an "Elixir of Life" with her picture on the bottle.

Her story is inseparable from Victoria's. Though she played a tinny treble to Victoria's deeper bass, the tunes they worked their charms with were usually duets. Tennessee's Spiritualism was a matter of business, and when she didn't need money she let it alone; Victoria never let it alone, it was in her blood. Tennessee was more casual about her husbands and lovers; she got what she wanted without any fuss, because she didn't want anything as much as Victoria wanted everything, and the world needn't know about it. She was gayer, and prettier and not so beautiful as her stormy sister; she, too, was fascinating, but when she was young she was coarse.

Coarseness was an asset to a cure-all outfit, in which Brother Hebern was a cancer-doctor without any medical training, and Roxy brewed elixirs in her kettle with spirit-help, while Buck Claflin brewed any scheme for cash.

They got medical histories from their first patients, whose discarded prescriptions from real physicians they used on others. In the beginning, in every town they went to, they sent out small boys to distribute advertising hand-bills; and too soon after they were settled in some dim rooming-house with a sign in the window, they had to decamp because they couldn't afford a license or a bribe for the police. But after a while they were advertising in the newspapers and staying at the best hotels.

They prospered. Victoria joined them occasionally, but the testimonials in the newspapers were addressed to Tennessee, and here is one of them:

"A CARD

"Out of justice to MISS TENNESSEE CLAFLIN (a natural born Clairvoyant) and a duty I owe to myself and community I have thought proper to make the following statement:

"On or about the 10th of November inst., I was informed . . . that Mr. Bambrough, . . . residing at No. 41 Long Street, was fast recovering from his perilous situation; he had been quite indisposed for some two or three years, and within two or three months past had two paralytic strokes, the last of which nearly deprived him of the use of his limbs as well as that of his mind, and good physicians said . . . his stay on earth was of short duration, and such was my opinion when I last saw him . . . I heard that he was recovering and I went immediately to see him and found him . . . recovering, and soon MISS TENNESSEE CLAFLIN came in and commenced operating upon him with her hands and prescribing medicine, etc., and I sat with astonishment and looked at him and her for some minutes, and he seemed to be so much better and in his right mind . . . and can now visit among his old neighbors as usual. . . . I . . . put myself under her . . . treatment as I considered myself in a dangerous situation . . . and her operations and medicine gave me immediate relief. . . . This young lady who is only fourteen years of age, is now stopping at the United States Hotel on High Street, Columbus, Ohio, where she may be consulted upon all matters pertaining to life and health.

E. Bacus, Sr., No. 38 Rich St.,
Columbus, Nov. 24, 1859."

In Indianapolis Victoria was a part of the cure-all outfit. But her baby was ill, and later she described the vision she had then. ". . . Just after my infant son's recovery . . . While sitting in the parlor of the house which we occupied I had this baby boy on my lap. I was alone, and I beheld Jesus standing in the doorway. His arms were outstretched showing me His hands and feet. I saw the scars of His crucifixion . . . a light blue scarf was around Him. He was visible for several minutes. My whole future was foreshadowed in that time."

What clues to Victoria's inner life those visions were! Now with her itch for greatness she had to tend to sick children, while sister Tennessee went to the heights of underground fame. Restless behind the bars of womanhood, she must have been tired of her jailer too. We can imagine how Canning Woodhull's gentle goodness maddened her, and how his social superiority made her feel small, though she learned from him the ways of gentility that her family never learned. But when he drank to forget what he dared not remember, she despised him and left him. Brought up to know she did right because she did it, her exalted visitant needed to lull no scruples, but He showed her that He had scars, too, and He foreshadowed that great future, so often promised in the otherwhere. He dispelled her moments of doubt.

In Ottawa, Illinois, Tennessee's fame turned sinister.

The *Ottawa Free Trader* of July 4, 1863, announced that the:

"AMERICAN KING OF CANCERS—Dr. R. B. Claflin is stopping at Mr. M. D. Calkin's home in South Ottawa. He claims to be the King of Cancers and all kinds of chronic diseases, fever sores, bone diseases, scrofula, piles, sore eyes in the worst stages, heart and liver complaints, female weaknesses, consumption, inflammatory rheumatism, asthma, neurolgia, sick headache, dropsy in the chest, and fits in various forms.

"The doctor also guarantees a cure in all cases where patients live up to directions. The poor dealt with liberally.

"Cancers killed and extracted, root and branch in from 10 to 48 hours without instruments, pain, or the use of chloroform, simply by applying a mild salve of the doctor's own make. . . ."

Two weeks later the *Free Trader* advertised, the "wonderful child (who) . . . has so astonished people through her wonderful cures and mysterious revelations during her travels in the United States."

The Claflins did well enough in Ottawa to rent the Fox River House, the town's oldest hotel for a cancer infirmary, where the "cult of love" was taught incidentally. Testimonials from patients were printed in the newspapers, including one from a Mrs. Rebecca Howe, which stated that she had been cured of a cancer of the breast.

But Mrs. Howe wrote to the *Ottawa Republican,* on June 4, 1864:

"TO WHOM IT MAY CONCERN—Miss Tennessee Claflin, having published a card addressed to the public, touching her treatment of myself for cancer, which statement was prepared by Miss Claflin herself, and which is in many respects false and untrue and calculated as I believe to mislead the public and may result if uncontradicted in wrong and injury to others to the same extent that I myself have suffered. I deem it but an act of duty to say that I have been imposed upon by her statements which have proved to be wholly false and untrue. I am not only not cured, but much worse than I was when I first submitted to her treatment. Every step of her treatment has been accompanied by extreme pain and aggravation of all the symptoms and I have grown worse day by day. I make this statement realizing the fact that I have but a short time to live, and that it is my wish to prevent, as far as I am able, the injury which might otherwise be inflicted upon innocent sufferers, who might be induced by the statement purporting to have come from me, to apply to Miss Claflin, whom I believe to be an impostor, and more, and wholly unfit for the confidence of the community.

Signed, Rebecca Howe.
Margaret Ward, witness."

After Mrs. Howe's letter was printed, a committee of local doctors visited the infirmary and said the sick got neither care nor food. Dr. Joseph Stout said he had never seen such suffering and filth. And when Rebecca Howe died, Tennessee was indicted for manslaughter, an indictment still to be seen in the courthouse at Ottawa, written in faded ink, on paper scorched from a fire.

"State of Illinois, La Salle County, S.S.—The people vs. Tennessee Claflin. Of the June term of the Circuit Court of La Salle County in the year of our Lord one thousand, eight hundred and sixty-four.

"The grand jurors chosen, selected and sworn . . . in the name and by the authority of the people of the state of Illinois, upon their oaths, present that Tennessee Claflin, late of said county, on the first day of November in the year of our Lord 1863, and on divers other days and times between that day and the seventh of June, in the year of our Lord 1864, . . . upon the right side of the breast of one Rebecca Howe, . . . then and there being divers quantities of deleterious and caustic drugs to the jury aforesaid unknown, then and there feloniously and wilfully did apply and place by means whereof a large amount of flesh upon the right side of the breast of her, the said Rebecca Howe was . . . wholly eaten away, consumed and destroyed, . . . the said Rebecca Howe . . . became . . . mortally sick, sore and distempered of her body, . . . Rebecca Howe . . . did languish and languishing did live on, which said 7th day of June . . . in the county aforesaid, . . . of the said deleterious and caustic drugs so by Tennessee Claflin applied . . . Rebecca Howe died and so the jurors . . . upon their oaths aforesaid do say that the said Tennessee Claflin, the said Rebecca Howe, . . . did kill and slay, contrary to the form of the statute in such case made and provided, and against the peace and dignity of the same people of the state of Illinois. . . ."

. . . . . .

The *Free Trader* of June 18, 1864, recorded the

"SUDDEN DISAPPEARANCE OF TENNESSEE CLAFLIN. Miss Tennessee Claflin clairvoyant, doctress, &c., whose ability to perform miracles in the way of wonderful cures has been somewhat largely advertised in the local press hereabouts for the last six months and who has opened a 'magnetic infirmary' at the Old Fox House in Ottawa Center suddenly disappeared about a week ago. There are said to have been some fifteen patients in her 'infirmary' two weeks ago, all of whom she had 'paroled' except four who were too sick to leave. These were cancer cases, and were literally deserted, having no notice of her intentions to leave them. They were in the most horrible condition and were taken charge of by humane persons in the vicinity . . ."

Still in her 'teens, Tennessee was only a golden goose, chained by the force of his will to a father who extorted golden eggs and never cared where they came from, chained by her own devotion to a witless mother who believed in all those cure-alls and a united family.

The out-fit went to Cincinnati from Ottawa and advertised in the *Free Trader* that Tennessee would send her patients medicine from there!

In Cincinnati, a family started housekeeping on Mound Street at the corner of Sixth, and from their rear windows, they saw a strange picture. Three women were bending over a kettle that hung from a tripod in a back yard near by. The women stirred, and tested and poked at the embers, weirdly suggesting Macbeth's three witches, with a difference. One was a hag, but another was a pretty dimpled girl with jolly blue eyes and a don't-care air, the other was a stormy young beauty.

On the front window of the witches' dwelling, a sign read "Tennessee Claflin, and Victoria Woodhull, Clairvoyants." But curiosity turned to irritation when summer came, for through opened windows, day and night, came loud sounds of family strife.

No doubt the Claflins battled some over the cancer-salve and the spirits, for as Victoria grew older and more influential, the salve disappeared from their annals and the spirits prevailed.

While Miss Mary Alice Egbert was visiting in Cincinnati, she lost a gold belt buckle and went to see Tennessee Claflin. After Miss Egbert paid the usual fee she was told where she lost the buckle, but Tennessee wouldn't tell where she could find it, unless Miss Egbert paid more. Miss Egbert departed, in doubt. General Grant's father went to the Claflins for spiritual healing, and wrote a poem to celebrate a reunion of the sisters, Victoria, Tennessee and Utica, in which he rhymed tipsy with gypsy.

But people began to say the Claflins ran a house of assignation, and they said it in the courts of law. Tennessee figured in an adultery suit and a blackmail suit, which brought out so much evidence that prominent Cincinnatians asked the family to leave town.

About 1866 they turned up in Chicago with spirit manifestations and magnetic doctoring for sale; on Wabash Avenue, and afterwards on Harrison Street.

There, too, the neighbors complained of the family rows, and suspected their magnetic doctoring; so Victoria took Hebern, Tennessee, and Tennessee's first husband, John Bartels, whom she had married in Chicago, on a tour through Arkansas, Missouri, Kansas and Tennessee. The sisters told fortunes and gave Spiritualistic seances, and the men gambled. Bartels was a professional sport.

Tennessee kept her marriage secret because it would hurt business, and the attentions she received from other men irritated Bartels.

"One day we had a fierce row over ten dollars," he said later. "I wanted to know where Tennie got the bill and she wouldn't tell. After that we quarrelled pretty much all the time. We finally came back to Chicago, driving into town in circus style with a band and outriders. By that time Tennie was tired of me and I of her. The women had made a fortune on that trip. They gave me twenty thousand dollars on the understanding that I was to keep out of the way and not bother them any more."

But that return to Chicago in circus style with a band and outriders was Victoria's first parade. We can picture her sitting straight in a high carriage, in an acre of purple cloth, for woman wore acres then and

MISS TENNESSEE

THE WONDERFUL CHILD.

HAS ESTABLISHED A

MAGNETIC

INFIRMARY

AT No 265 WABASH AVENUE.

HICAGO. ILL.

ONE OF THE OLD HANDBILLS

Victoria favored purple, and she always wore a white rose at her breast. Her blue eyes would have blazed with delight under the tilted flat-crowned hat of the period. For she inevitably confused amazement with the admiration she craved. The gaping crowds must have thrilled her.

Chicago was full of strange sights in those days. And back in Harrison Street the neighbors still complained.

They couldn't prove that joy was sold there though they were certain of it. So the eviction papers were served on Victoria Woodhull for fraudulent fortune-telling.

Victoria had none of Tennessee's silly vulgarities, none of those pathetic leers with which those who have been degraded by sex try to degrade it. She was too intelligent, too healthily erotic to have sold it, anyway, when she didn't want it, unless she was terribly needy, and the price was high. Then she could escape unpleasant moments in a self-hypnosis; she was made that way.

Prostitution was not a pleasant profession in those days. According to a piece that appeared in *Woodhull & Claflin's Weekly* later:

"... At present the profession of prostitute is illegal. If seen to stop and speak to a man, to prevent arrest she gives the patrolman $3.00 to $10.00 a week and the privilege of visiting her gratis. She pays $10.00 to $15.00 for board, and for every visitor an additional tax of from 50c to $2.00 to landlord. The amount of degradation and bodily injury to which you must daily submit to meet these combined charges may be imagined ... police captains and police sergeants

. . . (demand) $20.00 to $30.00 when these officers need money. Wine is furnished them when wanted and they are accorded the privilege of frequenting without charge such inmates as they may select. Any person taking offense with them may have their house 'pulled' as disorderly. Police officers are sent and everyone in a designated building, including the men on a visit, are taken before the justice, who fines each girl and man $10.00, and the keeper of the establishment from $100 to $20. . . . Advantage of licensing prostitution and houses of prostitution is their entire independence from the police (and) Weekly visits from medical men to each girl, as in Europe . . . Prostitution exists and will exist so long as society maintains its present ideas and organization. As it cannot be extinguished, its evils should be palliated."

From Chicago the Claflins went to St. Louis; and when one of their relatives joined them there, she saw a strange man with luxuriant side whiskers.

"Why who is that?" she asked Dr. Woodhull.

"That's Colonel Blood," said he. "He's Vickey's husband."

"Where do you come in!"

"We don't live together any more," said Canning Woodhull, quietly.

The Tilton biography explained the situation:

" . . . Col. James H. Blood, Commander of the Sixth Missouri Regiment, who at the close of the war was elected City Auditor of St. Louis, who became President of the Society of Spiritualists in that place, and who had himself been, like Victoria, the legal partner of a morally sundered marriage, called one day on Mrs. Woodhull to consult her as a Spiritualistic physician (having never met her before), and was startled to see her pass into a trance, during which she announced, unconsciously to herself, that his future destiny was to be linked with

COLONEL JAMES H. BLOOD

hers in marriage. Thus, to their mutual amazement, but to their subsequent happiness, they were betrothed on the spot by 'the powers of the air.' The legal tie by which at first they bound themselves to each other was afterward by mutual consent annulled—the necessary form of Illinois law being complied with to this effect. But the marriage stands on its merits, and is to all who witness its harmony, known to be a sweet and accordant union of congenial souls.

"Colonel Blood is a man of a philosophic and reflective cast of mind, an enthusiastic student of the higher lore of Spiritualism, a recluse from society, and an expectant believer in a stupendous destiny for Victoria . . ."

Most of the honors he claimed belonged to Sullivan Blood, an older St. Louisan; but Colonel Blood was a Civil War veteran, with five bullet holes in his body, and he was a sincere Spiritualist.

Spiritualism was an organized religion then, as well as a conviction and a practise; many (like the Pauline Church of the 'forties) believed in a regeneration of the world through theories of social freedom, which were delightful but impractical. Colonel Blood was half philosophical anarchist, half state socialist, with a flavor of mysticism. He believed in a curious kind of reincarnation, in free love, and in fiat money, that recurrent dream of printed currency based on the faith and resources of a nation, not redeemable in gold or any standard. Its advocates were called Greenbackers after the Civil War.

Colonel Blood brought causes into Victoria's life; he gave her cosmic touch its claws. Said he, "When anyone can't understand me well enough to know that I am working for the human race and not for Colonel

Blood, I don't care to have very much to do with them," and his life proved that he meant it.

He worshipped Victoria, and no doubt her Greek visitant united them through their own desires.

A handsome man, with a fine face, a splendid physique, and military carriage, was Colonel Blood, a gallant, kindly adventurer, whom everybody liked.

Canning Woodhull liked him.

Poor Canning Woodhull had given up his profession and his family to be near Victoria on any terms. He was devoted to his children, too, and wanted to look after them. And when the situation, which violated everything he ever had heard of, was particularly unbearable, he got drunk and forgot it.

But when Victoria was depressed, he would take her in a room alone; and when she came out, the Colonel would ask, "Do you feel better, Vicky?"

"I'm getting over it," she'd say.

Canning Woodhull, sober, was a father to her now, a comforting father to consult with, the father she never had had. Moreover, Woodhull's worship was a sop to her vanity. In his weakness he took the place of a son too. Often when she fondled her boy Byron, he'd push her away because he didn't know her.

The boy was a tragedy, though the girl, Zulu Maud was her constant joy.

But her early itch for greatness had grown with the slurs it fed on until no personal happiness would do. She had to show Homer how great she was, and Cincinnati. She had to show Ottawa, where small boys had jeered at her and Tennessee. Chicago still smarted, and now in St. Louis, there were encounters with the police.

There was a Mrs. James H. Blood and two little Bloods; and shortly after the Colonel's singular betrothal to Victoria, he conveniently dropped his last name, and as James Harvey, Esquire, he toured the Middle West with her.

The Colonel believed that the end justified the means, in a good cause of course, but he was the judge of the cause. He believed that might made right too. Victoria believed that anything she did was right, because she did it.

But the world never feeds its philosophers gratuitously. Victoria and the Colonel travelled in a covered van with a ball-fringed top, and Victoria called herself Madam Harvey and told fortunes; Colonel Blood drummed up trade.

It must have been a blissful vacation from Victoria's brawling family, and any contemptuous crowd. They stopped on the outskirts of small towns and saw none but enchanted customers.

Victoria had extra perceptions that made her an uncanny fortune-teller. As a blind man feels things the blindfolded would bump into, so she felt tensions in the atmosphere; she saw color changes, muscle movements ordinary people wouldn't see. She told a Western judge that his daughter, then a healthy girl, would die within a year, and the girl died, which may have been a coincidence. Other prophecies failed.

Men could get a woman's viewpoint from her, on many things they couldn't mention to their wives and mothers. Women told her what they dared not tell anyone without her background.

In those days sex was considered a shame and a scourge. Colonel Blood taught Victoria that it was a right and a rapture, for that was his conviction, as well as his practice.

He welded the chaos of her early life into a philosophy. He believed in her destiny, too. He was a mystic and an optimist.

But Mrs. Blood traced her roving Colonel after awhile, and the Harveys had to come back to St. Louis to pay every cent they had made for his freedom. There was a double divorce; and in the court house at Dayton, Ohio, is the curious record of a marriage license issued to James H. Blood and Victoria Claflin, on July 14, 1866. If the marriage were performed, the minister made no return; the record does not show that they were legally married.

Two years later Victoria was in Pittsburgh; and while she was sitting at a marble table, her favorite spirit visitor appeared in his Greek tunic. For years he had said she would emerge from poverty and live in a mansion, that she would win great wealth in a city crowded with ships, he had insisted that she would become the ruler of her country; but he never had revealed his identity. Now he wrote "Demosthenes" on the table in an indistinct writing that grew so bright it filled the room and frightened her. Then he commanded her to go to New York City, to a house at number 17 Great Jones Street, which would be ready for her. Whereupon she had a vision of the house.

She went to New York; she hurried to 17 Great Jones Street; she found the hall, the stairways, the rooms and the furniture that she had seen in her vision. She wandered into the library and idly picked up a book. To her "blood-chilling astonishment" it was the "Orations of Demosthenes." So Victoria said.

Chapter Four

"TOMATO SOUP FOR THREE"

NEITHER Colonel Blood nor Demosthenes was a good provider. And when all the hungry Claflins flocked to Great Jones Street, Buckman took his golden goose to Commodore Vanderbilt, who was the logical prey of fake healers.

The Commodore was seventy-five years old then and sick; naturally he fired doctors who couldn't cure him and hired any mystic who promised to. The Commodore fired any man who didn't do his job. And he believed diseases could be caused and cured by spells chanted over a miniature or a lock of hair. It was easy for Cornelius Vanderbilt to believe in miracles, because he was one. He had started as a Staten Island ferryman, and at twenty-three he was the captain of a ferry-boat; at sixty-three he owned twenty steamships and forty steamboats; and at seventy he went into the railroad business and mastered it. Now he was the monarch of finance, because he was the boldest, the hardest, the ablest of them all.

He kept his magic out of the railroad business, as well as his fondness for high-stepping horses and fair fragility, inclinations the public knew about, however. He was a familiar figure, sitting erect in his buggy, driving his white-footed trotters down Broadway every morning, his longish white hair blowing in the wind, above a big white cravat and black clerical clothes.

He saw everyone who called on him, so it was easy for Buck Claflin to get an audience for Tennessee, who was magnetic healer as well as fair fragility. In fact, Tennessee was a little plump, but men liked them plump in those days.

Magnetic healers were supposed to give their patients vital force through contact. They claimed to create electricity by the laying-on of hands. They likened themselves to a battery, the right hand being the positive, the left the negative force.

Tennessee magnetized the Commodore during the most active and useful period of his life; apparently she did him no harm. He liked it well enough to ask her to marry him. Said he, "I intended to have done so, but the family made other plans." Which was an evasion; none but old Cornelius ever made plans in his family.

He had planned to conquer conventional society because it shuddered at "that coarse Mr. Vanderbilt." He never was invited to those distinguished dinners at Cyrus Field's or Philip Hone's (where philosophical discussion would have bewildered him) nor even to the "soirées" of a flashier "élite." Conventional society would have shuddered at Tennie C. too, so he married Miss Frank Crawford, a young gentlewoman from Alabama, who was socially acceptable anywhere.

But when Buckman took Tennessee to call on the bridegroom, Cornelius kissed her in front of his dignified wife. "You might have been Mrs. Vanderbilt," he said somewhat exuberantly.

Afterward he agreed to back a Napoleonic scheme, probably originated by Colonel Blood, who was a student of the Corsican. When Colonel Blood's fortunes waned, he tried to brighten them with a dashing coup,

TENNIE C. CLAFLIN IN THE SEMI-MASCULINE COSTUME SHE AND VICTORIA SOMETIMES WORE

like Napoleon's coup d'état. Sometimes it turned into a pointless trick; this time it triumphed.

On January twentieth, 1870, the *New York Herald* announced a sensation in Wall Street. Two fashionably dressed lady speculators, whom nobody knew, had appeared. Everybody wondered where they got their knowledge of stocks. They said they were staying at the Hoffman House and that they intended to become habitués of Wall Street. Two days later the *Herald* marked the progress of Women's Rights' agitations by the appearance of these "Queens of Finance", and though in those days newspaper comment was supposed to disgrace any woman who wasn't an actress or an agitator, the *Herald* printed a note from them, indicating that they didn't shrink from publicity:

"We were not a little surprised at seeing our appearance in Wall Street noticed in your columns of today. As we intend operating as mentioned, we should be glad to make your personal acquaintance when convenient. Woodhull, Claflin & Co." They enclosed two cards, delicately engraved, "Mrs. Victoria C. Woodhull, Hoffman House, Parlors 25 and 26, Mrs. Tennessee Claflin, ditto."

In the same issue was a description of the oil paintings, statuary, chairs and piano in Parlor 25, as well as a motto in a glazed frame, "Simply to Thy cross I cling," near the photograph of Commodore Vanderbilt.

The reporter questioned Tennessee. "It is a novel sight to see a woman go on the Street as a stock operator, and I presume you find it rather awkward?" he asked.

"Were I to notice what is said by what they call society," said Tennessee, "I could not leave my apartment except in fantastic walking-dress and ball-room costume. But I despise what squeamy crying girls or powdered, counter-jumping dandies say of me. . . . We have the counsel of those who have more experience than we have, and we are endorsed by the best backers in the city."

Victoria's "sanguine, nervous temperament" impressed the reporter, so did her keen eyes, her diamond ring, and the single rose in her hair. She told him that Woodhull, Claflin and Company had a project for working a silver ledge company in Nevada.

"The firm has been in business for three years, and it has made seven hundred thousand dollars," said she, "but what do present profits amount to when it costs us over twenty-five thousand dollars a month to live?"

Woodhull, Claflin & Company had made a fortune out of the Commodore's tips on Black Friday during the September panic. It took a fortune to harbor Roxanna, Buckman, Polly Sparr and her husband and two sets of children, Margaret Ann Miles and four children, lovely Utica Brooker, (the youngest Claflin, who was named after John Snyder's daughter,) as well as Victoria's daughter and her boy Byron, Victoria, Tennessee and Colonel Blood, who was the "company" of Woodhull, Claflin & Company, which supported the lot. Moreover, having tasted luxury, they liked it and demanded it. But this was glorious news to get to Homer, and Ottawa, and Cincinnati, St. Louis and Chicago. No wonder Victoria confided in the metropolitan press!

Victoria never took Colonel Blood's name. Tennessee never had called herself Bartels, either; when she married him, her name was a trademark too valuable to lose. Of course, both marriages were a little vague, but it may have been Victoria's faith in her future fame that influenced her to keep the name which sounded best. Tennessee soon shortened Tennessee Celeste to Tennie C.

She paid business calls for the firm.

It was Tennessee who deposited Vanderbilt's check for seven thousand dollars with Henry Clews and Company. A few days later she drove up in a cab and told Mr. Clews she had a "point" from a high source. Mr. Clews had no more faith in "points" than he had in pretty women in Wall Street, but she had a winning smile and she was close to Vanderbilt. He listened. She wanted to buy a thousand shares of New York Central. But New York Central was a stock the Commodore might manipulate. Was this a Vanderbilt trick to load him with the stock and crack the market? Anyway, Mr. Clews didn't want to be associated with Woodhull, Claflin & Company. He tapped his office bell and sent word to the cashier to make out Miss Claflin's account.

Tennie smiled. She went to the Fourth National Bank and presented her check. Then she came back to Mr. Clews.

"Mr. Clews," said she, sweetly, "the bank wishes to have me identified."

Mr. Clews was courteous, as well as wary, and he sent one of his boys to the bank to identify her. In this way, he sealed her credit and appeared to be one of the sponsors of Woodhull, Claflin & Company, to his intense annoyance.

Such conservative bankers were suspicious of the "Lady Brokers", or the "Bewitching Brokers" as they often were called. But when they opened their office at 44 Broad Street, every financial house sent a representative to call. Vanderbilt's power was behind them. Newspapers cooed over their beauty and charm; reporters described their dark blue empress walking-dresses, and noted the gold pens behind lovely ears. They were the first female brokers in the world; they were beautiful; they were a sensation. Crowds followed them through the streets. Visitors besieged them; they had to put a sign on the wall: "All gentlemen will state their business and then retire at once."

The women who drove downtown in their carriages used the rear entrance to Victoria Woodhull's private office, which was separated from the front by a richly carved walnut partition, topped with ornamented glass. They might find her at a green baize covered walnut desk, eating early strawberries sent in by some friend on the Street; or happily pasting newspaper clippings about the "Queens of Finance" in a scrapbook. Sometimes Buck Claflin sat beside her, an incongruous figure, in high leather boots, with his beard trimmed to a point, a malign representation of "Uncle Sam". But everyone admired Victoria's bright face lit by such soft blue eyes. They were charmed by her flute-like voice, and none failed to find her energy infectious. She vitalized everyone who met her.

Actually those sensational sisters were received with a remarkable lack of hostility at a time when the conventional frowned on any woman who even believed

THE LADY BROKERS DRIVING THE BULLS AND BEARS OF WALL STREET. TENNIE C. HOLDING THE REINS, VICTORIA THE WHIP

(From a cartoon in the *New York Telegraph*, February 18, 1870)

in woman's suffrage, when women were not allowed in restaurants without a male escort after six o'clock. In this same year, Mrs. Chickering, an elderly gentlewoman, happened to be in New York overnight without her husband. She went from hotel to hotel before one bold landlord gave her shelter,—and put a negro porter on watch outside her door all night.

In such an era of male bluster, men grew fierce whiskers and swore horribly; they drank and gambled and conspicuously played with prostitutes. It was manly to be rough and tough. It was womanly to be pure and sweet, much too weak ever to be trusted alone, far too tender for anything but childbearing, cooking, laundry work and capturing a husband. This rôle was as hard to live with as it was to live up to, for such determined innocence was dull.

It was not surprising that gentlemen had to be asked to 'state their business and retire' at 44 Broad Street, or that the Commodore was often seen with the exciting pair. Apparently the new Mrs. Vanderbilt preferred religion to society. She influenced the Commodore to give money away; she brought a clergyman into the house to advise him. She made him call a real doctor when he was ill. She didn't try to make his house a social center. Probably the Commodore's social whim was short-lived anyway; and with the Claflin sisters he could be natural. Tennessee guffawed appreciatively when he said the ladies bought his stocks to get his likeness on the certificates. She was his "little sparrow," who slapped him on the back and told him to "Wake up, old boy." The Commodore was tired and old, and both sisters stimulated him. Victoria summoned the spirits, which was fascinating;

THE BEWITCHING BROKERS ACCORDING TO MATTHEW HALE SMITH IN "BULLS AND BEARS OF NEW YORK"

Spiritualism and whist were his recreations. The Commodore was no fool; he paid his money, and he had his fun.

At last, after writhing under slurs in obscurity, Victoria Woodhull saw her name in the big New York papers. With the faith of the uneducated in mere print, she, who had craved importance, thought she had achieved it. Forever afterward she associated vindication with publication in the newspapers. She formed the habit of telling all to a listening world.

". . . During our experience of fifteen years, while we have almost universally received the counsel, support and approval of the opposite sex, our own has universally thrown dirt on us," said she, in the *New York Herald* for February 13, 1870, "such being our experience, we are not of those who affect to believe our sex is despoiled of most of their rights by the domineering will of man, but on the contrary, if we may assert, many are illy prepared to make the best use of greater opportunities. As soon as the sex is prepared to perform all the calls and duties of life, the right to do so cannot be withheld, and if so, we ourselves propose to fight for it, if need be. Without secession, we propose revolution, whenever the chains of conservatism drop too slowly and leave us chafing under their restraints too long, or deny us the means of applying possessed capacity."

Victoria's approach to reform was not subtle.

The Claflins lived at 15 East 38th Street now, in a glitter of gilt. Gilt chairs upholstered in satin with lace tidies, statuary on gilt pedestals and oil paintings in gilt frames were multiplied by countless mirrors extending from floor to ceiling, set in white and gilt tracery on the walls. Victoria demanded order when she had servants, and the place was exquisitely kept. But the family brawled as usual. Utica Brooker seemed to hate her prominent sisters. Utica, the most beautiful Claflin, was undone. She was the youngest, and like her sisters, she had married a nice young man who wanted a home. But she wouldn't leave her family in St. Louis, nor the small part she had there in a stock company, when Thomas Brooker wanted her with him in Quincy, Illinois, so he left her. They were divorced. And Utica took to gin and malice. And Victoria shared Tennessee's reputation, though she didn't deserve it. She begged Tennessee to be less prodigal with her favors. Tennessee was devoted to Victoria, but she wouldn't change her merry little ways.

In spite of her family Victoria struggled on to fulfill her destiny, a destiny into which an American philosopher now entered.

He was Stephen Pearl Andrews, a son of the Baptist minister who had led the contest to break away from the established church of Massachusetts. With rebellion in his blood, young Stephen Pearl went from Amherst College to Louisana where he taught in a young ladies' seminary and studied law. Louisiana lawyers needed to know Latin, Spanish and French, and Andrews interested himself in languages. There, too, he became an abolitionist.

But a lone abolitionist couldn't hope to reform Louisiana. Stephen Pearl Andrews decided to go to Texas,

STEPHEN PEARL ANDREWS

then an independent republic to which, after its revolt from Mexico, many Southern slave-holders had moved. Andrews practised law in Houston. He waited until the price of cotton fell, and with it the value of slaves, before he mentioned abolition. Then he suggested it as a practical measure; and as such, it was received with enthusiasm, until he went to Galveston where organized opposition defeated it. He went to England with Louis Tappan, to ask the anti-slavery society there to advance loans to buy the Texas slaves, but this mission failed. However, there was enough excitement to alarm the South and hasten the annexation of Texas.

Meanwhile, Stephen Pearl found a common element in Swedenborg and Fourier, which Swedenborg called the "Doctrine of Correspondence" and the French philosopher called "Universal Analogy." Andrews discovered echoes of sameness relating spheres of being to one another, and founded a "Universal Science," on them. He decided that every sound must have a different meaning which could be discovered and fixed into a universal language. He found those meanings, and called the language "Alwato." It was Stephen Pearl Andrews who introduced phonographic writing, now called short-hand, into the United States. He wrote books about it and tried to get it adopted into the educational system.

He also learned Chinese, and wrote a Chinese text-book, besides two French text-books. And when his first wife died, he married a woman who was a qualified physician. To aid her and to enlarge his scientific scope, Andrews went to the New York Medical College, and got his medical degree.

He studied the social doctrines of Josiah Warren, one of Robert Owen's disciples who believed in the sovereignty of the individual. Andrews recommended a complete reconstruction of society, an "Institution of a Unitary Government" for the whole world under the guidance of a new and supreme institute of humanity, which he named "The Pantarchy."

Unfortunately, Andrews' "Basic Outline of Universology" was nine hundred pages of profound mysticism, which few read and fewer could understand. Andrews was nearly sixty in 1870, a quiet, dreamy, bearded philosopher, an active member of the New York Liberal Club, to which his friend Horace Greeley and other conservative libertarians belonged. Andrews was too quiet, too profound, too politic, to get his radical schemes to a public ear attuned to the sensational.

The public was listening to "The Lady Brokers"; and when Andrews met Victoria Woodhull, he saw the ideal trumpeter for his ideas. What she had learned from Colonel Blood, she already used impressively. Her voice was musical and captivating. Sometimes, in general conversation, her mind seemed to halt as if it were elsewhere, until she got interested, excited, then sentences poured forth; two crimson spots, like a pair of red roses, dashed into her cheeks; her sad face lightened; her eyes glowed like blue stars. Her vitality leaped out like a flame.

She worshipped learning, and here was a man who knew more than Colonel Blood. Colonel Blood believed in "social freedom" but Andrews had lived at "Modern Times" for awhile, a community on Long Island, based on Warren's "individual sovereignty," where property was the product of individual industry, where exchange was free, and so was love. Andrews was the author of "The Science of Society," admired by all reformers in America and England. He had had a triangular discussion with Greeley and Henry James in the *New York Tribune* on love, marriage and divorce, which was famous at the time. He was a celebrity. Now he had long philosophical discussions with Colonel Blood who said the end justified any means. Andrews claimed some ends justified some means. Victoria didn't know whether she was a means or an end, but she knew that she was justified in anything she did, because she was different. Nothing she did was wrong because she did it. But it would be a more comfortable world if others did as she did, if she always were admired instead of being scorned.

Andrews told her about the free love faith. Colonel Blood was a free lover too, but he took it for granted, and talked rather clinically about it; more fervent about labor problems and fiat money.

Andrews said the state had no more right to interfere with morals than with religion. But only a confusion of ideas could degrade free love to licentiousness. Moreover, freedom was only fitted for the wise, for those who could use it with moderation, without encroaching on the freedom of others. But why shouldn't superior natures exhibit a type of beautiful society, instead of being enslaved by the limitation of the inferior majority?

Victoria told Stephen Pearl Andrews about Demosthenes, and he was interested. He had investigated Spiritualism and half believed in it. She told him her visitant had foreseen that she would emerge from poverty and live in a mansion, that she would win great wealth in a city crowded with ships. He had told her that she would become the ruler of her country also!

Any hardy philosopher would say, "Why not?" to such diverting audacity, which, incidentally, was a good opening blast for a trumpeter. And on April the second, 1870, the *New York Herald* printed Victoria C. Woodhull's "First Pronunciamento," written by Andrews and Blood, with a few homely, pungent phrases that must have been her own.

" . . . As I happen to be the most prominent representative of the only unrepresented class in the Republic, and perhaps the most practical exponent of the principles of equality, I request the favor of being permitted to address the public through the medium of the *Herald,*" said she, "while others of my sex devoted themselves to a crusade against the laws that shackle the women of the country, I asserted my individual independence; while others prayed for the good time coming, I worked for it; while others argued the equality of woman with man, I proved it by successfully engaging in business; while others sought to show that there was no valid reason why women should be treated, socially and politically, as being inferior to man, I boldly entered the arena . . . of business and exercised the rights I already possessed. I therefore claim the right to speak for the unenfranchised women of the country, and believing as I do that the prejudices which still exist in the popular mind against women in public life will soon disappear, I now announce myself as candidate for the Presidency.

" . . . This is an epoch of sudden changes and startling surprises. . . . The blacks were cattle in 1860; a negro now sits in Jeff Davis' seat in the United States Senate. . . .

"Political preachers paw the air; there is no live issue up for discussion. . . .

" . . . The platform that is to succeed in the coming election must enunciate the general principles of enlightened justice and economy.

" . . . I anticipate criticism; but however unfavorable the comment this letter may evoke I trust that my sincerity will not be called in question. I have deliberately and of my own accord placed myself before the people as a candidate for the Presidency of the United States, and having the means, courage, energy and strength necessary for the race, intend to contest it to the close."

This letter evoked little unfavorable comment. A humorous public which had looked to George Francis Train's eccentricity, and Jim Fiske's rascality for entertainment, now got it from the "Lady Brokers." And Victoria was delighted by more newspaper fame.

The *Herald* asked Tennessee for her financial opinions. In a reaction against Victoria's new intellectual friends who didn't like her, Tennessee said:

". . . For myself, I have at least one financial opinion, and that is that gold is cash; and as a consequence, that to have plenty of it is to be pretty nearly independent of everything and everybody, even that most terrible personage, public opinion, and that very interesting and well informed individual, Madam Grundy. . . ."

A series of papers on "The Tendencies of Government" signed by Victoria C. Woodhull, appeared in the *Herald*. They were treatises on primitive government, Comte's formulas, and the progress of the world. They skimmed the history of ancient Egypt and Assyria, and touched on Ancient Greece, Rome and Modern Europe. They gave pleasant reasons why the

United States should be the centre of a universal government. When the world developed into one system of government, when it adopted a universal language, the one country that had arrived at perfection would control the world.

Stephen Pearl Andrews rarely wrote such readable material. It is a fact that every man who wrote over Victoria's signature, every reporter who interviewed her, everyone who came in contact with her, expressed themselves with more than their usual vividness, while they were under her spell.

According to an editorial on May 27, 1870, the *Herald* was impressed by "The Tendencies of Government."

" . . . It is evident that Mrs. Woodhull is imbued with at least one very sensible idea . . . that fitness is the first prequisite of qualifications entitling the seeker to enjoy the position sought for. This it is, doubtless, which has led her not only to study and perfect herself in the nature of the functions which she seeks to exercise . . . but, to give her opinions to the people, that they may judge of her ability and the correctness of her views.

" . . . Mrs. Woodhull offers herself in apparent good faith as a candidate, and perhaps has a remote impression, or rather hope, that she may be elected. . . . The public mind is not yet educated to the pitch of universal woman's rights. At present man, in his affection for and kindness toward the weaker sex, is disposed to accord her any reasonable number of privileges. Beyond that stage he pauses because there seems to him to be a something which is unnatural in permitting her to share the turmoil, the excitement, the risks of competition for the glory of governing . . ."

Then the sensational sisters tackled one of their rights in their own way.

In 1870, women were not allowed in restaurants without a male escort after six o'clock. At seven, Victoria and Tennessee went to dinner at Delmonico's.

"Tomato soup for two," said Victoria.

The waiter coughed. He stood on one foot and then the other.

"Why don't you get the soup!" said Victoria sharply.

"I beg your pardon, madam, but it is after six o'clock, and there is no gentleman with you."

"You go and send Charlie Delmonico here to me," said Tennessee.

Mr. Delmonico admired the sisters and they were valued patrons. In those days of prosperity, they entertained lavishly.

"Now, I'll tell you what we'll do," said Mr. Delmonico. "You pretend to be talking to me, and I'll walk out to the door with you, and people will think you just dropped in to speak to me. That will make it all right."

"Make what all right?" asked Victoria.

He walked toward the door and Tennessee followed him. "I can't let you eat here without some man," he told her. "It would start an awful precedent."

Tennie giggled. "Don't let me embarrass you."

She beckoned to a cabman who sat on his box at the door.

By this time people in the restaurant were standing up to watch.

"Come down off your box and come in here," said Tennie to the cabman.

She marched him down the center aisle.

"Now waiter," said she, "bring tomato soup for three."

"TOMATO SOUP FOR THREE"

Chapter Five

HUMPTY-DUMPTY

THE free love movement, which had started in America in the 'thirties, was flourishing in 1870. It had its own preachers, its poets and its colonies. It published newspapers and organized excursions and picnics. All the papers were full of it.

According to a loose estimate, there were four million Spiritualists in America then. Spiritualism was the first step from orthodoxy, and many Spiritualists regarded marriage as a doctrine of affinity to be made or unmade at will. Some believed that Heaven could be entered only with one's natural mate. Others, not all of whom were Spiritualists, simply held that the state had no jurisdiction over the affectional relations of the individual. Such was the creed of Stephen Pearl Andrews and the group of radical intellectuals who were his followers. They advocated a sort of state socialism, a "unitary" government, in which children, property, or anything in the economic field would be governed by the state, while the individual governed his own nature, free to vary his destiny or pursuits without any social restrictions. This group called itself the "Pantarchy," and Stephen Pearl was its "Pantarch."

The object of the "Pantarchy" was to sustain Andrews so that he might complete his scientific and philosophical discoveries, to give practical illustrations of the right working of his principles, and to lead the way to a great and beneficent revolution.

By way of sustaining Andrews, Victoria Woodhull asked him to stay at 15 East 38th Street while his wife was away; the Sparrs had had to be "dumped out" as Tennie put it, and there was room for him.

So Victoria met women who threw bouquets at her instead of dirt. She charmed the women of the "Pantarchy." Some were professional lecturers, one was a pioneer trained nurse, several were fanatical on social questions, but all were well-born, cultured gentlewomen. They preached what she had practised; they ennobled what she had been slurred for. At last, she, who always had been an outsider, found friends. She belonged.

But the "Pantarchy" wasn't enough for Victoria Woodhull. She wanted a larger field and more publicity. Since the newspapers had other people to write about, why shouldn't she have her own paper in which her name constantly could appear? Woodhull, Claflin & Company had money; and Colonel Blood wanted an organ for his views, which agreed with most of Stephen Pearl's.

On May 14, 1870, the first issue of *Woodhull & Claflin's Weekly* came forth, a sixteen page sheet, with "Upward and Onward" on the cover above advertisements of important financial houses procured by Tennie C. The *Weekly* deprecated "personalities, wilful misstatements or scurrility in journalism, because they lower the tone of the press, and injure its just influence with the people." It promised to be "primarily devoted to the vital interests of the people, and will treat of all matters freely and without reservation. It will support Victoria C. Woodhull for president with its whole strength; otherwise it will be untrammeled by party or personal considerations, free from all affiliation with political or social creeds, and will advocate Suffrage without distinction of sex."

Newspapers called it a "handsome and readable paper." One commentator added:

"There are at least two advocates of the woman movement that endeavor to show by example and precept that the fair sex with ordinary fair play and industry can take care of itself. We refer to the lady brokers who recently created a stir among the bulls and bears of Wall Street by setting up a china shop, so to speak, right in the midst of that disorderly locality. . . . They do more and talk less than the two divisions of female agitators put together."

At that time Julia Ward Howe and Mrs. Livermore represented the ultra conservative suffragists in *The Woman's Journal* of Boston. Susan B. Anthony, and Elizabeth Cady Stanton and Laura Curtis Bullard were more liberal in *The Revolution;* but both groups officially were unaware of Victoria Woodhull's existence.

It is possible that Victoria Woodhull's desire for the presidency made her a suffragist. Her femininity (and Tennessee's) had been her fortune, but without the vote, it was a barrier to this supreme vindication, the ultimate answer to the old contempt. Indeed, the presidency could have seemed no more remote to Victoria Woodhull than her past was. No wonder she had no sense of proportion.

Of course she was the prey, or the intended prey, of women who exploited female solidarity. A woman compositor complained in the newspapers that she found six male clerks at 44 Broad Street and no women except Victoria Woodhull, who was bewitching until she asked for work on the *Weekly*.

"We won't have our paper spoiled by women," said Mrs. Woodhull.

The Princess Editha Gilbert Montez sued Woodhull, Claflin & Company for a ring with three diamonds in it, which she claimed to have deposited at 44 Broad Street. She also claimed to be the daughter of Lola Montez and the King of Bavaria, and had tried to give lectures on her origin. The lectures had been a failure, and now the Astor House clamored for payment of a royal board bill.

Victoria, in a neat brown Holland duster over a black silk dress, fanned herself with a Japanese fan while she testified:

"I am a broker. I know the lady. She came to my office, I think about the time mentioned. She never gave me any jewels or money. I gave her five dollars to pay her board bill to keep her, as she said, from a house of prostitution. She never went to Washington on my business. (As she claimed.) She was entirely lost to truth, and I thought likely to involve me and my friends. I think the girl never had a diamond or knew what a diamond was. She asked me to get her before a New York audience to have her claim as the daughter of Lola Montez supported. In this I assisted her. I warned her against making statements about her mother being poisoned by a gentleman at Flushing; and his retaining her diamonds."

Judge Dowling dismissed the complaint and turned the complainant over to the Commission of Charities and Corrections.

For two months, *Woodhull & Claflin's Weekly* was a fairly gentle woman's paper. Its editorials urged woman to learn to be independent. "Then she will never be thrown on the mercy of the world, nor driven to conditions against which her soul revolts." A translation of "In Spite of All," by George Sand, was its first serial. "As soon as daughters obtain sufficient age, put them to practical tasks, as you do your sons," suggested the second number. It chided Elizabeth Cady Stanton for giving a lecture to "Ladies Only". "It is a pity for women to set the example of discourtesy." In June it began to attack the fashions. "Calves, hips and breasts are padded to make the form more deceptively voluptuous, and thereby appeal more directly to the passions of men." A bold editorial on the social evil appeared on July 2nd, deploring midnight raids, the source of ecclesiastical rents, and recommending police licenses and rigorous visitation. "This is not authorizing sin by statute. It is simply recognizing social and physiological facts." In the same issue was an indication that the *Weekly* could be a weapon:

"When Vanderbilt and Fiske get to work and make sport for the people, how we simple ones laugh. We are told first how Mr. Fiske, most daring of speculators, cornered that profound calculator, the Commodore, on grain transportation at ridiculously low rates; the grain turned out to be cattle, carried over the Central at prices that won't pay for car grease. . . . Meanwhile flour and beef are no cheaper; somebody is making money and sure it is that when Behemoth and Leviathan make up their difference, which they surely will, the public will have to pay for the sport. . . ."

Beautifully printed on the best paper, the *Weekly* was an extravagant enterprise. The Claflins wouldn't economize for it; and though Colonel Blood, who did most of the work at 44 Broad Street, had transferred his energies to it, it had been too colorless to attract a large circulation. Without Colonel Blood, less money came into Broad Street, and the Commodore may have been remiss about tips. After this playful tap, (or a visit from Tennessee) the Commodore was commended for taking the southern mails on his private steam line without remuneration, for presenting the steam frigate "Vanderbilt" to the government, for being ". . . that indomitable, self-shrouded Commodore Vanderbilt, who stands alone in his sphere, the envy of little minds, and the gigantic scoffer of the impudent malice of his enemies."

On September tenth, the *Weekly* started muckraking:

> " . . . We entered upon the 'walks of money, 'change' to do a legitimate business in American securities. . . . We discovered . . . frauds . . . contemplated by petroleum and shoddy bankers, who like scum had risen to the surface in boilings of the dishonest cauldrons of the war. We have employed the ablest detective talent . . . and we are prepared with the names of each party, the description and extent of the frauds perpetrated . . . the amount of bonds and shares in many cases which gratuitously and dishonestly went to each banker, congressman and state legislator. . . . We shall not hesitate to give names, acts, transactions. . . ."

Indeed, many honest men must have welcomed some muckraking. War, with what orators call its purifying flame, had left more than its usual smear of smut. Moreover, with the national expansion of public utilities came a corrupt Congress, corrupt state legislatures, and corrupt city bosses, of whom Tweed of New York was the most infamous only because he had the richest pickings. Suspicious gifts were received in Washington; relatives were boldly favored. State legislatures threatened to introduce outrageous bills to make affected interests pay for peace. A judiciary enslaved by private capitalists permitted the most flagrant stock watering, wildcat selling and railway wrecking. Greenback inflation also stimulated business to excesses, which should have shaken Colonel Blood's belief in fiat money; but at the time, the rascality of capitalism might have blurred anybody's economic thinking.

Woodhull & Claflin's Weekly steadily supported "Victoria C. Woodhull for president, with its whole strength," and it didn't neglect her private life either. She was incapable of writing most of the essays she signed. Stephen Pearl Andrews or Colonel Blood wrote them. But she constantly was consulted, she was the *Weekly's* vitality, its inspiration; she was in sympathy with everything in it that she could understand. The articles on free love, prostitution and abortion certainly expressed her views; for she echoed them in private conversation, and later in public. They began in October with, "Where boundless love prevails . . . : the mother who produces an inferior child will be dishonored and unhappy . . . and she who produces superior children will feel proportionately pleased. When woman attains this position, she will consider superior offspring a necessity and be apt to procreate only with superior men. Her intercourse with others

WOODHULL & CLAFLIN'S WEEKLY.

PROGRESS! FREE THOUGHT! UNTRAMMELED LIVES!

BREAKING THE WAY FOR FUTURE GENERATIONS.

Vol. 4 No. 1.—WHOLE No. 79. NEW YORK, NOVEMBER 18, 1871. PRICE FIVE CENTS.

will be limited, and the proper means will be taken to render it unprolific . . ."

In September the *Weekly* printed a letter from Sarah F. Norton, one of the members of the "Pantarchy," who also was a suffragist.

"I have been busily thinking over your account of that call and its apparent object from Susan B. Anthony, together with the fact that for a long time I have intended to tell you the same disagreeable things that she did. . . . Those men who said the vicious things of you as reported by Miss Anthony are, be assured, men who cannot gain access to you and that is their way of retaliating. . . . Those others who are not 'going to get into scrapes by having anything to do with Woodhull and Claflin' are men who have been taught caution by their previous scrapes with what are generally regarded as 'nice women'. . . ."

Apparently downright Miss Anthony had gone to Victoria to tell her why the National Woman Suffrage Association couldn't work with her. Miss Anthony started something.

The New York papers were not forgetting the sensational sisters. Victoria was in the ascendent now, which didn't bother Tennessee who cared less for prominence than for her merry little ways.

According to the *Weekly* for October 8, a reporter from the *New York Sun* went to 15 East Thirty-eighth Street. ". . . Tennessee with the impulsive gaiety of a gypsy seized the *Sun* reporter and hurried him through the splendid apartments. She speaks with such rapidity that her words seem on a gallop to overtake each other. Her blue-gray eyes flashed with a singular magnetic fire." She showed him "some of the costly garments in which she and her sister sometimes dazzle the multitudes that flock around them", and told him about her clairvoyant feats. Then Victoria Woodhull dressed in a handsome print silk dress invited the reporter into a "Cinderella fairy chamber".

"'I see,' she said, 'you admire my dress. Let me show you the dress I intend to wear in the streets of New York, and at my banking house in Broad Street.'"

"She tripped out of the room, Tennie in the meantime engaging the reporter's attention", and when he turned to see where Victoria had gone, she stood before him in pants of dark blue cloth reaching to her knees, where they buckled over light blue stockings. Her dark blue blouse was knee-length. She wore a shirt-front, collar and cravat, and her hair was cut short like a boy's.

After a pause, the reporter said, "Mrs. Woodhull, if you appear on the street in that dress the police will arrest you."

Red spots dashed into Victoria Woodhull's cheeks. She folded her arms and drew herself erect. "No, they won't," she said, "when I am ready to make my appearance in this dress, no police will touch me."

Evidently Victoria had chosen this for her presidential costume. She knew that a president of the United States was not subject to arrest.

And then Victoria Woodhull met General Benjamin Butler, who was a strong rung in the male ladder she climbed on.

A short stout man was Ben Butler, with a large bald head, a round body and short thin legs. He looked like a gnome, or the king of the gnomes, for there was

GENERAL BENJAMIN F. BUTLER

HER CAMPAIGN BUTTON

power in his domed brow, in his vulture's nose, in every line of his combative face. While his right eye-ball wandered as if on some mission of its own, his left glared warily, with a one-eyed effect that must have suggested Buck Claflin to Victoria. Indeed, Ben Butler had some of Buckman's unscrupulousness with none of his repose.

Butler was a born antagonist. While he was in command of New Orleans after the Civil War, he ordered his soldiers to treat the Southern women as women of the town, if they didn't stop being impertinent. They turned their backs on every Northerner who passed. Remarked Butler, "These women evidently know which end of them looks best." They named him "Beast Butler." But New Orleans never had been as clean, as orderly, nor as healthful.

Ben Butler had wit and courage; he had a brilliant mind and great charm for eminent men who weren't afraid of him. "It is only when they cannot imitate it, that they complain of my sharpness," he said, as if words had to be weapons. During the Civil War, he freed the negroes who entered the Union lines as contraband of war; he always was their advocate. After the war, he was a "Greenbacker" like Colonel Blood, a believer in currency without a fixed standard, which probably brought him in touch with Victoria Woodhull. *Woodhull & Claflin's Weekly* was echoing Colonel Blood's views.

Moreover, Butler was in favor of woman suffrage, and when Victoria told him about that visit from Susan B. Anthony, it was like him to plan a trick, and like Victoria to get an impetus from scorn to triumph by trickery. Her audacity, her beauty, her charm appealed to Ben Butler; her pariah flavor must have aroused him.

On December 21st, 1870, Victorial Woodhull arrived in Washington with a memorial, praying Congress to enact such laws as were necessary to enable women to exercise the right to vote already vested in them by the Fourteenth Amendment to the Constitution of the United States. It was presented in the Senate by Harris of Louisiana, and in the House by Julian of Indiana, referred to the Judiciary Committee and printed.

It was not a coincidence that the National Woman Suffrage Association were to open their third annual convention in Washington on the morning that Victoria Woodhull was to address the Judiciary Committee of the House of Representatives, an official recognition none of them had achieved. The suffragists were amazed when they read about it in the newspapers.

Susan B. Anthony told Mrs. Isabella Beecher Hooker that they ought to go to the hearing and find out what Mrs. Woodhull was going to do. Mrs. Hooker emphatically refused. But she was Senator Pomeroy's guest at the time, and the Senator said, "This is not politics. Men never could work in a political party if they stopped to investigate each member's antecedents and associates. If you are going into a fight, you must accept every help that offers."

The National Association decided to postpone their convention until the afternoon; and on the morning of January 11, 1871, the Honorable A. G. Riddle escorted Miss Anthony, Mrs. Hooker and Paulina Wright Davis into the judiciary room, where they saw Victoria Woodhull. She wore a plain dark dress with

VICTORIA WOODHULL PRESENTING HER MEMORIAL BEFORE THE JUDICIARY COMMITTEE OF THE HOUSE OF REPRESENTATIVES IN WASHINGTON

(From *Frank Leslie's* of February 4, 1871)

a blue necktie, her short brown hair curled under an Alpine hat. She looked so pale, they wondered if she were going to faint; and when she began to read her voice trembled and broke. Suddenly her face flushed; it lighted; beauty gilded it. Her voice cleared, and gathered deep musical tones. Her grace, her engaging manner captivated every man and woman there. Her charm leaped out as if it had antennae.

Judge Riddle addressed the committee after she finished, and Miss Anthony said, ". . . I wish, General Butler, you would say 'contraband' for us. . . ."

That afternoon the suffrage convention opened at Lincoln Hall, and on the platform with Paulina Wright Davis, Isabella Beecher Hooker, Josephine Griffing and Miss Anthony sat Victoria Woodhull and sister Tennessee.

Mrs. Hooker introduced Victoria, saying that it was her first attempt at public speaking, but with her heart in the movement she was determined to try. Victoria came to the front of the platform leaning on Mrs. Hooker's arm. Again her voice trembled and cleared as if at the sound of itself. She apologized for her nervousness, read her memorial and gave a report of her interview with the Judiciary Committee. They had assured her of a favorable report; they said the heart of every man in Congress was in the movement.

During the rest of the convention Victoria Woodhull sat still, so still that a Philadelphia correspondent compared her to "one of the forces in nature behind the storm, or a small splinter of the indestructible; and if her veins were opened they would be found to contain ice."

What thoughts must have filled that stillness! She had spoken at the Capitol of the nation, the first woman ever to speak there officially; she had triumphed over women who had spurned her. They wanted to be friendly now. But suppose some man came along, who had known her and Tennie, in Ottawa, or Chicago or Cincinnati?

The National Association devoted the time usually spent on resolutions, to speeches on woman's right to vote under the Fourteenth Amendment, the amendment that declared that all persons born or naturalized in the United States were citizens thereof, with the privileges of citizens, including the rights of the elective franchise. On account of the "Woodhull Memorial" the National Association decided to assert their rights instead of fighting for them, under a separate amendment. Women were urged to apply for registration and to sue for it in the courts if it were withheld. Many believed the suffrage battle was won. The Republican Party flirted with the new issue, arousing the wildest hopes.

In conservative Boston, the American Woman Suffrage Association shrieked at the National Association's alliance with Victoria Woodhull. Men, shocked at their new convert, swamped the suffragists with letters of protest.

Elizabeth Cady Stanton, who was on a lecture tour, answered one of these, characteristically:

"In regard to the gossip about Mrs. Woodhull, I have one answer to give all my gentlemen friends: When the men who make laws for us in Washington can stand forth and declare themselves pure and unspotted from all the sins mentioned in the Decalogue, then we will demand that every woman who makes a constitutional argument on our platform shall be as chaste as Diana. If our good men will only trouble themselves as much about the virtue of their own sex as they do about ours, if they will make one moral code for both men and women, we shall have a nobler type of manhood and womanhood. . . .

"We have had women enough sacrificed to this sentimental, hypocritical prating about purity. This is one of man's most effective engines for our division and subjugation. He creates the public sentiment, builds the gallows, and then makes us hangmen for our sex. Women have crucified the Mary Wollstonecrafts, the Fanny Wrights, the George Sands, the Fanny Kembles of all ages; and now men mock us with the fact, and say we are ever cruel to each other. Let us end this ignoble record and henceforth stand by womanhood. If Victoria Woodhull must be crucified, let men drive the spikes and plait the crown of thorns."

Later Mrs. Stanton wrote to Lucretia Mott: ". . . I have thought much of Mrs. Woodhull and of all the gossip about her past, and have come to the conclusion that it is great impertinence in any of us to pry into her private affairs. To me there is a sacredness in individual experience which it seems like profanation to search into or expose. This woman stands before us today as an able speaker and writer. Her face, manners and conversation, all indicate the triumph of the moral, intellectual and spiritual. The processes and localities of her education are little to us, but the result should be everything. Most women, who like some tender flower, perish in the first rude blast, think there must be some subtle poison in the hardy plant which grows stronger and more beautiful in poor earth and rough exposure, where they would fall faded, withered and bleeding to the ground. . . ."

Susan B. Anthony, once won all won, declared that Mrs. Woodhull's antecedents were as good as most Congressmen's. Mrs. Woodhull had youth, beauty and money, and an argument any of them might be proud of. Indeed, sturdy Miss Anthony said she would welcome all the infamous women in New York if they would make speeches for freedom.

The Revolution, the organ of the National Association (edited by Laura Curtis Bullard) gave all the credit for the success of the Washington convention to Victoria Woodhull. This convention had attracted new and valuable allies. "Mrs. Woodhull is a lady of talent and enterprise and although the bitter strife of slanderous tongues has assailed her . . . her conduct has been such as to commend her to such women as Mrs. I. B. Hooker, Mrs. P. W. Davis, and others, and this ought to be enough to silence every envious voice of detraction. . . ."

Susan B. Anthony went on a western tour with a lecture called "The New Situation," based on the "Woodhull Memorial." In January the Judiciary Committee reported it adversely, deciding that Congress did not have the power to act. But there was a minority report in its favor, signed by Benjamin Butler and William Loughridge of Iowa, one of the strongest arguments ever written on woman's right to vote under the constitution. Believing that another committee would act differently, the women were not discouraged.

Susan B. Anthony wrote to Victoria, "Bravo! My dear Woodhull. Your letter is here. . . . Glorious old Ben! He is surely going to pronounce the word that will settle the woman question, just as he did the word 'contraband' that so summarily settled the Negro question. . . . Go ahead doing, bright, glorious, young and strong spirit, and believe in the best love and hope and faith of S. B. Anthony."

And Mrs. Stanton wrote her from Tenafly, "I have watched the grand work inaugurated by you in Washington this winter. . . . I read your journal with great pleasure. It is the ablest women's journal we have had yet, discussing as it does the great questions of national life in which it will be necessary for us one and all soon to have clear and pronounced opinions."

The Mercantile Library Association of New York City asked Victoria Woodhull to deliver her "Constitutional Argument." She lectured on suffrage at Cooper Institute to a feminine audience that clapped when she said women were under men's subjugation as the slave used to be. But she was only beginning to get her platform presence, her return to the emotional authority with which she had preached in Homer from the "Mount of Olive."

Next she read a long document on capital and labor at the Labor Reform Convention at Cooper Institute. This must have been written by Stephen Pearl Andrews who had organized a group called "The New Democracy" in 1869, which advocated the referendum and a voluntary socialism (in the *New York Tribune*). "The New Democracy" sent an address written by Andrews to the General Council of the International Working Men's Association in London, pointing out that the (American) National Labor Union was behind the times. "Our organization," said he, "can rightfully claim, both through ideas and by immediate personal affiliations, to be the direct successors . . . of the industrial congress and labor and land reform movement of twenty years ago in this country." The "New Democracy" disbanded in 1870 to reorganize as two American sections of the International, sections nine and twelve. Section twelve became the leading American section. Representing the principles of Stephen Pearl Andrews, it was under the nominal leadership of Victoria Woodhull and Tennessee Claflin.

Vanderbilt, Butler, Andrews or Blood composed all the tunes Victoria played; but she played them with her own expression. Like a musician she rendered the work of others; like an actress she performed in dramas she didn't write. And she chose to do so; she easily could have been the pampered mistress of the rich.

Victoria's first foothold had come through the Commodore, by way of Tennessee. Now she pulled Tennessee into her activities, though Tennessee could not, or would not, adapt to them.

When the New York suffragists called on Victoria, they were enchanted with her mind and manners. But on the way home, one distinguished agitator rebuked her husband.

"My dear," he said mildly, "when you take me into a house where a damsel as plump and pretty as Miss Tennie C. sits on the arm of my chair and leans over until I suspect there is very little if anything underneath the thin mother hubbard she is wearing,—then how can you blame any man for putting his arm around the damsel to verify such a suspicion?"

HENRY WARD BEECHER

(From *A Biography of Rev. Henry Ward Beecher,* by Wm. C. Beecher and Rev. Samuel Scoville, published, 1888, by Charles L. Webster & Co., N. Y.)

COMMODORE VANDERBILT

(From *Certain Rich Men,* by Meade Minnigerode, published, 1927, by G. P. Putnam's Sons)

Most of the liberal thinkers of the day came to 15 East 38th Street to see Stephen Pearl Andrews. They too, were delighted with Victoria, and shocked by Tennie C.

Victoria's family were not a help. She said they extracted money for silence about the two husbands she had at 15 East 38th Street. Actually the situation was blameless, but the public wouldn't find it so. After a long disappearance, Canning Woodhull had turned up in New York, needy and ill from drink, cast off by his own family. With no possible motive except kindness and affection, Victoria gave him a home. He couldn't have been of any erotic interest to anybody. When he wasn't drinking, he looked after his daughter Zulu Maud and took care of the unfortunate boy Byron.

Miss Anne L. Swindell, a school teacher who had come to New York to invest her savings, brought Victoria and Tennie into court again. She had called on the "Lady Brokers" because their *Weekly* advertised that they would help working women. She said she told Mrs. Woodhull she didn't want a speculative investment, and that Mrs. Woodhull assured her they guaranteed women against losses.

Victoria took the stand.

"I am a member of the firm of Woodhull, Claflin, and Company," she said, "and chief directress of the *Woodhull and Claflin Weekly*. I was in the office of the firm at the time the transactions which are the subject of this suit were first opened. . . . I told her it was a risky business, and advised her if she had any money to keep it—the advice I would give any woman, unless she understood the business. . . . I told her 'this may positively result in a loss . . .' After this she came to the office and gave me the money; I accepted it at once and gave it to the colored boy and told him to take it to the Gold Room. Miss Swindell knew at the time that the money was to be invested in gold. . . ."

"Did you tell her that if she lost her money in gold speculation that you would repay her?"

"I did not; I told her I would guard her money as carefully as I would my own; she understood the matter as well as I did, and spoke of the fluctuation of gold. . . ."

"Have you not advertised yourself as a candidate for the presidency?"

"That's not your business, sir; it has no bearing on the case; if the court thinks it has, I shall answer."

There was laughter in the court-room.

Said Miss Swindell's counsel: "Women candidates for so distinguished an office as the Presidency of the United States cannot have time to remember the smaller business matters."

"Perhaps you might not," said Victoria sweetly.

"I am not a candidate for the Presidency."

"Well, I should think not, indeed!" Then Victoria got excited. "You asked the other witnesses if they were strong minded women; now, I'm a strong minded woman, and I would feel insulted if you men thought I was anything else; I claim to be a strong minded woman and I feel proud of it. . . ."

On the third of May, 1871, Victoria had a talk with Elizabeth Cady Stanton, and Mrs. Stanton indiscreetly told a story about some distinguished friends in a neighboring city, whose lives conformed to Victoria's social theories. Heroic Mrs. Stanton was human; who doesn't like to tell gossip? Moreover, Mrs. Stanton was a gracious person, sensitively responsive to another's feelings; she wanted to say what Victoria wanted to hear. And with her background, she couldn't imagine anyone using such a story.

What a contrast her background was to Victoria's, anyway! And yet she, too, was spurred by early slights, though hers were gentle slights. At four, she was brought in to see a new sister and to hear, "What a pity it is she's a girl", and she never forgot it. At eleven when her only brother died she tried to comfort her father, and he said, "Oh, my daughter, would that you were a boy!" She studied Latin, Greek and Mathematics, with a class of boys in the village academy, and when she won a prize in Greek she joyfully took it to her father. "Ah, you should have been a boy," he said. She couldn't go to college; because she was a girl she had to go to Miss Willard's Seminary.

Her mother was the daughter of an eminent colonel in the Revolutionary War, her own father was an eminent judge; Victoria's people were trash. Elizabeth Cady was brought up in a comfortable, orderly household; Victoria in squalor.

It was in 1840, at the World's Anti-slavery Convention in London, when the women delegates were denied votes, that Mrs. Stanton and Lucretia Mott decided to form a society to advocate rights for women. They held their first convention at Seneca Falls in 1848. Three years later, Mrs. Stanton met Susan B. Anthony, who fired the thunderbolts she forged, while she brought up seven children. ". . . How many men," she wrote Susan, ". . . would marry, if woman claimed the right to say when she would become a mother?" And, ". . . My whole soul is in the work, but my hands belong to the family." When her family were old enough, she went on the lyceum circuit. This remarkable woman was a profound scholar and a brilliant speaker. She was as wise as she was witty, but she was impulsive. And impulsively she talked to Victoria Woodhull, who charmed her.

Victoria bewitched Isabella Beecher Hooker. Mrs. Hooker addressed her as, "My Darling Queen," and wrote a letter saying, "My sister Catherine says she is convinced now that I am right and that Mrs. Woodhull is a pure woman, holding a wrong social theory, and ought to be treated with kindness if we wish to win her to the truth. Catherine wanted me to write her a letter of introduction, so that when she went to New York she could make her acquaintance and try to convince her that she is in error in regard to her views on marriage. . . . When she sees her she will be just as much in love with her as the rest of us. . . ."

It was a devilish coincidence that Catherine Beecher called on Victoria to reform her a few days after Victoria's talk with Mrs. Stanton. They went for a drive in the park, and this tiresome, prating, puritanical sister of Henry Ward Beecher's patronized Victoria and attacked her on the marriage question. This arid authoress tried to reform a Victoria who was going to reform the world!

Victoria bluntly told her the names of others who shared her free love views and practised accordingly.

They didn't have enough moral courage to admit it openly. None of those names were strange to Catherine Beecher.

Shocked, amazed and horrified, Catherine Beecher was unconvinced, but she was not in love with Mrs. Woodhull.

The Suffrage Anniversary was celebrated at Apollo Hall in New York on May 11 and 12, 1871. In New York, where Victoria Woodhull was too well known, many women objected to sitting on the platform with her. Mrs. Stanton seated her between Lucretia Mott and herself, "to give her respectability."

Newspapers called it "The Woodhull Convention." Victoria colored it, with her "Great Secession Speech."

". . . If the very next Congress refuses women all the legitimate results of citizenship; . . . we shall proceed to call another convention expressly to frame a new constitution and to erect a new government. . . . We mean treason; we mean secession, and on a thousand times grander scale than was that of the South. We are plotting revolution; we will overthrow this bogus Republic and plant a government of righteousness in its stead. . . ."

Then Victoria got into full swing as an orator. Suppose she didn't write her speech; swept through her personality, it electrified Apollo Hall!

Even gentle Lucretia Mott was moved and won, though that saintly Quakeress had sat next to Victoria under protest. Paulina Wright Davis must have been hypnotized, or she never would have read some intricate resolutions prepared by Stephen Pearl Andrews, at which the papers howled, "free love." Horace Greeley had condemned "The Woodhull" and the *Weekly* in the *Tribune;* on May 12, he said:

"We toss our heads in the air for the Woodhull! She has the courage of her opinions! . . . This is a spirit to respect, perhaps to fear, certainly not to be laughed at. Would that the rest of those who burden themselves with the enfranchisement of one-half our whole population now living in chains and slavery had but her sagacious courage."

Four days later, Roxanna Claflin appeared in Essex police court. "Judge," said she, "my daughters were good daughters and affectionate children till they got in with this man Blood. He has threatened my life several times and one night last November he came into the house in Thirty-eighth Street and said he would not go to bed until he had washed his hands in my blood. I'll tell you what that man Blood is. He is one of those who have no bottom in their pockets; you can keep stuffing in all the money in New York; they never get full; if my daughters would just send this man away as I always told them, they might be millionairesses and riding around in their own carriages. I came here because I want to get my daughter out of this man's clutches; he has taken away Vickey's affection and Tennie's affection from poor old mother. S'help me God, Judge. I say here and I call Heaven to witness that there was the worst gang of free lovers in that house in Thirty-eighth Street that ever lived. Stephen Pearl Andrews and Dr. Woodhull and lots more of such trash."

"Keep quiet, old lady," said her counsel.

"Yes, yes, I'll keep quiet, but I want to tell the Judge what these people are . . ."

Daughter Polly (now Mary) Sparr corroborated these statements. She was asked, "What relation other than that of mother and daughter exists between your mother and Tennie?"

"Something I can't explain, something mysterious and unnatural. There is a different feeling between Tennie and my mother than between any other mother and child I know."

"When did you first notice this feeling."

The question was objected to. Blood said he was Mrs. Woodhull's husband, and that he knew nothing of a woman in Brooklyn who called herself his wife. He denied that he had ever threatened Mrs. Claflin. "One night last fall when she was very troublesome, I said, if she was not my mother-in-law, I would turn her over my knee and spank her." He continued, "I married Mrs. Woodhull in 1866."

Counsel asked, "Was Mrs. Woodhull divorced when you married her?"

"I do not know."

"Were you not afterwards divorced from Mrs. Woodhull?"

"Yes, in Chicago in 1868."

"How long were you separated from her?"

"We were never separated. We continued to live together and were afterwards remarried."

"Have you seen Dr. Woodhull?"

"I see him every day. We are living in the same house."

Counsel asked, "Do you and Mrs. Woodhull and Dr. Woodhull occupy the same room?"

There was no answer.

His own counsel said, "Please tell the court that

Dr. Woodhull lives in the same house and who supports him."

"The firm of Woodhull, Claflin and Company has supported the whole of them," said Colonel Blood. "Mrs. Woodhull's boy received a fall when he was young. He needs his father's medical care and treatment."

All this was aired in the papers.

The next day, Victoria and Tennie appeared in court.

Victoria testified: "Colonel Blood never treated my mother otherwise than kind; sometimes when she became violent he would utterly ignore her presence. . . . The most I ever heard him say was when she would come up to the door and abuse him frightfully as if she were possessed by some fiend, 'If you don't let that door alone, I'll go out and push you from it.' I never knew him to put his hands on her. She left my house on the first of April and went to the Washington Hotel to board. All bills for her maintenance were paid by Woodhull, Claflin and Company. . . . Sparr and his wife induced my mother to leave for their own protection and to excite public sympathy. I have always pitied my mother; she always seemed to have a desire to have her own way and seemed to know better what her children wanted than they did themselves. My father is still living with me. Sometimes, she (mother) would come down to the table and sit on Mr. Blood's lap and say he was the best son-in-law she had. Then again she would abuse him like a thief. . . . The whole trouble was mother wanted to get Tennie back to going around the country telling fortunes, and Sparr and his wife were always telling mother that as long as Blood was around she could not get the girl back. . . ."

Victoria went on to tell how Woodhull, Claflin & Company supported the Sparrs and the Mileses.

Then Tennessee came to the stand. She looked earnestly at the judge, greeted Colonel Blood's lawyer with a friendly nod, stared at the opposing counsel, and gave twenty-five reporters a melting glance.

She said she was a martyred woman. She said Colonel Blood treated her mother too kindly; she didn't see how he stood all her abuse. "My mother and I always got on together until Sparr came to the house. Sparr has been trying to blackmail people through mother. I have been accused of being a blackmailer. . . . I have a lot of letters here supposed to be written by my mother for the purpose of blackmailing different eminent persons in this city. My mother cannot read or write. They were written by this man Sparr. . . ."

"You and your mother have been on most intimate terms?"

"Yes, since I was eleven years old. I used to tell fortunes with her, and she wants me to go back with her to that business. But Vicky and Colonel Blood got me away from that life, and they are the best friends I have ever had. Since I was fourteen years old, I have kept thirty or thirty-five deadheads. Some people in Cincinnati interfered to save me from my good old mother. I am a clairvoyant; I am a Spiritualist. I have power and I know my power. . . . Commodore Vanderbilt knows my power. I have humbugged people, I know. But if I did it, it was to make money to keep these deadheads. . . . I believe in Spiritualism, myself. . . . You better ask some more questions, do! But Judge, I want my mother. I'm willing to take my mother home, now, or pay two hundred dollars a month for her in any safe place. . . . I'm single myself and I don't want anyone else with me but my mother."

During an argument between counsel and judge, Tennie suddenly dashed behind the railing, sprang towards her mother and clasped her in her arms. Mrs. Sparr tugged at the other side of Mrs. Claflin.

Colonel Blood went to Tennessee. "Retire," he whispered, "do retire, my dear. You are only making yourself conspicuous."

Tennessee obeyed, amidst excitement in the court room.

Canning Woodhull testified that Colonel Blood treated Mrs. Claflin well, but she treated him badly.

Decision was withheld.

Colonel Blood took Victoria and Tennie away in a carriage. Roxanna left with the Sparrs, and Canning Woodhull wandered away alone.

Said the *Cleveland Leader:*

"The unsavory piece of scandal telegraphed from New York . . . could hardly have caused much surprise to any one who had paid any attention to the record of Mrs. Victoria Woodhull. Her career as a trance-physician in Cincinnati, her brazen immodesty as a stock speculator on Wall Street, and the open, shameless effrontery with which she has paraded her name in circus-bill types at the head of her newspaper as candidate of the cosmo-political party for the Presidency in 1872—all this has proclaimed her as a vain, immodest, unsexed woman, with whom respectable people should have as little to do as possible. The one unfortunate fact . . . the only one which will justify a public newspaper in alluding to the vile story at all, is that Mrs. Woodhull has for the last six months made herself a prominent figure in the Woman Suffrage Movement. . . . And now that she has gone to the bad, and her shameful life has been exposed, it will follow that the enemies of female suffrage will point to her as a fair representation of the movement. . . . At Cincinnati, years ago, she was the same brazen snaky adventuress that she now is. . . . She is a suffrage advocate because being so made her notorious and her paper profitable."

This "man-fiend," said the *Weekly,* was "welcome to all the reputation you have made from your experiment of vilifying Mrs. Woodhull." The *Weekly* had reported Victoria's triumphs in Washington and New York; it reported her troubles now. Colonel Blood, with five bullet holes in his body, always outflanked the enemy. Led by him, Victoria never skulked.

The issue dated June 3, 1871, came out earlier according to the *Weekly's* custom. It reprinted Henry C. Bowen's attack, from *The Independent.*

"No subject discussed during anniversary week excited so much attention as the question of suffrage for women. . . . The excitement was not a little fanned by the sudden revelation of facts in the private life of Mrs. Woodhull. The facts were no secret before, but legal proceedings brought them into the press. . . ." Mr. Bowen admired Mrs. Stanton, Miss Anthony and Mrs. Hooker but thought them unwise to "have given a prominent place to Mrs. Woodhull, about whose private affairs all gossip is needless. *Woodhull & Claflin's Weekly* with its coarse treatment of all the sacred things of human life is enough to condemn anyone whose name is associated with it. . . ."

The *Weekly* said editorially that Mrs. Woodhull permitted her former husband to reside under the same roof as herself as a sacred duty to him and their unfortunate child.

". . . People should withhold the shafts which they would hurl at her . . . lest they be found fighting against a courageous devotion to principle which it is impossible for common minds to comprehend . . . or is it that Mrs. Woodhull is so unfortunate as to have unprincipled relatives from whom she has suffered everything but death, that Mr. Bowen takes exception to her as a leader in the cause of women? . . . Mrs. Woodhull will always appear when justice calls, even if that be in the police court. . . . She is a lifelong spiritualist and owes all she is to the education and constant guidance of spirit influcnce. . . . She also believes in and advocates free love in the high, the best sense . . . as the only cure for the immorality, lewdness, and licentiousness which may corrode the holy institution of the Sexual Relation.

". . . Victoria C. Woodhull's personal and individual private life is something entirely distinct from her public position. Daniel Webster, William Pitt were bon vivants; they were also great statesmen. . . . If Mrs. Woodhull has valuable ideas . . . what has her past history to do with them?

". . . Three weeks ago we stated in good faith that we did not profess to deal in personalities and private histories. We meant what we said then, and we mean what we say now and we say now just the contrary. We are converts through the merciless treatment we are receiving to the necessity of carrying the war into Africa, and we issue this preliminary protocol in view of an early formal declaration of war. . . . Civilization is festering to the bursting point in our great cities, and notably in New York and Brooklyn. . . . At this very moment, awful and herculean efforts are being made to suppress the most terrific scandal in a neighboring city which has ever astounded and convulsed any community. . . .

"We have the inventory of discarded husbands and wives and lovers, with dates, circumstances and establishments.

"Bankers in Wall Street and great railroad men come early on the schedule. Confidences which are no confidences abound. . . ."

At bay, a tigress snarled.

The two branches of the suffrage party met to call Miss Anthony and others to account for the alliance with Mrs. Woodhull and for the apparent endorsement of her free love doctrines on the platform of the National Association.

Chapter Six

"BECAUSE I AM A WOMAN"

SCATTERED over the country, chiefly among social reformers, *Woodhull & Claflin's Weekly* had about twenty thousand subscribers. To make Victoria's purpose plain to a larger public, she sent what was called a 'card' to the *New York Times* and the *World.*

"Because I am a woman," said she, "and because I conscientiously hold opinions somewhat different from the self-elected orthodoxy which men find their pride in supporting . . . self-elected orthodoxy assails me, vilifies me, and endeavors to cover my life with ridicule and dishonor. This has been particularly the case in reference to certain law proceedings in which I was recently drawn by the weakness of one very near, and provoked by other relatives.

"One of the charges made against me is that I live in the same house with my former husband, Dr. Woodhull, and my present husband, Colonel Blood. The fact is a fact. Dr. Woodhull, being sick, ailing and incapable of self-support, I felt it my duty to myself and to human nature that he should be cared for, and although his incapacity was in no way attributable to me. My present husband, Colonel Blood, not only approves of this charge, but co-operates in it. I esteem it one of the most virtuous acts of my life. The various editors have scandalized me as the living example of immorality and inchastity.

"My opinions and principles are subjects of just criticism. I put myself before the public voluntarily. . . .

"But let him who is without sin cast his stone. I do not intend to be the scapegoat of sacrifice, to be offered up as a victim to society by those who cover over the foulness and the feculence of their thought with hypocritical mouthing of fair professions, and by diverting public attention from their own iniquity and pointing their finger at me. . . . I advocate free love. In the highest and purest sense, as the only cure for the immorality . . . by which men corrupt . . . sexual relations. My judges preach against 'free love' openly, practice it secretly. . . . For example, I know of one man, a public teacher of eminence, who lives in concubinage with the wife of another public teacher of almost equal eminence. All three concur in denouncing offenses against morality. . . . So be it, but I decline to stand up as the 'frightful example.' I shall make it my business to analyse some of these lives and will take my chance in the matter of libel suits. . . ."

Whereupon Theodore Tilton went to see Victoria.

With penetrating affection Horace Greeley called Tilton "Boy Theodore." Like a perennial adolescent, Theodore Tilton was stubborn and easily swayed in turn. In turn he was strong and weak, heroic and sentimental, an idealistic fanatic and a dramatic poseur.

He was born with a silver tongue, but without a silver spoon. He was the son of a carpenter who managed to send him to the Free Academy, but he had to leave before he graduated and go to work. He started as a reporter on the *New York Tribune,* where he was known as a steady young man, a good shorthand writer. He refused a higher salary at the *Herald,* because he would have to work on Sundays. At twenty, he married Elizabeth Richards, a pretty Sunday School teacher in Plymouth Church, Beecher's church, in Brooklyn. Soon Theodore left the daily press for religious journalism and joined the editorial staff of *The Independent,* for which he had reported the sermons of Henry Ward Beecher.

His purple pen suited the period, just as his long blond mane did. It was a florid, hirsute time, when the lyceum bloomed. Preachers, prophets, politicians and poets went on lecture tours. Tilton was an inspiring speaker, and his lectures brought an additional income, which he needed for a large and growing family.

To his charming home in Brooklyn with "And whatsoever house ye enter, ye shall first say, 'Peace to this house' " written over the door, came the ardent thinkers of the day. Tilton had been a fiery abolitionist. Abraham Lincoln had been his friend. He was a leader of the Woman's Rights Movement. Mrs. Stanton, Miss Anthony, Laura Curtis Bullard and many others were devoted to him. He had made his first platform hit introducing Henry Ward Beecher to lyceum audiences. He worshipped Beecher.

Next to himself, Theodore probably loved his wife, a pretty birdlike creature, with soft hazel eyes, a soft warm mouth and a quiet bewitching charm. Steeped in the teaching of Henry Ward Beecher for fifteen years, she was the fruit of his erotic fervor, the flower of his creed.

When her pastor called her house a "placc of peace," and said, "What a pretty house this is! I wish I lived here," she felt as if Christ had blessed it. Evidently, in her emotions, Beecher's image merged with Christ's anyhow.

Henry Ward Beecher was magnificent in his way.

Every Sunday ferry boats, (called Beecher boats) brought throngs from New York to Brooklyn to stand for hours in front of Plymouth Church, filling the streets far up and down, waiting for the ten minute

THEODORE TILTON
(From the portrait by Thomas Le Clear, N. A.)

bell. Then tardy pewholders lost their seats. People crouched on the stairs and filled the vestibule to see a small door in the rear platform slide open, and a chair suddenly pushed aside, as Beecher, wrapped in a long cape, bounded before them. They liked to watch him fling his soft hat on the floor, smell a vase of flowers and sweep the huge church with a long sharp glance.

He was a short, stocky man, compactly built, with a youthful, florid face that burned in the heat of discourse. When he thundered, he stood erect, his eyes flashing as he thumped the table, made of wood from Gethsemane.

Then he would give his peculiar little shrug and tell a story about a drunken man before a judge, and be that drunken man, and make them laugh or cry; or he might be an artisan clinching rivets inside a steam boiler, true to every sound and gesture to illustrate some point.

He was the epitome of religious intoxication, the climax of the revival spirit, toned down by the urban touch, tuned up to a plane of artistry.

Beecher and all his generation had been brought up to fear God, the Terrible Punisher, in shrinking dread of Hell. At Plymouth Church Beecher said one needed only "the all-inspiring love power" to be saved. He had found something for his own needs, and he was generous with it. He developed a mystical theology of universal love as broad as it was vague. With it he fought the doctrine of punishment, which his people wanted to fight; and from his articulate rebellion they took comfort and conviction.

Moreover, Beecher and all his generation had been brought up to associate beauty and joy with the Devil.

Beecher, in his own childhood, never had one toy. Now he collected precious stones and played with them; he bought paintings and fine rugs, and reveled in music; and he went to Tilton's pretty house, especially when his friend Tilton was away.

His own house was harsh enough, with a jealous shrew on the hearth. His wife personified every Puritan trait he wanted to forget.

And since God was love, it was an expression of divinity. To deny it was not only unpleasant to himself, but dangerous to his theology. And it was easy to persuade Elizabeth Tilton that what she demurely called "nest hiding" was ecstasy according to Heavenly plans.

Maybe nest hiding was beyond Elizabeth Tilton's emotional means. Or pleasures sometimes rankle as they fade. Moreover, Elizabeth was subject to soul throbs. So was Theodore. They wrote fervid, tortured letters to one another about their souls, for the transition from Puritanism to Paganism was a shaking enterprise at best. Elizabeth was exacting too. Theodore was self-important. Women with better brains than hers adored him. Maybe she wanted to hurt him. Or maybe it was sheer love of drama. Whatever her motives were, in July, 1870, she told Theodore all about her affair with Henry Ward Beecher, insisting, incidentally, that she was as pure as she ever had been.

With a spurt of Christian fortitude, Theodore forgave her. He forgave his idol Henry Ward Beecher, and resolved, heroically, to do absolutely nothing.

But a silver tongue couldn't keep still, any more than his purple pen could. When Theodore began to lose faith in the church, he lost it publicly. When he began to think about love, marriage and divorce he had to write an editorial about them in the *The Independent,* though it was a religious paper. In the issue for December 1st, 1870, he announced that when "Love departs, marriage ceases, and divorce begins. This is the essence of Christ's idea." It was the essence of free love, too; but Theodore denounced free love, and then said that anyone who wasn't ideally married should be divorced, though further on he said the ideal marriage was beyond man! His readers were as confused as he was, and took it out in being shocked.

And then, what was the use of being a hero, if nobody knew about it?

One day, Mrs. Stanton, Miss Anthony and Mrs. Bullard met the Tiltons at the office of *The Revolution,* the suffrage paper that Theodore helped to edit. Through a misunderstanding, Miss Anthony went home with Mrs. Tilton, and they dined together, while Theodore dined at the Bullards' with Mrs. Stanton. There he told the story of his wife's infidelity, as a phase of social life of interest to reformers.

It interested them. The next evening, when Mrs. Stanton told Theodore's story to Miss Anthony, Susan, too, had a story to tell. Elizabeth Tilton had quarrelled with Theodore over the mistake about dinner. They got excited. Both spoke of having broken their marriage vow. Miss Anthony went to her room. Elizabeth dashed after her, Theodore, enraged, in pursuit. She rushed into Susan's room and bolted the door. When Theodore pounded on it, Miss Anthony said, "If you enter this room, it will be over my dead body!"

And Mrs. Stanton told Victoria Woodhull about this unhappy scene.

There were so many factors in that Brooklyn romance. As soon as Henry Ward Beecher heard about Elizabeth's confession, he decided to break Theodore Tilton because his knowledge was a menace. In danger, Beecher was merciless and clear; he left his mysticism to theology. And he, who had loved Theodore Tilton hated him now, because he felt that he had wronged him. Found out, Beecher forgot that the "all-inspiring love power" was a saving grace.

He conspired with Henry C. Bowen to oust Theodore Tilton from the *Independent*. Henry C. Bowen had told Tilton confidentially that they had the same grudge against Beecher. He, too, had forgiven Beecher, but he, too, hadn't forgotten. However, Bowen wasn't ready to break Beecher yet. Bowen had stock in Plymouth Church and Beecher made it a good investment.

Of course Bowen had to hate Tilton because he had confided in him. And while Tilton had made a success of *The Independent,* Bowen's paper, that editorial on "Love, Marriage, and Divorce," had upset its readers.

Tilton had a wife, four children, and no money. In his extremity, he turned to his friend Frank Moulton, who tried to arrange matters intelligently. Moulton had an immediate influence over Beecher, and Beecher promised him to urge Elizabeth to love her husband again.

Frank Moulton was a practical man with a sense of

fair play. He persuaded Beecher to provide some capital for *The Golden Age*, a new magazine Tilton wanted to start.

Elizabeth Tilton renewed her marriage vow.

Time passed.

Then Victoria Woodhull's "Card" appeared in the *New York Times* and the *World*.

Tilton and Beecher conferred with Frank Moulton about this enemy to their new peace. They decided that Tilton should make a friend of Victoria Woodhull; that he should put her under obligations to silence her.

When Theodore came into her office, Victoria theatrically handed him a copy of her "card" in the *Times*.

"I wish you would read it aloud," she said.

Tilton read, "Because I am a woman . . ." and he shuddered as he read on.

"Do you know, sir, to whom I refer in that card?" Victoria asked him.

"How can I tell to whom you refer in a blind card like this!" blustered Tilton.

"I refer, sir, to the Reverend Henry Ward Beecher and your wife. . . . I read by the expression on your face that my charge is true."

Afterward Theodore Tilton said that Victoria Woodhull's enemies, outside her own household, were strangers. "To see her, is to respect her—to know her is to vindicate her."

Moreover, Elizabeth Cady Stanton, Miss Anthony, even gentle Mrs. Mott, the women Theodore honored, were enchanted with Victoria Woodhull, which hastened Theodore's enchantment. He dedicated himself to making a friend of Victoria with an intensity that earned its reward.

In June he described the leading suffragists, in "A Legend of Good Women," for the *Golden Age*.

"Victoria C. Woodhull is a younger heroine than most of the foregoing . . ." said he. ". . . If the woman's movement has a Joan of Arc, it is this gentle but fiery genius. . . . Little understood by the public, she is denounced in the most outrageous manner by people who do not appreciate her moral worth. . . . She is a devotee . . . a seer of visions . . . a devout communionist with the other world. . . . Her bold social theories have startled many good souls, but anybody who on this account imagines her to stand below the whitest and purest of her sex will misplace a woman who in moral integrity rises to the full height of the highest."

He went on to say that, "Isabella Beecher Hooker, a sisterly confederate of Mrs. Woodhull, is rapidly earning the best reputation in the Beecher family. Her courageous . . . advocacy of woman's enfranchisement, including not merely woman's political but social freedom, is a new proof that a Calvinistic education, if once the soul which it narrows gets broadened, furnishes an intensity of moral conviction . . . it is somewhat singular that Mrs. Stowe (Harriet Beecher Stowe), who does not know Mrs. Woodhull, is writing furiously and unwarrantably against her in the *Christian Union,* while Mrs. Stowe's sister, who does know her, is acting bravely as Mrs. Woodhull's chief co-worker. . . ."

Soon Theodore Tilton was spell-bound too. He, too, was deaf and blind. Neither he nor Mrs. Hooker ever was dumb. And Victoria needed a champion more than an enemy. Her family had almost undone her.

The Commodore was too canny to stick to a family that took its brawls to court where anything might be aired. Others edged away from Woodhull, Claflin & Company.

Victoria took Theodore through her house to show him how bare it was, though people said it was a house of ill-repute. All the glitter and gilt were gone; only necessary furniture was in the occupied rooms. Theodore decided that she was a traduced woman.

He rewrote General Butler's report on "The Woodhull Memorial" for her as a speech in a popular form. He took her to see Elizabeth.

Elizabeth Tilton glowered. She resented having a woman of Victoria Woodhull's reputation in her house.

"Elizabeth, Mrs. Woodhull knows all."

"Everything?"

"Everything," said Theodore.

Elizabeth forced herself to be friendly. She asked Victoria to sit by her side on a low chair, while she sewed on a small checked silk dress for one of the children.

Before she realized it, she was telling Victoria Woodhull her inmost thoughts. Nobody ever did resist the Woodhull witchery when Victoria turned it on. And at last Elizabeth found a woman who understood how she could love Theodore and her pastor too.

"It is just such a revolution in society as would permit the peaceable adjustment of such cases, that I am working (for)," said Victoria.

Elizabeth got up and found a book of poems and gave it to her, and wrote, "To my friend Victoria C. Woodhull, Elizabeth R. Tilton," on the fly-leaf.

It was not long before Elizabeth Tilton detested Victoria Woodhull, because she had fascinated Theodore. No pure wife, however unfaithful, could stand for that.

During the summer of 1871, Victoria and Theodore went rowing together on the Harlem River; they drove out to Coney Island and went in bathing there; they spent long evenings alone on the cool roof of the house in Thirty-eighth Street.

Later Victoria told a reporter from the *Chicago Times* that ". . . he was my devoted lover for more than half a year, and I admit that during that time he was my accepted lover. A woman who could not love Theodore Tilton, especially in reciprocation of a generous, impulsive, overwhelming affection such as he was capable of bestowing, must indeed be dead to all the sweeter impulses of nature . . . for three months we were hardly out of each other's sight. . . . He slept every night for three months, in my arms. . . ."

Victoria gave him a roll of notes and a sketch of her life, which Colonel Blood had written. It was too didactic, and she asked Theodore to revise it. He rewrote it instead, almost at one sitting, in a fine frenzy.

It told a fantastic story of Victoria's childhood. It made a monster out of Canning Woodhull to justify her divorce to a public that wouldn't stand for divorce from a man. She was a candidate for the presidency, in her own mind and in the *Weekly*, and she never hesitated to create a past which she thought would fit her present. Hounded heroines were popular in the 'seventies.

If Canning Woodhull had an imagination and a sense of humor, he might have added some details. He was a member of the household then. And according to a more detached observer than Theodore Tilton was, he never denied Victoria anything he could give her.

But Victoria complained, "You have left out the most important parts. . . ."

"What!" said he, "do you want me to say that you have called a dead child to life?"

"Yes, I do, for to read my life and leave out that incident would be to play the part of Hamlet with Hamlet omitted."

In the back parlor at 15 East Thirty-eighth Street, all through one summer night Theodore worked on the manuscript. He wrote how Victoria ". . . during a severe illness of her son, left him to visit her patients, and on her return was startled with the news that the boy had died two hours before. 'No,' she exclaimed, 'I will not permit his death.' And with frantic energy she stripped her bosom naked, caught up his lifeless form and sitting thus, flesh to flesh, glided insensibly into a trance in which she remained seven hours; at the end of which time she awoke, a perspiration started from his clammy skin, and the child that had been thought dead was brought back to life—and lives to this day in sad half-death. It is her belief that the spirit of Jesus Christ brooded over the lifeless form, and re-wrought the miracle of Lazarus. . . ."

He quoted a letter from Colonel Blood, which described their Spiritualistic habits. "At about eleven or twelve o'clock at night, two or three times a week, and sometimes without nightly interval, Victoria and I hold parliament with the spirits. . . . Victoria goes into a trance, during which her guardian spirit takes control of her mind, speaking audibly through her lips, propounding various matters for our subsequent investigation and verification, and announcing principles, detached thoughts, hints of systems, and suggestions for affairs. In this way, and in this spiritual night-school, began that . . . instruction by which Victoria has risen to her present position as a political economist and politician. . . ."

At breakfast, Theodore read his "account of Mrs. Woodhull" to her family. "They pronounced it perfect."

Did Buckman join the admiring chorus when he heard that, ". . . the father, at times a Mephistopheles, waits till the inspiration of cunning overmasters his parental instinct, and watching for a moment when his ill word to a stranger will blight their business schemes, drops in upon some capitalist whose money is in their hands, lodges an indictment against his own flesh and blood, takes out his handkerchief to hide a few well-feigned tears, clasps his hands with an unfelt agony, hobbles off smiling sardonically at the mischief he has done, and the next day repents his wickedness. . . ."

There was some truth in Colonel Blood's account of their Spiritualistic habits. No doubt the learned, brilliant talk Victoria heard from Stephen Pearl Andrews and his friends seeped into her subconscious mind and came forth, colored with her personality, when she went into a self-hypnosis.

Colonel Blood was a consistent Spiritualist, as well as a consistent free lover, and Victoria's worshipper. He drudged to feed Victoria's fame because she wanted fame, and because her fame might feed the cause of social freedom, his other dream. He had enough philosophic calm, as well as enough self-confidence, not only to live his faith but to feel it. He did not sacrifice his ego for Victoria's happiness because she wanted variety. It gratified his ego for Victoria to live according to his lights. And he had reasons to know that she always would come back to him.

The test of the Colonel's devotion to Victoria was his endurance of Roxanna Claflin.

One morning in June he rushed out of 15 East Thirty-eighth Street, with Victoria and Tennie, Roxanna in pursuit.

"You bloody ruffian, you imp of a devil," yelled Roxanna after him. "You vile free lover, you have ruined my da'ater! I'll have yer life!"

Then she shouted, "My da'aters, come back to your mama! Mama wants you!"

Murray Hill was interested.

The Colonel came back to 15 East Thirty-eighth Street, and went inside.

Roxanna sank down on the stone stoop and when reporters swarmed she talked to them.

". . . Oh, my gals are virtuous. I've given them a Christian mother's example. . . . This Hell-hound Blood . . . said, 'Let's start a bank an' all the brokers on Broad and Wall Streets will deal with you an' take off their hats when yer carriage drives up.' Blood has suthin about him that infaturates and he infaturated my da'aters. Blood says to the gals, let's start a paper. Ye'll get lots of subscribers and when you ride out all them brokers will take off their hats to ye's. . . ."

A reporter suggested that the old lady might go under the stoop and get away from the sun.

"Oh, no," she said, "I'll wait here until my dear gals come home; then I'll run and clasp Tennie to my bosom and say her mamma is waiting and she'll kiss me an' let me in."

When Tennie came back, she ushered the whole crowd indoors. Throwing herself into a chair she ran her fingers through her short hair, and said, ". . . I'm nearly twenty-six years old and yet they treat me as if I had no rights above those of a child of five. I have been the ruin of my relations . . . by giving them blood until they became the merest leeches. For years they have lived this contemptible . . . life, and now enervated and useless like so many bloated corpses, they utter the screams of the infirm when I attempt to clear myself of the dead weight. We will show you up, we will put you in the newspapers, we will ruin you. This has been the cry at every attempt of mine towards independence. . . . I told such wonderful things as a child, that my father made from fifty dollars to a hundred a day at hotels simply by letting people see the strange clairvoyant child . . . not a day passes now but people come to me or write to me and say that what I told them as a child has come to pass. As I grew older and the deadheads accumulated around me, I was forced to humbug. I didn't want to but I was obliged to make money . . . mother was constantly in fear that I would marry and stop the income. I never had any happiness until I came to live with my darling sister Vicky. With Colonel Blood I made fourteen thousand dollars in six months. In all that time I bought myself only two calico dresses."

Victoria came in and said pathetically, "We don't want any scandal. But if we had had the nerve to do our duty years ago it would have been far better. . . . I believe Tennie ought to use the gift God has given her; but not in the mercenary way she was forced to use it. She has no right to prostitute her powers."

At French's hotel, Benjamin Sparr was found nearly nude, his head against the door panel, in a locked room, dead. He had died of apoplexy. And in the room was a pencilled letter, beginning, "Vicky, Colonel, and Tennie included. . . ."

The *New York Herald* printed a letter from Woodhull & Claflin to the Emperor Louis Napoleon.

"Sire:

"We desire to offer to your Majesty the first numbers of our *Weekly*.

"You, sire, are as wise as powerful; you can therefore appreciate and encourage the efforts of those who are honestly seeking to elevate their sex. . . . Woodhull & Claflin."

Chapter Seven

SOCIAL FREEDOM

IN 1871 Victoria Woodhull was not only a storm centre, she was the flag that people waved to express their own sentiments.

Said splendid Mrs. Stanton in *The Golden Age:*

"Some carp at the National Organization because it endorses Mrs. Woodhull. . . . What if foul-mouthed scandal . . . seeks to defile her? Shall we ignore a champion like this? Admit for the sake of argument what all men say of her is true—though it is false—, that she has been or is a courtesan in sentiment and practise. When a woman of this class shall suddenly devote herself to a study of the grave problems of life, brought there by profound thought or sad experience, and with new faith and hope struggles to redeem the errors of the past by a grand life in the future, shall we not welcome her to the better place she desires to hold? . . . The nature that can pass through all phases of social degradation, vice, crime, poverty and temptation in all its forms, and yet maintain a dignity and purity of character through all, gives unmistakable proof of its high origin, its divinity. . . ."

In the *Tribune,* Horace Greeley spoke for the crowd:

"Let her be one who has two husbands after a sort, and lives in the same house with them both, sharing the couch of one, but bearing the name of the other (to indicate her impartiality perhaps) and cause and candidate will be so fitly mated . . . that there will be no occasion even under the most liberal and progressive enlightened regime to sue for their divorce."

Now Horace Greeley was old enough to be irritated at the thought of any change. In 1842, when Albert Brisbane brought Fourierism to the United States, the *Tribune* was its organ. Greeley helped to support a "Phalanx" at Red Bank, New Jersey, which was a community according to Fourier's ideas. Though Greeley protested that it had been modified for America, Fourier's system could not be reconciled with the conventional concept of the family. For years Greeley had been an active member of the New York Liberal Club, a real open forum; he was a close friend of Stephen Pearl Andrews, who had expressed himself freely in the *Tribune.* Margaret Fuller was on the *Tribune* staff for awhile; she was no Madam Grundy. For years any radical idea might have been found in the *Tribune,* whether Greeley agreed with it or not. Now he was violently opposed to woman suffrage, divorce and Spiritualism; and Victoria Woodhull was a red flag for all three.

Woodhull & Claflin's Weekly tried to interpret him:

"Mr. Greeley's home has always been a sort of domestic hell. I do not mean that Mr. Greeley has proved an unfaithful husband. . . . On the contrary he has been held up . . . as a model husband in that particular, and for that reason the fault and opprobrium of domestic discord has been heaped on Mrs. Greeley.—(Referring to Xantippe and Socrates)—Who has ever troubled himself to inquire how much philosopher Socrates or philosopher Greeley has had to do with souring the temper, unstringing the nerves and completely disorganizing the machinery of a delicate woman's organization. . . . Whenever . . . a scold, a nervous, an unreasonable, or even a devilish tendency is developed in a wife, it is well to scrutinize closely the qualities of the husband. . . ."

Then the *Weekly* answered Mr. Greeley, saying,

"Men make very grievous blunders when they encounter free love women. I have myself had to repeatedly free myself of the presence of gentlemen of the press as too intolerable with their lascivious allusions and gross conduct . . . when these same 'gentlemen of the press' have gone home to indite pious and eloquent objurgations against free love. . . . In respect of my domestic relations . . . I was divorced from Dr. Woodhull for reasons which to me were sufficient, but I never was his enemy. He continued to need my friendship and he has had it. My children continued to prize and need his affection and presence, and they have had them."

The *Springfield Republican* said: "The time came when the Woman Suffrage Movement could not afford to carry this woman and her load of vicious thieves." Governor Hawley of Connecticut, wrote an editorial in the *Hartford Daily Courant,* for October 24, 1871 which he dubbed, "A DISAGREEABLE SUBJECT." "We have hesitated whether to advertise a certain disreputable weekly journal in New York which is edited by a woman, by denouncing its real character. It becomes, however, a duty to do it, when we see that the journal is taken and read by woman Spiritists and woman Suffragists, who may shut their eyes to its immorality, and who do introduce it into respectable households where there are virtuous girls . . ."

"There is never," went on Governor Hawley, "in this weekly which prints this stuff in prose and poetry, any editorial dissent from it. . . . It will not do to say that she (Victoria Woodhull) is not responsible for such communications in her paper . . . when we find women in effect declaring the suffrage to be only a means to what we regard as social demoralization, we naturally stop to think . . ." et cetera.

The *Weekly* answered those attacks. Editorially, Victoria said the Suffrage Movement never had carried her; she had given it new life! Moreover, how could love be anything but free? Free love was merely an obvious description, instead of a social conduct. This was Victoria's favorite dodge, when dodging was expedient. The highest sexual relations were monogamic. Victoria only protested against laws that compelled women to have relations with men for whom they had no regard. She protested against men or women who were pure because the law compelled them.

Victoria was not obscure now, but she was almost as much of a pariah as she used to be. Since she was eager for contacts with respectable people, by way of putting her under further obligations to keep the Beecher-Tilton secret, Tilton introduced her to Frank Moulton and his wife. They, too, were charmed with her. They agreed with Theodore that she was a genius, born and reared among rude influences. Refined society would develop her noble nature. They told all this to Henry Ward Beecher, whom Victoria wanted to meet.

Beecher's sisters wouldn't let her alone. She must have been a red flag to all they wished or feared. Harriet Beecher Stowe satirized her viciously in the *Christian Union,* and Victoria told Theodore she would hold Henry Ward Beecher responsible if they didn't stop.

". . . If you wish to answer Mrs. Stowe's attack," said Theodore, "do it in a way of superior gracefulness and gentleness. . . ."

But Beecher was panic-stricken until a "superior graceful" answer was published in the *Weekly*. For he couldn't keep his sisters quiet.

So Tilton wrote to Victoria.

"My dear Victoria:

"I have arranged with Frank that you shall see Mr. Beecher at my house on Friday night. He will attend a meeting of the church at ten o'clock and will give you the rest of the evening as late as you desire. You may consider this fixed. Meanwhile on this sunshiny day I salute you, with a good morning. Peace with you. Yours, T. T."

Later Beecher said Victoria rushed to greet him like a spider to a fly. She held out both hands as was her custom. She knew the power of her touch.

They talked of marriage, and Beecher called it the grave of love. He said whenever he married a couple he felt condemned. But if he said such things publicly, he would preach to empty seats.

Victoria understood him. He didn't have to persuade her that God was love. She knew it. And she wanted Beecher for another rung in that male ladder she climbed on. He was the most important man of his time in the religious field. If he vouched for her, everybody would. Besides she borrowed a phrase from Phrenology and said that Beecher had "Amativeness 8". On a scale of one.

Beecher probably wanted Victoria because she was beautiful and desirable. He wanted to secure her silence too.

Victoria didn't know that a victory over Beecher sometimes was a defeat.

During this period, Theodore Tilton wrote "Tempest Tossed", a novel in which a man, and wife, and child and nurse were marooned on a deserted ship for seventeen years. The peace of it must have seemed ideal to Theodore. They lived on canned food, with which the vessel was amply supplied, and drifted around in the Caribbean Sea until the end of a splendid yarn.

Victoria had told Theodore not to whine over his wife's affair with Beecher, a natural event in the social revolution now taking place. She said, "the dreadful suzz" was "merely a bogus sentimentality, pumped in his imagination, because our sickly religious literature and Sunday School morality and pulpit Phariseeism had humbugged him all his life into the belief that he ought to feel and act in this harlequin and absurd way on such an occasion." She tried to show him that, "a true manliness . . . would glory in protecting the absolute freedom of the woman who was loved . . . and that the true sense of honor in the future will be, not to know even what relations our lovers have with any and all persons than ourselves—as true courtesy never seeks to spy over or to pry into other people's private affairs."

But when Victoria came into the room and saw Colonel Blood with his arms around another woman, she threw a pair of shears at them. She believed in freedom for everybody, but Colonel Blood, the one man she would not share.

And after Victoria met Beecher, Tilton wrote "Sir Marmaduke's Musings":

"I won a noble fame,
But with a sudden frown,
The people snatched my crown,
And in the mire trod down
My lofty name.

. . .

"I clasped a woman's breast
As if her heart I knew,
Or fancied would be true.
Who proved—alas, she too!
False like the rest.

. . .

"So, lest I be inclined
To render ill for ill—
Henceforth in me instill,
O, God, a sweet good will
To all mankind."

When Elizabeth Tilton read this in *The Golden Age,* she wept and said Theodore might as well have mentioned her name.

Meanwhile Victoria's public life went on. She tried to vote in her district, and when she wasn't allowed to, she wrote a letter to the *Times,* claiming her rights under the Constitution.

The Victoria League nominated her for the Presidency of the United States in 1872. The Victoria League was created by the *Weekly,* and in the *Weekly* Victoria accepted the nomination, saying, among other things, ". . . It is true that a Victoria rules the great

VICTORIA C. WOODHULL AT THE POLLS, NOVEMBER, 1871, ASSERTING HER CONSTITUTIONAL RIGHT TO VOTE
(From a sketch by H. Balling)

rival nation . . . on the other shore of the Atlantic, and it might grace the amity just sealed between the two nations, and be a new security of peace, if a twin sisterhood of Victorias were to preside over the two nations. . . . I have sometimes thought . . . that there is . . . something providential and prophetic in the fact that my parents were prompted to confer on me a name which forbids the very thought of failure; and as the great Napoleon believed in the star of his destiny, you will at least excuse me, and charge it to the credulity of the woman, if I believe also in fatality of triumph as somehow inhering in my name. . . .

Victoria C. Woodhull."

Tennessee decided to run for Congress from the Eighth Congressional District in New York.

A large crowd from Wall Street, including Henry Clews, came to hear her address her would-be constituents, who were Germans. Her speech was brief, but her voice was singsong and indistinct, her German execrable.

". . . I am the first woman who has ever presented herself before an appreciative public in this or any other country with words of such significant import," she began modestly. ". . . It may surprise you that I resort in the first instance to the German people. . . . I am descended from the German Stock and feel instinctively attracted to those of that nationality. . . . I know that the Germans are especially receptive to cosmopolitan ideas . . . Under the amendments, women are already entitled to vote. . . . It is part of my object to make this case a test."

Woodhull, Claflin & Company published "The Origins, Tendencies and Principles of Government," by Victoria C. Woodhull, and "Constitutional Equality, A Right of Woman", by Tennie C. Claflin. Both were nicely bound in brown cloth.

Victoria's book included the *Herald* papers, some weighty conclusions on capital and labor, and others on "Tendencies and Prophecies of the Present Age", which were revised from *The American Workman.* Its readers probably thought them learned and deep instead of vague and confusing. They had that curious metaphysical attitude towards "elements" that muddled the era, but they probably helped to make Victoria Woodhull a goddess of learning as well as a queen of beauty in the minds of American workmen. Into their homes went her loveliest photograph; and when historians for the American Labor Movement went around the country to gather documentary material, they found one of those photographs treasured by every old labor leader.

When Tilton's "Account of Mrs. Woodhull" appeared as a "Golden Age Tract," *Harper's Weekly* said: "If apples are wormy this year and grapes mildew, and ducks' eggs addle, and bladed corn be lodged, it may all be ascribed to the unhallowed influence of Mr. Tilton's life of V.W."

Its extravagant grotesqueries shocked Theodore's lyceum audiences; its casual attitude towards the Woodhull-Blood union appalled them. Which Theodore would have forseen if he could have seen anything but Victoria when he wrote it. She had a way of blinding men.

It damaged Victoria's reputation instead of restoring it. Tilton's "Account of Mrs. Woodhull" was not good campaign literature, and yet it brought Victoria a presidency.

Hitherto Victoria had had no connection with any state or national association of spiritualists. But her spirit adventures in the Tilton biography moved the National Society of Spiritualists to invite her to their Eighth Annual Convention in Troy. They were thrilled by that "Golden Age Tract."

They were so thrilled by its subject when they saw her and heard her at Troy, that they elected her president of the association. And Victoria had another eager audience.

She told the readers of the *Weekly* that ". . . the new president of the National Society of Spiritualists begins her presidency with a profound sense, not only that she has been made the surprised recipient of the chief honor of her life, but that she is thus called officially to the most congenial service which her soul's ambition could desire on earth."

Later an editorial appeared in the *Weekly* to tell how ". . . these irreverent persons, and the malicious press will awake some morning . . . to learn with surprise, if not with dismay, that the armies of Spiritualism with whom they have long been battling with apparent success have been organized into a solid phalanx ready to be hurled upon them to once and forever destroy their too long continued resistance to the onward march of the world of ideas . . ." A few weeks later the *Weekly* explained the mission of spiritualism. ". . . One of the first facts of spiritualism is to make the spirit life more tangible. . . . It demonstrates the fallacy of the existence of the orthodox heaven and hell. . . . The churches and the politicians may sneer at the intentions of the spirit world, but they will do well to remember that it is in arms and impatiently waits the signal to move upon their stronghold. . . . All will be action and whoever joins not in the movement, will be crushed beneath its weight."

Victoria threatened a hostile world with a host militant from the otherwhere!

At Vineland, New Jersey, "The Equal Rights Party" held a convention, which resolved to support "The Victoria League," and its candidate, Victoria C. Woodhull, for the Presidency of the United States. Most of the members of "The Equal Rights Party" were readers of the *Weekly,* Spiritualists, "Pantarchians", or stray radicals.

At Cleveland, Ohio, Victoria spoke to three thousand Spiritualists on Woman Suffrage. As usual many went to condemn and stayed to call her a "rapt idealist," with "impassioned thought," a "sibyl of politics and spiritualism."

At Plymouth, Massachusetts, she told the state Spiritualist Convention that "Children are the points to which our most earnest efforts should be directed. . . . They have something more than minds to be developed, they have souls as well, and bodies in which they must perforce reside. Each should receive its proper and equal share of culture. . . ." She urged parents to instruct their children. "If our houses of prostitution were searched and their inmates questioned, none would be found whose mothers had the good sense to teach them the objects and functions of their sexual systems. . . ." And, "Children . . . are made curious to just the extent the means of satisfying that curiosity is difficult. . . . This results in a morbid condition of the mind about it. . . ."

Meanwhile William West published a manifesto in *Woodhull & Claflin's Weekly* on behalf of section twelve of the International Workingmen's Association, known as the Woodhull-Claflin section. The manifesto was issued without the authority of the central committee. Section one of the International protested against this "appeal to the citizens of the union" which advocated woman suffrage, sexual freedom, universal language and the "Pantarchy." Fourteen sections met and dissolved the central committee and then reorganized a federal council to exclude section twelve, inasmuch as section twelve were neither wage laborers nor interested in labor questions.

Assembled workmen always upheld the family and the home. The German and Irish sections protested to the London Council against Victoria Woodhull and Tennie C. Claflin's practise and advocacy of free love. Karl Marx expelled the one delegate who voted to retain section twelve in the council. Section twelve organized a council of its own.

When it was announced that Victoria Woodhull was going to lecture on "The Woodhull Memorial" at Hartford, Connecticut, the home of Governor Hawley and Catherine Beecher, a letter appeared in the *Hartford Courant,* for November eleventh.

"A Lady of Hartford" stated that the ladies of that city were confronted with a moral problem: could they support a woman who maintained that when a wife and mother loved elsewhere, she should forsake her family for that love, who maintained also that a woman who fulfilled conjugal duties after that specific love was gone, was guilty of prostitution. "Can any Christian woman . . . sanction in any way the efforts of such a woman . . ." asked "A Lady of Hartford," obviously referring to sentiments Victoria had expressed to Catherine Beecher.

On November 13th, "Fair Play" reminded the readers of the *Courant* that Mrs. Woodhull had addressed an audience of four thousand people in Cleveland. Many had disagreed with her views, but none could find fault with the character of her speech. She had said nothing to offend. "She is too much of a lady for that." Moreover, her lecture in Hartford would be based on those political and social questions advocated by "that portion of the woman suffrage party which she leads" concluded "Fair Play" who sounded like Colonel Blood.

The next day, "A Citizen of Hartford" wrote to the *Courant* to say that while the disreputable conduct charged against Mrs. Woodhull was the kind that never can be proved by eye-witnesses, her opinions, her character and her past history were well-known, and so was her "violation of decorum" in her intercourse and language with men.

"As to her past character and history as given by her friend of the *Golden Age*, it has not been favorable to the cultivation of feelings of delicacy and propriety.

". . . she is acting according to her principles in living as a wife with a man from whom she has been divorced . . . that they might bear a testimony against legal marriage in their present union.

". . . and she has associated with herself in business and seeks to introduce into society, a sister who exceeds her in indecencies.

". . . Will the citizens of this place patronize such a person when she comes expressly to seek the ballot in order that laws may be made to promote such principles and practices?"

Whereupon seven hundred citizens went to hear Victoria Woodhull at the Hartford Opera House. While Theodore Tilton's audiences wanted uplift from the editor of a religious paper (many thought him a minister), Victoria's audiences went to be shocked. They must have been disappointed in her political discourse at Hartford, until she read that letter from "A Citizen of Hartford."

"My friends," she cried, "I had intended to say something in reply to Miss Catherine Beecher's article . . . but I remember that it is a purely personal attack, differing from the recent one of Governor Hawley's, which called in question something more than a personality. Miss Beecher told me . . . she would strike me. She has done so, but now, instead of returning the blow, I will present her with my other cheek, with the hope that even her conscience will not smite her for speaking so unkindly of me as she has. . . . She may profess Christ, but I hope I may exceed her in living his precepts."

It was said that Beecher paid cash for those coals of fire.

Victoria believed in social freedom. She found an ecstasy in causes far beyond the notoriety she got from them, the ecstasy of losing oneself to gain the infinite, the ecstasy of defying futility with power. Such volcanic power had to come from primitive passion to appeal so elementally; it had to be terribly sincere to be so intense. She had to be excited to excite her hearers; she had to burn with every flame she kindled. Her oratory was paroxysmal, jammed with such passionate impulses to proclaim, that when she released them she jerked people out of the everyday world.

Stephen Pearl Andrews wrote the speech called "Social Freedom," and Colonel Blood probably wrote a letter that went to Henry Ward Beecher:

"Dear Sir:

"For reasons in which you are deeply interested as well as myself and the cause of truth, I desire to have an interview with you, without fail, at some hour tomorrow. Two of your sisters have gone out of their way to assail my character and purposes, both by the means of the public press and by numerous private letters written to various persons with whom they seek to injure me and thus to defeat the political ends at which I aim.

"You doubtless know that it is in my power to strike back, and in ways more disastrous than anything that can come to me; but I do not desire to do this. I simply desire justice from those from whom I have a right to expect it; and a reasonable course on your part will assist me to it. I speak guardedly, but I think you will understand me. I repeat that I must have an interview tomorrow, since I am to speak tomorrow evening at Steinway Hall and what I shall or shall not say will depend largely on the result of the interview. Yours very truly, Victoria C. Woodhull.

"P. S. Please return answer by bearer."

Colonel Blood was fervent about social freedom now that he fought for it. He was a fighter by nature. And in his philosophy Victoria and the cause justified any means. That guarded note was a plain threat, but if it worked and Beecher introduced Victoria's speech on "Social Freedom" at Steinway Hall, Victoria would soar, and so would the cause.

But the great preacher would fall, and he knew it; he wouldn't be a rung on anybody's ladder.

Alone with Beecher in his study, Victoria argued.

"I should sink through the floor," said he, "I am a moral coward on this subject and I know it; and I am not fit to stand by you, who go there to speak what you know to be the truth. I should stand there a living lie."

Beecher got up on the sofa, on his knees beside her, and taking her face in his hands, he begged her to let him off.

In disgust she left him. She had no patience with cowardice; one trait she never had. And doubtless it hurt her vanity that she had caught one fly who got no web on his wings. And the man who hurt Victoria's vanity had to suffer.

Beecher took that ominous letter to Frank Moulton, with all his other troubles. Moulton, his confidant as well as Tilton's, was working for peace without hysteria.

Moulton arranged for Beecher to meet Victoria at his house. Tilton rushed there when he heard about the letter. He told Beecher to introduce Victoria without involving himself; he could say that he disagreed with her views but believed in her right to express them; thereby, said Tilton, Beecher would fix Victoria's gratitude. He said this might be Beecher's last chance to save himself from ruin. Both realized that Victoria threatened to illustrate her theories with the Beecher-Tilton story.

But Beecher only moaned, "Oh . . . if it must come, let me know of it twenty-four hours in advance, that I may take my own life. I cannot, cannot face this thing!"

Such a senile threat, such a whine for pity must have worked on somebody in Beecher's past. He used it so often. But emotional appeal was his forte.

It was Victoria's also, and it didn't impress her. She turned on her heel and said, "Mr. Beecher if I am compelled to go upon that platform alone, I shall begin by telling the audience why I am alone and why you are not with me."

Huge posters announced:

"FREEDOM! FREEDOM! FREEDOM!

"In Its Last Analysis

"The Social Relations

"If it is good in the Religious and Political Sphere

"Who shall deny that it is good in

"THE SOCIAL SPHERE?

"For the express purpose of silencing the voices and stopping the pens of those who, either ignorantly or willfully, persistently misrepresent, slander, abuse and vilify her on account of her outspoken advocacy of, and supreme faith in, God's first, last and best law,

"VICTORIA C. WOODHULL
"WILL SPEAK AT
"STEINWAY HALL
"MONDAY NOVEMBER 20
"AT EIGHT P.M. ON
"'THE PRINCIPLES OF SOCIAL FREEDOM'
"INVOLVING THE QUESTION OF
"FREE LOVE, MARRIAGE, DIVORCE AND
"PROSTITUTION

"She wishes it to be distinctly understood that freedom does not mean anarchy in the social relations any more than it does in religion and politics; also that the advocacy of its principles requires neither abandoned action nor immodest speech.

"Horace Greeley, Governor Hawley of Connecticut,
"and the Boston Exclusives
"are specially invited to seats on the platform.
"All her lesser defamers should secure front seats."

The night of November 20th was wet and stormy, but by seven o'clock the entrance to Steinway Hall was jammed. The stairs swarmed with people. In the dimly lighted hall, cat-calls and rough by-play annoyed the respectable.

One red-haired girl bounced in, threw off her shawl, and raised her voice: "I hope, by gosh! I haven't come here for nothing in all this rain."

Victoria and Tennie received the reporters in an ante-room. Victoria wore a dark dress, a fresh tea rose at her neck. With suppressed fire she told a *Herald* reporter she was glad to see him. "That paper has never misrepresented me, and I know it won't now," she said.

Tennie agreed. She too, was dressed in black, and with a dextrous movement as sudden as her speech, she showed a tiny pair of feet encased in gaiters.

Victoria presented the *Herald* reporter with a tea rose.

Then Theodore Tilton came in with Frank Moulton.

It was ten minutes before eight. In the hall, three thousand people waited.

Flushed with excitement, Victoria took hold of Tilton's arm. "There isn't a brave man in the circle of two cities to preside at my meeting!" she said.

She didn't have to remind him of what would happen if she went on the platform alone.

Members of the "Pantarchy" trooped in to encourage Victoria. Stephen Pearl Andrews bade her "Godspeed."

Victoria started for the hall. Tennie followed her, with the reporters. Suddenly Tilton strode ahead.

Frank Moulton cried out, "Are you going to introduce Mrs. Woodhull to the audience, Tilton?"

"Yes, by heaven," said the blond poet, "since no one else has the pluck to do it!"

"Now, Vicky, be calm," Tennie warned her, loudly, and the audience clapped.

Tennie went to a box on the right of the stage, with some ladies of the "Pantarchy." In the left stage box, sat sister Utica Brooker with her friends.

Victoria walked timidly onto the stage, and from every seat, from every foot of standing room, came deafening applause. A hundred men stood and leaned over the platform.

Theodore Tilton led Victoria forward, and said:

"Ladies and gentlemen: Happening to have an unoccupied night, which is an unusual thing for me in the lecture season, I came to this meeting actuated by curiosity to know what my friend would have to say in regard to the great question which has occupied her so many years of her life. I was met at the door by a member of the committee who informed me that several gentlemen had been applied to particularly within in the circuit of these two or three neighboring cities; to know whether they would occupy the platform and preside on this occasion. Every one had declined, one after the other, for various reasons, the chief among them being—first, objections to the lady's character; I know it, and believe in it, and vouch for it. (Applause and a few hisses.) As to her views, she will give them to you herself in a few minutes, and you may judge for yourself. It may be that she is a fanatic; it may be that I am a fool; but, before high heaven, I would rather be both fanatic and fool in one than to be such a coward as would deny a woman the right of free speech. (Applause.) I desire to say that five minutes ago I did not expect to appear here. Allow me the privilege of saying that with as much pride as ever prompted me to the performance of any act in fifteen or twenty years, I have the honor of introducing to you Victoria C. Woodhull, who will address you upon the subject of social freedom."

In a clear, even voice Victoria sketched the fight for individual freedom since the sixteenth century. Stephen Pearl Andrews hovered around the foot of the stage, following her words on a manuscript.

When she came to the present time, she lifted her curly head, like a horse champing at the bit. Charged with feeling her voice deepened, and a thrill went through the crowd, as she said: ". . . The court holds that if the law solemnly pronounces two married, they are married. There is no analogy in nature.

. . . The law cannot compel two to love. . . . Two people are sexually united, married by nature, united by God. . . . Suppose after this marriage has continued an indefinite time, the unity between them departs. Could they any more prevent it than they could prevent the love which came without their bidding? . . . All compelling laws of marriage are despotic, being remnants of the barbaric age in which they were originated, and utterly unfitted for an age . . . so enlightened in the general principles of freedom and equality, as is this."

Two crimson spots burned on her cheeks. Her blue eyes blazed like black fire. There was no use for Stephen Pearl to follow her words on the manuscript now. Few of them were there.

"Suppose a separation is desired because one of the two loves and is loved elsewhere? . . . If the union is maintained by force at least two of them, probably three are unhappy. . . . It is better to break a bad bargain than to keep it. . . . All that is good and commendable now existing would continue to exist if all marriage laws were repealed tomorrow."

The audience burst into wild applause and cheered. Then hisses crept in, and more hisses. The applause got louder, the hisses fiercer.

Victoria flashed to the front of the platform. "If any gentleman or lady in the audience who is hissing—" she said.

"It is not a gentleman or a lady," a voice interrupted her.

"If the gentleman or lady will come on the platform with me," Victoria went on, amidst shouts of "Hurrah!"

Victoria's own sister, Utica Brooker arose, in the left stage box. She turned the prettiest face imaginable to the audience, and calmly, resolutely, said in a sweet clear voice, "May I speak to her?" She asked Victoria, "How would you like to come into this world without knowing who your father or mother was?"

Victoria's spell shattered. And those to whom free love was anathema, hating themselves for having yielded to it, applauded Utica wildly. She was their deliverer. Men shouted. Women waved handkerchiefs.

But Victoria was not dismayed. She leaned over the edge of the platform and waved her slender arms. "There are thousands of noble men and women in the world today, who never knew who their fathers were," she cried.

Again hand-claps vied with hisses.

Utica sat down, alone in the box. Her friends had melted away.

Victoria continued her speech: "You are shouldering on free love the results that flow from precisely its antithesis, which is the spirit, if not the letter of your marriage theory, which is slavery and not freedom. . . . I have a better right to speak, as one having authority in this matter . . . since it has been my province to study it in all its various lights and shades. Hundreds, aye thousands of desolate, heart-broken men as well as women have come to me for advice. . . . The tales of horror, of wrongs inflicted and endured . . . compelled me to consider whether laws which were prolific of so much crime and misery . . . should be continued. . . . I came to recommend the grant of entire freedom to those who were complained of as inconstant; and the frank asking for it by those who desired it. My invariable advice was: 'Withdraw lovingly, but completely all claim and all complaint as an injured and deserted husband or wife. . . . Be kind to and sympathise with the new attraction, rather than waspish or indignant. . .'."

Again Utica arose. Because she was so pretty, because men were uncomfortably stirred by her stormy sister, they applauded her.

Victoria's friends called for a policeman to put Utica out, which was not paradoxical for advocates of social freedom who believed that one person should never infringe on another's rights. And they knew that Utica hated her prominent sister; she might say anything.

An officer sheepishly entered her box. Utica stood and waited, a satirical smile on her dainty lips. Victoria went on with her speech. When the policeman laid a big hand on Utica's arm, Victoria's audience cried, "Shame!" But as the policeman tried to get Utica out of the box, she looked him full in the eyes, and bewitched him with a smile. He let her alone.

"Three cheers for Brooker! Brooker! Brooker!" yelled the crowd.

Victoria beckoned to Theodore. He looked frightened, but he got up from his chair, and Victoria led him to the footlights. She pulled at him until he began to speak.

"There sometimes occurs a moment," said he, "in public meetings when a chairman has to have all his energies about him. You have seen a policeman step into the balcony and lay his hands upon a woman. . . ."

"Put him out!"

"Brooker!"

"Brooker! Brooker!"

They wouldn't listen to him.

Victoria went to the right side of the stage where her friends were. "Tennie, can't you get Utie to go out?" she asked.

As the uproar subsided a little, Theodore said that it was right enough for the lady to speak. "I am her sister," interrupted Utica. But Tilton continued, "I am in the chair. I would myself ask her to come down on the platform and address you, (cries of "Yes! Yes!") for I believe in free speech, but as this meeting was called for the lady who was speaking when this rather pleasant interruption occurred, shall I again introduce her?"

Victoria stepped to the front. Tilton returned to his seat, his hands in his hind coat pockets. Utica sat down.

A fury now, Victoria was vehemence unrestrained. Words not in the printed speech poured on the audience like a hot blast. She said free love would be the religion of the future. She said it was the natural sequence of social freedom.

"Are you a free lover?" somebody shouted.

"YES! I AM A FREE LOVER! (Howls, hoots, hisses and cheers broke loose, and above it all, Victoria's voice rang like a bell) I HAVE AN INALIENABLE, CONSTITUTIONAL, AND NATURAL RIGHT TO LOVE WHOM I MAY, TO LOVE AS LONG OR AS SHORT A PERIOD AS I CAN, TO CHANGE THAT LOVE EVERY DAY IF I PLEASE! And with that right neither you nor any law you can frame have any right to interfere; and I have the further right to demand a free and unrestricted exercise of that right, and it is your duty not only to accord it, but as a community, to see that I am protected in it. I trust that I am fully understood, for I mean just that and nothing less."

The hall fairly rocked.

"I deem it a false and perverse modesty that shuts off discussion and consequently knowledge, upon these subjects. . . . So long as they (women) knew nothing but a blind and servile obedience . . . to the will and wish of men, they did not rebel; but the time has arrived . . . wherein they rebel, demanding freedom, freedom to hold their own lives and bodies from the demoralizing influence of sexual relations that are not founded in and maintained by love. And this rebellion will continue too, until love, unshackled, shall be free to go forth, it shall be respected as holy, pure and true. . . . None too soon will the yoke fall by which the unwilling are made to render a hypocritical obedience to the despotism of public opinion, which, distorted and blinded by a sham sentimentality, is a false standard of morals and virtue, which can only be fostered and cultivated by freedom of the affections.

"Free love, then, is the law by which men and women of all grades and kinds are attracted to or repelled from each other, and does not describe the results accomplished by either. These results depend upon the condition and development of the individual subjects.

". . . Promiscuity in sexuality is simply the anarchical stage of development wherein the passions rule supreme. When spirituality comes in and rescues the real man or woman from the domain of the purely material, promiscuity is simply impossible . . . the very highest sexual unions are monogamic . . . the highest kind of love . . . is utterly freed from selfishness . . . whose highest gratification comes from rendering its object the greatest amount of happiness, let that happiness depend on whatever it may. . . . An affection that does not desire to bless its object instead of appropriating it by a selfish possession to its own uses, is not worthy of the name of love. . . .

"I dearly prize the good opinion of my fellow beings. I would so gladly have you think well of me. It is because I love you all . . . that I tell you my vision of the future . . . that I . . . disturb your confidence . . . in the old dead . . . past. . . .

". . . The love that I cannot command is not mine; let me not disturb myself about it, nor attempt to filch it from its rightful owner. . . . Shall I forcibly capture the truant and transfix it with the barb of my selfish affection and pin it to the wall of my chamber? Rather let me leave my doors and windows open, intent only on living so nobly that the best cannot fail to be drawn to me by an irresistible attraction."

None who heard Victoria Woodhull on the night of November 20th, 1871, doubted her sincerity. And if some of the light was Stephen Pearl Andrews', all of the heat was hers.

Afterward Theodore Tilton said, "It was not the printed speech that did the damage, it was the interjected remarks in response to the audience; she said violent things." In Plymouth Church a group wanted to expel Tilton for his association with "The Woodhull." They didn't know that he purposely was expelling himself by prolonged absence, according to the church rules. But in the lecture field, his engagements were cancelled, invitations were withdrawn. He met repugnance and prejudice everywhere.

And the Claflins had to leave 15 East Thirty-eighth Street and live in a boarding house. Society rejected social freedom. All outside support from Wall Street or elsewhere was withdrawn. Though the scandal that ruined Theodore in the lecture field made Victoria a sensational success there, her family and the *Weekly* were drains no lecture receipts could stop. And still they kept up the *Weekly*.

Chapter Eight

"THE WOODHULL"

IN *Woodhull & Claflin's Weekly* women could read about a lady contractor in New Hampshire, or a postmistress at West Point or any milestone on the road to feminine freedom. The *Weekly* probed the social evil when other papers ignored it, though commercialized prostitution was as blatant in the 'seventies as it was vicious. The famous abortionist, Madam Restell, plied her trade in a Fifth Avenue mansion, and she and her colleagues published guarded advertisements in leading journals, which never dealt with the subject otherwise except when one of its victims was found coffined in a trunk. The *Weekly* dealt with it constantly and seriously, and suggested that women be taught physiology. It reprinted the famous letters Henry James exchanged with Andrews in the *Tribune,* and a correspondence with Carlyle on the labor question. It exposed insurance frauds and bond swindles. The strike in the anthracite district of Pennsylvania was analysed in the *Weekly,* and a public which couldn't have been reached elsewhere was asked whether the high price of coal was due to the strikers' demands or to the exactions of the carrying company! The *Weekly* condemned writers who had inspired France to fight Germany for territory the peasants would bleed for. It expressed the enlightened radicalism of its day; and yet it aired any gabble about clairvoyant healing, and promised incredible milleniums; it published any letter commending Victoria Woodhull, and it was used as a weapon. Like Victoria herself it was silly and venomous and sublime.

In the issue of December 16, 1871, appeared a letter from "Mary Bowles" to Victoria Woodhull:

" . . . The brave words uttered at Steinway Hall . . . have touched the hearts of thousands of degraded women with a thrill of joy and hope . . . that speech is the cause of my addressing you.

"I was reared in more than ordinary comfort . . . and was not . . . left wholly uneducated. But at twenty years of age, by a train of circumstances . . . an uncongenial marriage, an abandonment, inexperience, desperation, total want of comprehension and sympathy by my own family—by my own folly, if you will—I found myself the inmate of a house of ill-repute in this city. . . . I conceived an intense indignation . . . for society which had condemned and excluded me, and for men especially, in their mean and hateful treatment of women of our class—intimate with and caressing us in private, and coolly passing us without recognition before the world. . . .

"I discovered in myself a shrewd business capacity, and after a few years . . . I found myself the successful mistress of a house of the kind of what I had been an inmate before.

" . . . From the time that I opened my house . . . a first-class house—I have kept a . . . record of the men who have visited it. I had no distinct thought of ever using the information against them, but it gave me, somehow, a sense of power over them, which was a happiness to me. I finally procured a large ledger, and subsequently a second . . . and entered in a business way the names and residences and some of the incidents of each visit of all the visitors at my establishment . . . they deceived me, and I went so far as to keep a man engaged in tracking them to their homes, offices or hotels, and ascertaining who they were. . . .

"My business has been successful but I am tired of it. I am arranging to break it up and to go . . . to Europe. . . . If you, in the prosecution of your blessed mission as a social reformer, have any need to see more behind the scenes and to understand the real state of New York society better, I will give you access to my two big books, or would even leave them with you in my absence. You will find in them . . . doctors of divinity to counter-jumpers and runners for mercantile houses. . . .

"With love and admiration, Mary Bowles."

Tennie answered this letter.

"My dear sister:

"My sister Victoria is at the West on a lecturing tour, and it falls to me to answer her letters. . . . Perhaps I, even more than Victoria, am interested, as a specialty, in the social question. She has taken on herself more fully the political career . . . when I was a little child, the spirits announced that Jesus Christ was born to save the world, and I was born to convince the world. . . . My mother has always treasured that saying in her heart, and believes that I was born to accomplish some wonderful mission. . . . To me, it has never seemed as anything, until of late, it has begun to come often in my mind that, perhaps, I may be called on to . . . shame the world out of its cruelty to unfortunate women. . . . I don't see or feel the difference between them and . . . the men who debauch them. . . . I live on Murray Hill, quite among the respectables, and am visited continually by all classes, from the family of the President, and from clergymen and their wives, and the presidents of colleges, down to the most humble, and I shall be happy to receive you at my home alone, at any time, with others of your class; and shall be . . . willing to accompany you on the street, or dine with you at the restaurant as if you were in all respects, the first ladies in the land.

" . . . I curse and denounce a virtue which is forced on women as slaves, by men who are themselves confessedly steeped in the same vice. . . . I have to associate with male prostitutes in my business, in the family, everywhere, and if I then condemn and avoid women of equally bad character am I not glaringly false and traitorous to the dignity and equality of my sex . . .?

" . . . In respect to the books you speak of, I do not know what use can be made of them, for my sister and myself have scrupulously adopted the policy of avoiding personalities when possible. But the time may come when that policy will have to be abandoned, for our enemies do not scruple to resort to them in the most scandalous manner.

"I will arrange through your messenger and otherwise on that subject.

"Very truly your friend, Tennie C. Claflin."

Afterwards Tennie admitted that she had written the "Mary Bowles" letter as well as the reply, and she had several motives for writing them. She sincerely resented the social attitude towards prostitutes, and the exoneration of the men concerned; moreover, the Claflins needed money, and that horrible ledger might be alarming enough to produce some. Nobody knew who Mary Bowles might be! Or maybe it was all sheer audacity.

Tennie was not shy in those days. She appeared before Judge Shandley at Jefferson Market Court, and charged her father, Buckman Claflin, and her mother, Anna Claflin, with disturbing the peace. She complained that they had ignored a summons she had procured in the morning. She merely wanted their removal from the house, where they annoyed her and other residents. She offered to pay twenty-five dollars a week for their board elsewhere.

An officer was sent for them. With a faith in the law only equalled by her sister's faith in the newspapers, Tennie seemed to think a summons would settle all her family troubles. Buckman's children had seen him take everything to court, but Tennie might have known he wouldn't be taken there. The officer came back without him or Roxanna.

The newspapers reported this entertaining performance without comment. It needed none.

When Tennie C. made her debut as a public speaker, a mob of ten thousand people swarmed into the Academy of Music to hear her. Women in costly capes jostled against women in shabby shawls or gaudy silks. Bankers, merchants, hack-drivers and boot-blacks clamored for seats. The manager sent word to the police that the building was tottering.

It didn't fall, though Tennie said marriage was an unnatural state.

The lecture was called "The Ethics of Sexual Equality" and it was a sensible speech, appallingly frank for 1872. Tennie C. had learned to speak since her Congressional fiasco; her voice was pleasing and clear. She never had Victoria's hypnotic power but she had her own charm and a spirit of irony that won her audience. They cheered when she ridiculed marriage, and, as her hack drove off, they gave her a "regular tiger".

Meanwhile *Woodhull & Claflin's Weekly* teased and tortured Henry Ward Beecher.

On January 6th, 1872, it said editorially that nobody had as much influence as Henry Ward Beecher despite his radical theology. It regretted that a table which the spirits had used for communication had been removed from Plymouth Church, the church that was destined to enact a great rôle in the cause of spiritual truth. All that could be done to shut it back would only make it more startling when it came! The *Weekly* regretted that Mr. Beecher lacked the moral courage to introduce spirit-life into the lifeless creeds of the established church.

No wonder Mr. Beecher sought Elizabeth Tilton and the all-inspiring love power again. No wonder he said he knew he was going to die soon. He said it in the pulpit and he said it to his friends.

And if "The Woodhull" extorted money from him as his family always claimed, in the *Weekly* for April 6, 1872, might be found her defense.

It was an editorial comment on an article in the *New York World,* in which a woman who had tried to get money out of a parson "by so-called false pretences" was attacked.

The woman who "avenges the oppressions of her sex by what is called blackmailing," the *Weekly* compared to Rob Roy, "the great Scottish blackmailer" who "was urged to this resort as his only means of sustaining himself against his enemies.

" . . . Since men . . . are howling unmercifully against those of my sex who have recourse to this only method of righting themselves," the writer, ("One who knows" according to the signature) was "in just such a frenzy", detesting "the villainy which tries to shield itself by raising an outcry against the natural defense of its victim . . . these women who resort to blackmailing have by base treatment of the other sex had all the love of their natures converted into hate. . . . As long as man is only a cunning animal and exercises no other faculty in his intercourse with such women as he dares to outrage, can it be expected that they will not meet cunning with cunning, fraud with fraud. If the laws will not protect women, they must protect themselves by the same crude justice that invented the blackmail system of the Scottish borders.

" . . . The term beat (describes) . . . an individual who adopts every device to cheat women out of those favors which so many of them are forced to sell as their only means of maintenance . . . he will declaim of the beautiful woman he possesses 'all for love'. . . . Let every beat who has been blackmailed remember how many more times by his cheating of women he has deserved a repetition of this treatment. . . .

" . . . I know a man of wealth . . . a deacon of the church. . . . He is an ignorant fellow, fond of that bawdy talk which is pure obscenity, without any relief of wit or humor. . . . A young girl . . . being absolutely forced to obtain money at any cost, made up her mind to go to an assignation house. Never having been to such a place before she requested me to go with her. As I believe that all places should be known to the wise, I did not hesitate to accompany her. She was there introduced to Shank, who after treating us to wine, retired with my companion. This rich and pious deacon gave to this necessitous girl, to her terrible disappointment, but half the price usual in the house. She complained to me, and but for my remonstrance he would not have given the balance, which he afterwards did.

"Away with the nonsense about personalities! This attempt to cover up the crimes of individuals against defenceless women is criminal. General statements are of no avail. The mask must be stripped from the visages of these hypocrites and night prowlers, who are raising in the newspapers the cry of blackmail to cover up their own scoundrelisms, that women may not be able to say to them effectively, so as to touch that fear of the world's opinion, which is their only conscience and restraint, 'Let him who is without sin among you, cast the first stone.' Indeed, I say to my sex, 'Have you been deceived, maltreated, abandoned, or to comprise it all in one word—beat, write out your experiences, state the plain truth, give names and incidents with all possible particularity. Send these statements to *Woodhull & Claflin's Weekly* that they may be published and sent broadcast over the land; that like Cain wherever one of these men go, his infamy may follow him, so that the publicity of his crime may incite him to retrieve his disohonor, or deter others from his acts. . . .'"

Such a hearty invitation was evidence that "One Who Knows" was closer to the *Weekly* than a mere correspondent.

In December Victoria Woodhull marched in the memorial demonstration of the International Workingmen's Association, in honor of Rossel and his companions, who were executed at Versailles by the Thiers Government. Stephen Pearl Andrews and Theodore Tilton, too, were among the six hundred who walked silently from Cooper Union to Thirty-fourth Street. In the procession went a funeral canopy, drawn by six gray horses draped in black. "Honor to the Martyrs of the Universal Republic" was painted on the wagon, and inside was a platform on which a mahogany coffin stood draped in red. All the Internationals wore red ribbons or red ties; and Tennie C. carried one of the red banners.

Victoria repeated the "Social Freedom" speech in Boston where she told another howling mob that she was a free lover and that she had a right to change her love as often as she pleased.

And yet, when the National Suffrage Association convened in Washington on January 11th, 1872, onto the stage with Elizabeth Cady Stanton and Susan B. Anthony, stepped Victoria Woodhull, in a blue broadcloth suit with a double breasted chinchilla cloth coat.

The National Association now assumed, according to 'The Woodhull Memorial,' that women had a constitutional right to vote.

After Mrs. Stanton and Miss Anthony had addressed the Convention, Victoria told them about the relation of spiritualism to political reform. Like her English namesake, she used the third person.

" . . . The President of the National Association of Spiritualists stands as the present bearer of the standard of the Equal Rights Party. . . . She has, as gallantly as she knew how, breasted the dark clouds and storms that have risen over her path, but she has done so devoutly and reverentially, always recognizing that she is but an humble instrument of those who command the armies of Heaven and desire the conquest of the individuals of the earth; though sometimes weary and almost fainting by the wayside, by the help of the good angels she will neither permit the banner to trail in the dust, nor resign it until the victory is either won or another braver, stouter, and better shall be sent to bear it. . . .

" . . . All people in whose souls there has dawned a comprehension of the better government which shall descend from heaven, long foretold by prophets and seers, should rally to the overthrow of everything that is against the spirit of the new and the true. . . ."

Isabella Beecher Hooker said that if the spiritualists had brains enough to comprehend and soul enough to come up to the position to which Victoria Woodhull invited them, they would rule the world.

During the evening session, Victoria made a speech and proposed a "Constitution of the United States of the World", which was a sort of foretaste of the League of Nations.

Miss Anthony never shirked an issue. She didn't care about the history of any man or woman who worked for the movement. "I will take by the hand every prostitute I can find who seeks to escape the inequalities of that law which places all womanhood at the mercy of manhood." She said when she heard about a woman on Wall Street she wanted to see how a woman looked among the bulls and bears.

"Who brought Victoria Woodhull to the front? I have been asked by many, why did you drag her to the front?

"Now bless your souls, she was not dragged to the front; she came to Washington from Wall Street with a powerful argument and lots of cash behind her, and I bet you cash is a big thing with Congress. (Uproarious applause.) . . . If it takes youth, beauty and money to capture Congress, Victoria is the woman we are after.

"I have been asked, all along the line of the Pacific Coast, what about Woodhull? You make her your leader? Now we don't make leaders, they make themselves. If any can accomplish a more brilliant effort than Victoria Woodhull, let him or her go ahead and they will be leaders." (Applause.)

But Miss Anthony stated that they did not endorse temperance, labor reform or Spiritualism. Woman Suffrage was their platform.

Isabella Beecher Hooker recited a touching poem about a stained hand that might save man because it would work where white hands feared to go.

An attractive, earnest reformer was Laura Cuppy

Smith, who said she was not a hero-worshipper, but when she alluded to Victoria Woodhull, "my whole soul does homage to the principles of which I deem this grand woman to be the inspired representative."

In fact, though the convention attended to other matters, it is no wonder that Victoria thanked them for their approbation "with a heart too full for utterance". When they interrupted Stephen Pearl Andrews to call for "More Woodhull", after he had finished his speech, she said, ". . . there are many friends here who have come from distant places, having earnest words to say to you, and whom I, equally with you, should desire to hear. Thanking you for your appreciation and encouragement, I shall go home from this convention more determined than ever to push the car of progress."

But when Mrs. Addie Ballou of Wisconsin arose and nominated Victoria for the presidency of the United States, Miss Anthony said it was a little premature.

In the lobby of the Senate, Victoria met Matt Carpenter. Charging him with treachery to the cause of women, she threatened to organize them against him.

"The women of Wisconsin are all my friends," said Senator Carpenter.

"Yes?" said Victoria. "And if rumor speaks truly, you have lady friends belonging to other states."

Whereupon Carpenter suggested that she would get into Fortress Monroe if she were too free with her revolutionary schemes.

"All right," said Victoria. "If your people think that's a good thing to do, do it. I have no objections."

She told him they would get five hundred female orators to go around the country and tell the people about the characters of the men now misrepresenting them.

From there Victoria went to the home of William Ellery Channing. Mr. Channing and his wife were out, but their small daughter came into the sitting room to find an enchantress sitting on the floor playing blocks with her little brother. Victoria couldn't stay long enough to wait for their parents, but the children never forgot her. They thought her the most beautiful, the most fascinating person they ever had seen.

Then came *Harper's Weekly* with Victoria Woodhull cartooned as Mrs. Satan. A visiting Frenchman criticized American women, and Horace Greeley told him not to judge them by the "Woodhull Brigade of the Advanced Cohorts."

On the twentieth of February Victoria lectured at the New York Academy of Music on "The Impending Revolution."

The streets near the building were almost impassable by seven o'clock. The doors opened a half hour later, and people were wedged into the hall at the rate of a half-yard a minute. Women cried: "My ribs are going in!" "My pocket!" "My hoops!" and "My poor feet!" Men and women fell over one another. One of the gallery doors gave way. Speculators jammed through the crowd offering tickets, but the doorkeeper was too pressed to collect tickets anyhow. Throngs were turned away.

Victoria walked on the stage alone, while the crowd cheered and jeered. She looked charming with her curly hair floating nearly to her shoulders. She wore

"GET THEE BEHIND ME [MRS.] SATAN!"
(Victoria Woodhull cartooned by Thomas Nast in *Harper's Weekly* for February 17, 1872)

a black dress with three flounces and a panier, under a cutaway jacket, and a large blue neck-tie.

She smiled, flushed, and read distinctly from notes. She said the impending revolution was a struggle between the authority and injustice of the present, and the freedom, equality and justice of the future, based on the proposition that humanity is one. She blamed the slavery of the laboring classes on railroad and money monopolies, and on minority representation.

"A Vanderbilt," said she, "may sit in his office and manipulate stocks or declare dividends by which in a few years he amasses fifty million dollars from the industries of the country, and he is one of the remarkable men of the age. But if a poor, half-starved child should take a loaf of bread from his cupboard to appease her hunger, she would be sent to the Tombs. . . . An Astor may sit in his sumptuous apartments and watch the property bequeathed to him rise in value from one to fifty millions, and everybody bows before his immense power. . . . But if a tenant of his whose employer had discharged him because he did not vote the Republican ticket, fails to pay his month's rent to Mr. Astor, the law sets him and his family into the street. . . . Mr. Stewart, by business tact and the various practices known to trade, succeeds in twenty years, in obtaining from customers, whom he entraps into purchasing from him, fifty million dollars and . . . builds costly public beneficiaries, and straightway the world makes him a philanthropist. But a poor man who should come along with a bolt of cloth which he had smuggled into the country and which consequently he could sell at a lower price than Mr. Stewart, who paid the tariff, and is thereby authorized by law to add that sum to the price, would be cast into prison. . . . Now these three individuals represent three of the principal methods that the privileged classes have invented, by which to monopolize the accumulated wealth of the country."

While Victoria was speaking, a correspondent of *The American Spiritualist* saw a large band of spirits dressed in white, waving red and white flags over her head, a vision which signified liberty for the children of earth and equality for all.

But if the *New York Tribune,* the *Standard,* or the *Times* saw any visions, they didn't mention them, nor did they mention Victoria, nor "The Impending Revolution," nor her gigantic audience, which was a news story in itself. The *Sun* and the *World* described the audience, and referred to Victoria in passing. The *Herald* flippantly described Tennie C. flying from box to box, and said she had "few brains and much hair."

All of these papers had devoted nearly two columns to Victoria's "Social Freedom" speech. Though it was shocking it was exciting to attack marriage and the family; they must have considered an attack on property rights unmentionable.

Two days after the meeting the *Times* came out with a double leaded editorial called "A Lamp Without Oil," which suggested that while Mrs. Woodhull had been married more extensively than most American matrons, like the foolish virgins who provided lamps without oil, she tried to light the dark places of politics and ethics, without reason.

" . . . Her periodical exhibitions of bitter language upon the platform attract numbers of idle people . . . she is, moreover, the accepted representative of a large section of the party which advocates female suffrage, and as such is tacitly supported by men and women who dislike her parade of Communist fanaticism, and abhor her hostility to social morality. She is, therefore, capable of mischief in inflaming the unthinking hostility of the poor to the rich, and in fostering in the minds of the working men who applauded her during her recent lecture, the conviction that capitalists have no rights which working men are bound to respect.

"Mrs. Woodhull singles out for especial abuse, Messrs. Stewart and Astor—omitting to mention Mr. Vanderbilt among her rich oppressors of the poor. . . . When her best black silk and her jaunty sealskin jacket, her diamond rings and her golden necklaces, her dainty high-heeled boots, and her most cherished chignons have cracked and burned and melted in the fire, the intelligent workingmen of the city will at least credit her with a desire not to enjoy luxuries which she has not earned by manual labor. . . ."

It was particularly significant that Victoria Woodhull did name Mr. Vanderbilt among the oppressors of the poor. Moreover, in the many descriptions of her costumes, no jaunty sealskin jacket ever figured. And as she wore her hair short like the Empress of Austria and other women of her time, she certainly had no chignon. But a hostile press didn't bother with accuracy.

As Victoria's fortunes waned, her interest in Communism waxed. Back in Ohio, she had suffered because she was an outsider. Now she joined a cause for every phase, which meant a group to belong to, as well as a public to confide in, and a public to impress. Victoria was grimly gregarious.

Causes were not hard to find at a time when many who rebelled against the harsh religious training of the 'forties and 'fifties created outlets for the energy its mystic conflicts had induced. And Victoria led them not only because she was so vivid, not only because she picked ideas from such brainy men, but because she expressed herself directly. Her subjectivity was as simple as roast beef, and just as nourishing. No tortured twisting diverted any of her power.

When the unemployed held a mass meeting in Tomkins Square to celebrate the anniversary of the uprising of the Commune, leaders of the International joined the cries for "Vic Woodhull!" in spite of the split with section twelve. At the banquet in Houston Street that night, Victoria's plea for the political organization of labor was the first speech.

Canning Woodhull had been in the habit of taking morphine. When he got sick, his doctor stopped it and he died.

Utica Brooker told the doctor she didn't blame him. "But I intend to take revenge on the family," said she.

The coroner was informed forthwith that Dr. Woodhull had died under suspicious circumstances. He went to 118 West Twenty-third Street, where the Claflins lived now, and Margaret Ann Miles told him and the reporters that Utica Brooker and Mary Sparr were trying to do up the rest of the family. But a post-mortem examination showed that Dr. Woodhull had died of pneumonia.

All this was repeated to the readers of the *Weekly:* how "unscrupulous persons" not only had threatened to betray Canning Woodhull's presence in her house, they had done it relentlessly, when she rebelled against their tyranny; and how they ended their "insatiable vengeance in endeavoring to convey to the public that he whom we had sheltered and protected in defiance of public opinion during his life, had been foully dealt with by us in his leaving of it.

". . . The deceased . . . was one of the most skillful physicians . . ." his obituary went on to say, ". . . no clearer nor better testimony of the deep regard, aye, love, he had for our present husband, could be had than the care bestowed upon him during several violent attacks of sickness, and no better assurance of trust and confidence on his part than that he would permit no other physician to prescribe for him. These two people were not rivals. They were brothers; and in spite of all the attempts made to make them enemies, they remained friends to the last, he who is still with us, watching over the death-bed of him who has gone, with all the sleepless anxiety that danger imparts to those who love. . . ."

Nothing interfered with Victoria's cosmic plans.

During that spring of 1872 Miss Anthony was lecturing in the West. While she was waiting at a little railroad station in Illinois, somebody handed her a copy of *Woodhull & Claflin's Weekly*. To her amazement it announced that "the undersigned citizens," responding to the invitation of the National Woman Suffrage Association, proposed to hold a convention at Steinway Hall, New York, on May 9th and 10th, to form a new political party, to declare the platform of such a "People's Party," and to nominate candidates for President and Vice-president of the United States, "who shall be the best possible exponents of political and industrial reform. . . ." "The undersigned citizens" were,

Elizabeth Cady Stanton, Isabella Beecher Hooker, Matilda Joslyn Gage, and Susan B. Anthony.

Miss Anthony sent an indignant telegram demanding that her name be removed from a call to which it had been signed without her consent.

Nobody fooled such a wary campaigner! Some time ago she had written to Mrs. Stanton and Mrs. Hooker: ". . . Mrs. Woodhull has the advantage of us because she has the newspaper, and she persistently means to run our craft into her port and none other. If she were influenced by women spirits . . . I might consent to be a mere sail-hoister for her; but as it is, she is wholly owned and dominated by men spirits and I spurn the control of the whole lot of them. . . ."

The regular anniversary meeting of the National Association was to be held at Steinway Hall, New York, on the ninth of May. Miss Anthony hurried to New York and got Mrs. Stanton from Tenafly. As soon as the suffrage committee opened for its business session, Victoria Woodhull appeared and announced that the "People's Party" would convene jointly with the National Association. Miss Anthony said they would not. She denied them the use of Steinway Hall.

Completely bemused by Victoria, Isabella Beecher Hooker told Susan she was a bigot. Mrs. Stanton said she was narrow.

"The People's Party" engaged Apollo Hall.

The Suffrage Convention had a small crowd, and Mrs. Stanton resigned her presidency. Miss Anthony was elected in her stead; and just as she was about to adjourn the first evening session, Victoria Woodhull glided on the platform from the side, and moved that "this convention adjourn to meet tomorrow morning at Apollo Hall." An ally in the audience seconded the motion, but Miss Anthony refused to put it. An appeal was made from the decision of the chair. Mrs. Woodhull herself put the motion and it was carried overwhelmingly. Miss Anthony declared the proceeding out of order, as neither the seconder nor the majority voting were members of the Association. She adjourned the convention to meet in the same place the next morning, and as Victoria went on talking, she ordered the janitor to put out the gas.

About six hundred delegates gathered at Apollo Hall to form "The People's Party." They represented extreme radical organizations throughout the country. Some were *Weekly* readers who had become Victoria's followers. Some were free lovers, some were Spiritualists, some were Communists, and others were suffragists who had deserted Miss Anthony. And yet, a few were there because they thought she signed the call!

Judge Reymart of New York took the chair. Resolutions prepared by Stephen Pearl Andrews were read. "The Equal Rights Party" was adopted as a permanent name. And Victoria Woodhull was asked to address the evening session.

She addressed it fervently. Aroused by her fight with Miss Anthony, she drew her slender figure taut, her face flushed, her eyes gleamed and glowed. When she raised her arms with a tragic gesture, many thought of the great Rachel.

". . . From this convention will go forth a tide of revolution that shall sweep over the whole world . . . what does freedom mean? . . . the inalienable right to life, liberty and the pursuit of happiness. . . . What is equality? It is that every person shall have the same opportunities to exercise the inalienable rights belonging to the individual. . . . And what justice? That the alienable rights belonging to individuals shall be jealously guarded against encroachment. . . . Shall we be slaves to escape revolution? . . . away with such weak stupidity! . . . a revolution . . . shall sweep with resistless force, if not fury, over the whole country, to purge it of political trickery, despotic assumption, and all industrial injustice. . . ."

And then such words poured forth as only come from a mind aflame, and if it were alight with sparks from other minds, it was kindled by the throng she fired.

She paused and said clearly, "Who will dare to attempt to unlock the luminous portals of the future with the rusty key of the past!"

The audience sprang to their feet and cheered, responding as people always will to a winged phrase that flutters through every root and rhythm.

Judge Carter of Cincinnati stepped to the front of the platform, and nominated Victoria C. Woodhull for President of the United States. "All in favor of the nomination say aye," said he.

The hall roared "aye." Excited women sobbed. Men shouted themselves hoarse and jumped on their seats. Handkerchiefs waved, and hats. Crowds rushed in from the street to find out what the tumult was, and stayed to yell "Victoria!" too.

At last Victoria came back to the platform, and bowed with all her grace, though she was trembling.

"I thank you from the bottom of my soul for the honor you have conferred upon me tonight. I feel

VICTORIA C. WOODHULL NOMINATED FOR THE PRESIDENCY OF THE UNITED STATES BY THE EQUAL RIGHTS PARTY, AT APOLLO HALL, NEW YORK CITY, ON MAY 10, 1872
(Illustration from a pamphlet called "One Moral Standard for All," by M. F. Darwin)

it all the more deeply, as I have stood by you so long, sometimes meriting your applause, and sometimes encountering your rebuffs, but I have been always faithful to my principles and without saying more, I again thank you for the great honor you have shown me. . . ."

They wrangled over the candidate for Vice-president. Finally Moses Hull, of Louisville, Kentucky, nominated Frederick Douglass, the Negro reformer. ". . . We have had the oppressed sex represented by Woodhull, we must have the oppressed race represented by Douglass!"

A man shouted, "I move the nomination of Spotted Tail. Indians ought to have a voice here before the Negroes!" A woman yelled. "Let Colonel Blood go to Washington with Mrs. Woodhull. It is not well for man to be alone."

But it was decided that Frederick Douglass should be Victoria's running mate.

The *New York Herald* published a letter from Tennie C. to Joseph Tooker, Manager of the Grand Opera House:

"Dear Sir:

"I understand that the colonelcy of the gallant 9th Regiment of the National Guard made vacant by the death of James Fiske, Jr., still remains unfilled. . . . I protest that it would be a wrong to the memory of the dead leader to select as his successor any one who lacks the magnetic influence he possessed over his soldiers. . . . Your connection with the Grand Opera House brings you in social contact with the committee having the selection of colonel in hand. See the gentlemen please, and tell them I will accept the position and pledge myself, if elected, to give such impetus to recruiting, that in thirty days the 9th Regiment will be the foremost in the state.

"There can be no objection to me, save that I am a woman. Permit me to remind those who urge it that Joan d'Arc was also a woman. While I do not make pretentions to the same military genius she possessed, I may state that it has always been my desire to become actively connected with the service, and I have always gratified a passion for studying its rules and tactics, in which I am well versed.

"I have no doubt that this communication will at first sight occasion incredulity as to my intentions, but permit me to assure you I am deeply and forcibly in earnest in the matter.

"Yours very sincerely,

"Tennie C. Claflin."

Mr. Tooker turned the letter over to the captain of the regiment to which Mr. Tooker did not belong.

At this point the *Times* was entertained by the sensational sisters. "That there should be two such (in a family), jointly working at the same time, would surpass belief, did not the fact stare one in the face."

But they, or the idea of equal rights, must have alarmed the Grand Opera House. Though it had been rented for a mass meeting, it refused to allow the Equal Rights Party to hold one there.

Victoria formally accepted the presidential nomination in a long letter in which she (or Stephen Pearl Andrews, or Colonel Blood) stated that politics must give way to sociology and that her special function was breaking down the old to usher in the new; and that her spiritual pre-vision revealed views she looked on with dread. "Is it possible that they (the wealthy and well to do) can believe that the working men and women are not in earnest in their demands, and that nothing but a bloody commune will convince them?" She pledged herself to secure the success of the party.

The ratification meeting was held at Cooper Union on June sixth and every seat, every inch of standing room, was filled. Company A of the Veteran Guard, and Company C of the Spencer Grays, both colored troops, seated themselves on the platform. Mrs. Belva Lockwood and others spoke. Victoria delivered a stirring oration and she was followed by Captain Thomas Griffin of the Spencer Grays.

Captain Griffin referred to the "American noblemen" who had bled for so many years for his oppressed race, and how much they had accomplished. "But . . . through the unceasing efforts of two noble women, Woodhull and Claflin, despite discouraging opposition . . . the world has been forced to recognize the existence of this party that guarantees equal rights . . . to every intelligent, respectable being in the land, without regard to caste, condition, or sex." He said that colored military organizations in the city had tried for two years to organize a respectable battalion, but no "military gentlemen" would help them. Now ". . . a union of the separate bodies, numbering upwards of four hundred men, has been completed, and has resigned position in the command in favor of Miss Tennie C. Claflin as colonel of the battalion."

To the tune of "Comin' Thro' the Rye," Victoria's constituents sang:

"Yes! Victoria we've selected
For our chosen head:
With Fred Douglass on the ticket
We will raise the dead.

"Then around them let us rally
Without fear or dread,
And next March, we'll put the Grundys
In their little bed."

But they didn't. The Grundys were vigilant. Long before the next March the Equal Rights Party was in a little bed, from which it never arose.

Chapter Nine

CELL II, LUDLOW STREET JAIL

IN THE early annals of the Claflin sisters, the charge of blackmail appears as persistently as murder in the annals of the Borgias, to whom accusations must have been as casual as the deed was common. Fifteenth century Rome reeked with murder. After the Civil War, American cities reeked with blackmail too.

There had been the usual post-war fling, without any ethical reconstruction to insure it against disaster. Popular behavior was wanton while popular morals were rigid; which meant that half the people were in terror of being found out by another half, who gloated over sins they couldn't or wouldn't commit. The average person cared more for his reputation than his character, and on such an attitude blackmailers thrived.

Blackmailers wrote to men they never saw, threatening to expose indiscretions that never happened, and men paid and had to keep on paying. It was a side line for fortune-tellers, professional clairvoyants and many boarding-house keepers. Abortionists pried names out of their patients and got money from both. Pretty widows had kisses that "stung like adders" and hands that were "greedy of gold," according to a contemporary commentator.

Then any beautiful woman who seemed to live by her wits was accused of blackmail. Moreover, it is possible that members of Victoria's family signed her and Tennie's name to threatening letters. Tennie testified in court that one of them had done so. And if detectives had indictments for blackmail against the sisters as was claimed, why did they never serve them?

On the other hand *Woodhull & Claflin's Weekly* printed a defense of blackmailing, and it usually expressed Victoria's views. It denied, not too convincingly, a statement that Susan B. Anthony had made concerning five hundred dollars Victoria had tried to borrow from a Mrs. Phelps in May, 1872. According to this story, Mrs. Phelps didn't give her five hundred dollars because she didn't have it; but Victoria printed a slanderous circular about her and other suffragists from whom she had tried to get money. Miss Anthony was blunt of tongue and angular of body, but her integrity was unquestionable. And the sum of five hundred dollars and the slanderous circular appear in two other stories, one told under oath on the witness stand.

Victoria Woodhull and Theodore Tilton were both given to heroics. Such a theatrical relationship as theirs must have been couldn't last very long.

Victoria told him that within six months he would fall away from her.

"By all that is good, never!" swore the blond poet.

He was away on a lecture tour nearly all winter, and when he returned in June, Laura Curtis Bullard showed him the proof of an article put in type for *Woodhull & Claflin's Weekly,* assailing her reputation as well as other suffragists'. It was called "Tit for Tat."

The *Weekly* announced that if certain women didn't stop blackguarding Victoria Woodhull, she would print their private histories. If they wanted to disgrace her for supporting social freedom, they should sink with her for practising it.

Theodore Tilton strode into Victoria's office with the "Tit for Tat" article, and asked if she had written it or if she had had it written. She said she had a right to self-defense. A set of women were defaming her, and she would not tamely submit. But she promised Tilton not to publish the article in the *Weekly*.

However, those proof sheets were sent out. The women claimed they were offered immunity for five hundred dollars.

"But I haven't got five hundred dollars," wailed one distinguished agitator, who was conventional enough to know that a reputation attacked was a reputation ruined in those days.

"Don't bother about it," advised her husband. "Everybody knows you haven't been divorced, and when they say you have, and scandalously, who is going to believe it!"

"Lots of people believe anything they see in print." The thought of divorce scandalized the genteel then.

Again Theodore Tilton strode into Victoria's office. He told her that he had defended her when she was attacked. Now that she had attacked other women he washed his hands of her forever.

Victoria's account of this interview differed from Tilton's.

She said Theodore called on her the day before he left for the Progressive Republican convention at Cincinnati to tell her that he was going to report it for the *New York Tribune*.

"Theodore, you are lying again," she told him. "You are going to Cincinnati to nominate Mr. Greeley, and I see clairvoyantly, a coffin following him, in which you will be responsible for putting him, because you will be responsible for his death."

She said he left with a sad tenderness and that she never spoke to him again.

In fact Tilton's "Account of Mrs. Woodhull" was used as campaign material against Greeley. Cartoonists pounced on it. Greeley's presidential chances were materially lessened by his friendship for Tilton because of Tilton's connection with Victoria Woodhull, "a free lover", anathema to all those pure politicians. With a tenuity that would be amusing if it weren't so common, Greeley was definitely associated in the public mind with Victoria Woodhull and free love. And how he had fought both!

It was a strange coincidence that Greeley was put into his coffin very soon, but nobody knows whether Victoria clairvoyantly saw it beforehand, or afterward.

Later Victoria said that people were "poisoned" against her after the May convention and that, alarmed by the range of her social and political program, its enemies united to destroy her.

The Claflins were asked to leave Twenty-third Street, "because of the doctrines" they advocated, and because they exposed "the rottenness of the social condition." For the same reasons they could not find board elsewhere. They tried to rent a house, but the agents said, "We personally don't object to you, but you know there is such a prejudice against you, that really we can't do it."

The Hoffman House and other hotels refused to admit them. Finally they got rooms at the Gilsey, while

"THE WOODHULL"

Mr. Gardner, the proprietor, was away. When he returned, he said they had to go or all his family boarders would leave.

They claimed their rights as citizens and said they would not go unless a misdemeanor were proved against them.

Then Colonel Tennie C. went out to drill the Spencer Greys with four colored lieutenants who called for her in a carriage.

"Miss Tennie," said Mr. Gardner, "if you go off with those men in that carriage you need not come back here!"

Victoria and Colonel Blood came up from Broad Street to find their trunks and bags on the sidewalk. They were not allowed to get into their rooms. That night, with Tennie and the child Zulu Maud, they walked the streets because they had no place to go. Towards morning they thought of 44 Broad Street, but the building was locked. Finally they climbed over the transom of the outer door and got into their office. They slept there on the floor. For weeks it was their only shelter.

Suddenly their office rent was raised, a thousand dollars a year, the whole to be paid in advance. A monthly payment with security for the year was not acceptable, and nobody would rent them another office. After a sickening search, they found one at 48 Broad Street. Eventually relatives got a house for them.

With the issue of June twenty-second the *Weekly* had to suspend publication. In August Victoria Woodhull was sued for her debts. She testified that the clothes on her back did not belong to her; the furniture in her office was borrowed. She did not own any property of any kind.

Victoria, Tennie C. and Colonel Blood were financially ruined. They met nothing but bitterness everywhere.

Obviously financial ruin was not the fate of successful blackmailers. Were they ever blackmailers at all? Or did they make the mistake of trying to get small sums from too many people instead of big ones from a few? A correspondent to the *Boston Journal* of November 19, 1872, claimed that they demanded money from over thirty men on the threat of printed attacks. Some paid at first, others said, "Go ahead." One arose from his seat angry enough to take a woman by the collar, to lead her to the head of the stairs and tell her if she ever darkened his doors again he would fling her down, if he broke every bone in her body. The correspondent said these men had combined to destroy the sisters; there was not only safety, but respectability in numbers.

Victoria and Tennie certainly were persecuted during the summer of 1872, as well as later when there was another reason for it. Others who were advocating their views were not persecuted.

Nobody could draw an ultimate conclusion; anybody can weigh the evidence.

In September, worn, tired and discouraged, Victoria went to the convention of the National Spiritualists' Association at Boston. When the materialistic public hooted at the Tilton biography, these denizens of the otherwhere acclaimed it and her. Surely now that other friends had deserted, they would acclaim her again.

But Professor William Denton circulated a report among the delegates that she was in the habit of obtaining money under false pretences. He rallied her fighting spirit.

Around her, with the intuition of an expert fortune-teller, she felt an attitude of painful uncertainty and doubt.

She started for the platform to make her report, and confronted the expectant crowd. Her face was so charged with feeling that a shock swept through the audience. Tense, stilled, they waited, as if for a thunderclap.

And a mighty thunderclap it was! Afterwards Victoria said a gust of inspiration seized her, and took her out of herself. It was a gust of vindictiveness started by Buck Claflin's cruelty back in Homer; and it had gained more and more impetus in town after town. Victoria Woodhull never did anything she thought was wrong when she did it. Why should she suffer when coward souls went free? She had a sense of thwarted superiority. She believed in social freedom and practised it, and said she practised it. And other things she did to sustain herself that she might sustain the cause, an end that justified the means! So she thought.

She tossed back her curls, and burst into an indignant rhapsody. She swore, some said divinely, as she told in detail the story of the Beecher-Tilton affair, announcing in prophetic terms its bearings on the future of Spiritualism.

Flesh crept and blood ran cold.

Mrs. E. A. Meriwether described the scene in the *Memphis Appeal,* with a sectional preface which had the usual post-war slant:

Said Mrs. Meriwether: ". . . Every Northern paper calls her speech on September 11th obscene, though it was not that; it was such as would inevitably rouse the rage of many rich and powerful men. . . . Of course they will use their power to crush her to earth.

"Mrs. Woodhull's speech poured out like a stream of flame. . . . Editors, teachers, preachers, she spared not. . . . And those high and mighty Boston men shuddered and quaked too, for they seemed to dread she would seize their names and hold up their vices to be gazed at by the world. . . . Henry Ward Beecher suffered severely. . . . She said . . . he preached every Sunday to his mistresses, members of his church, sitting in their pews, robed in silks and satins and high respectability! . . . She believed it her mission to show up the shams, to uncover the hypocrisies. When she finished off Beecher, she came back to Boston and lifted some of its editors high in the air, and scorched them with her accusations. . . . Then in the most impassioned accents, she demanded if there was a single immaculate being in that hall, he should rise to his feet and cast on her the stones! Whereupon . . . a forlorn, seedy fellow, with a small carpet bag in his hand, rose to his feet and every eye turned on him. Mrs. Woodhull paused, and for a moment surveyed the forlorn figure claiming to be immaculate . . . that Boston audience broke into a shout of derisive laughter, then it hissed like a thousand snakes, then it howled, Put him out! Put him out! The astonished

Immaculate cowered down in his seat, and Mrs. Woodhull's fiery flame went on, until she suddenly stopped, and flashed from the platform and out at the side door just as swiftly as she had flashed in. . . ."

With the surest appeal a woman could make, she had shocked them, excited them, thrilled them and won them. They reëlected her president of the association and their hearts surged back to her.

One Boston paper guardedly said that Mrs. Woodhull had slandered a clergyman; the others merely called her speech obnoxious.

That Beecher-Tilton story had been whispered in newspaper offices over the country for some time, and all had refused to print it.

Now *Woodhull & Claflin's Weekly* resolved to fill the breach. Such a plea for social freedom would boost circulation, and perhaps Victoria thought it would impress the public as it had the Spiritualists, and win them back to her. The public was Victoria's obsession.

So the *Weekly* was revived with the issue of November 2, 1872. It told why it had been discontinued. "After carefully considering all these things, can anyone wonder that we have been compelled to turn on our accusers? Can anyone wonder, after our treatment at the Gilsey House, if we take the roofs off the hotels and expose the damned lechery that exists there so closely concealed? Can anyone wonder, after the personal treatment to which we have been subjected, if we strip the masks from the faces of our maligners and show them to be the rotten masses they would have it thought we were? . . .

"We have five hundred biographies of various persons, in all circles of life, many of which persons are the present oracles of society, the facts of which biographies are similar to those presented in this article. Many may deprecate the publication of such facts; but there is no other possible way out of the present social demoralization into which society is declining. People must be compelled to live just such lives as they want the public to think they live."

Then came "THE BEECHER-TILTON SCANDAL CASE. The Detailed Statement of the Whole Matter by Mrs. Woodhull," who proposed "as the commencement of a series of aggressive moral welfare on the social question, to begin this article with ventilating one of the most stupendous scandals which has ever occurred in any community. . . . I intend that this article shall burst like a bomb-shell into the ranks of the moralistic social camp. . . .

". . . Men and women tremble on the brink of the revolution, and hesitate to avow their convictions, while yet partly aware of their rights, and urged by the legitimate impulses of nature, they act upon the new doctrines while they profess obedience to the old. . . ."

She went on to say that she had heard of so many whose professions differed from their practises that unless she exposed them, she would be conniving at their hypocrisy. The Beecher-Tilton story was put in the form of an interview with a hypothetical reporter, and was supposed to have been suppressed in Boston.

When the "reporter" said, "You speak like some weird prophetess, madam," she answered, "I am a prophetess—I am an evangel, I am a Saviour, if you would but see it; but I too, come not to bring peace, but a sword."

She said she did not condemn Mr. Beecher, "with his demanding physical nature, and with the terrible restrictions upon a clergyman's life, imposed by that public opinion ignorant about physiological laws . . ." he probably had done his best. But she had "had every opportunity to know that he entertains, on conviction, substantially the same views which I entertain on the social question; that, under the influence of these convictions, he has lived for many years . . . in a manner which, the religious and moralistic public ostensibly . . . condemns; that he has permitted himself nevertheless to be over-awed by public opinion, to profess to believe otherwise than as he does believe, to have helped to maintain . . . that very social slavery under which he was chafing. . . . The fault with which I, therefore charge him, is not infidelity to the old ideas, but unfaithfulness to the new. . . . I am prone to denounce him as a poltroon, a coward and a sneak . . . for failing . . . to stand shoulder to shoulder with me and others who are endeavoring to hasten a social regeneration which he believes in."

Whereupon Victoria related the story Mrs. Stanton told her, a story Mrs. Stanton admitted afterwards, though some extravagant words she denied. Victoria certainly melodramatized that scandal, but the substance of it, the names, dates and major circumstances filled eleven columns, and it never was disproved in one of the longest court trials in the history of American law.

She said Theodore had told her how he had walked in the cemetery where a still-born child was buried and "stamped the ring with which we had plighted our troth deep into the soil that covered the fruit of my wife's infidelity," which may have been a detail invented by her histrionic imagination or one of Tilton's histrionic acts.

Eventually she offered Mr. Beecher an apology for interfering in his personal affairs. ". . . it is the paradox of my position that believing in the right of privacy and in the perfect right of Mr. Beecher socially, morally and divinely to have sought the embraces of Mrs. Tilton, or of any other woman or women whom he loved and who loved him . . . I still invade the most secret and sacred affairs of his life, and . . . expose him to the opprobrium and vilification of the public . . . What I do I do for a great purpose. . . . The social world is in the very agony of its new birth. . . . Somebody must be hurled forward into the gap. I have the power, I think, to compel Mr. Beecher to go forward and to do the duty for humanity from which he shrinks. . . ."

In conclusion, said Victoria, "The immense physical potency of Mr. Beecher and the indomitable urgency of his great nature for the intimacy and embraces of the noble and cultured women about him, instead of being a bad thing as the world thinks . . . is one of the noblest and grandest of the endowments of this truly great representative man. The amative impulse is the physiological basis of character. It is this which emanates zest and magnetic power to his whole audience through the organism of the great preacher. Plymouth Church has lived and fed, and the healthy vigor of public opinion for the last quarter of a century has been augmented and strengthened from the physical amativeness of Henry Ward Beecher. . . . Passional starvation, enforced on such a nature, so richly endowed

. . . is a horrid cruelty. The bigoted public, to which the great preacher ministered, while literally eating and drinking of his flesh and blood, condemned him, in their ignorance, to live without food. Every great man of Mr. Beecher's type, has had in the past, and will ever have, the need for and the right to, the loving manifestations of many women. . . ."

Adjoining this astonishing mixture of impertinence, vindictiveness and scientific diagnosis, which had at least a remote justification inasmuch as Mr. Beecher was an eminent teacher of morality, was "THE PHILOSOPHY OF MODERN HYPOCRISY—Mr. L. C. Challis the Illustration," which had no justification whatever.

Luther Challis was an unimportant broker whose private life could have been of no interest to the public. He had been a friend of Tennie C.'s. His story was preceded by a harmless column of Stephen Pearl Andrews' elemental meanderings about the generation of steam, and cess-pools in the social arena and the unfairness of the double standard. Wherewith, there ensued "in her own language," an account of certain happenings observed during the French Ball at the Academy of Music, by a lady who had gone there "incog". She did not stay "incog".

According to one of the newspapers, at the French Ball were "three thousand of the best men and four thousand of the worst women." Said the lady, "My sister and myself went closely dominoed. We had a box. After awhile I saw Mr. Challis and a gentleman with him whom I will call Smith, though his real name is one of the oldest and best in the annals of New York society. We made ourselves known to them, and they joined us, accompanied by two young girls not more than fifteen or sixteen years of age. These girls had come on fresh from school in Baltimore, and in the best society of New York had fallen in with these middle aged roués, and had in their innocence been led by them in the ways that lead to ruin. Wine was called for, and while the men drank but little, these young girls were plied with it, until I remonstrated and begged them not to drink any more. My effort to influence them was met with an insulting request from the men to let them alone. You may be sure I followed these girls up, and got the history of their connection with these men. They were seduced by them." Then followed a detailed and unprintable account of those seductions.

". . . We would ask why (men) should not be held up equally to the scorn of the world, instead of being called the 'worst women and the best men'."

Nobody knew how or why the brokerage firm at 48 Broad Street started up again when Victoria returned from Boston in September, nor where the money to revive the *Weekly* came from.

The day it appeared newsboys blocked Broad Street for hundreds of feet, the scandal issue was in such demand. By nightfall it sold on the streets for forty dollars a copy. Money poured into Woodhull, Claflin & Company; they were jubilant at the success of their coup.

In the evening friends came to 237 Fourth Avenue to rejoice with them. They found Victoria, Tennie, and Mrs. Miles in their spacious parlor, with Victoria's little daughter Zulu Maud and two young nieces. Zulu

Maud was reserved and shy, but the elder of the nieces, then about fifteen, was on the boards with Daly's Company at the Fifth Avenue Theatre. She sang ballads charmingly and entertained the company with recitations. It was a festive evening.

They reckoned without Anthony Comstock.

Anthony Comstock was a young dry-goods salesman who tried to fight the devil within by fighting his disciples without. The devil was a serious factor then. And Comstock was a man of action. He could control his acts, but he couldn't control his thoughts. "Whosoever looketh upon a woman to lust after her, hath committed adultery already in his heart," was his belief and his scourge. And he considered passion a disease, that ought to be wiped out.

At that time vice was violent and malignant in New York, and the obscene books and papers which were sold on the streets were supposed to increase it. Comstock knew they bred lust.

There had been the usual post-war centralization of power, and as usual repressive fanatics took advantage of it. In 1865 Congress passed a law which prohibited the circulation of obscene publications through the mail.

In 1868 one of Comstock's friends went astray; and when Comstock found that he had been reading erotic books, he took a police captain to his friend's bookseller, and bought a book as evidence and had the bookseller arrested and his stock seized. The police captain did not coöperate at first, and Comstock reported him to the commissioner. Somehow Comstock never was liked.

When the Young Men's Christian Association appointed a committee for the "Suppression of Vice," Comstock did its work.

He not only took the time and had the inclination, he had the sincerity of a thunderstorm and almost as much energy.

And in June 1872, a United States statute was passed declaring the transmission of obscene literature through the mails a misdemeanor.

Anthony Comstock saw the scandal issue of *Woodhull & Claflin's Weekly* at one o'clock in the evening. The next morning he gathered evidence and went to the District Attorney, who promised him a warrant for Woodhull & Claflin's arrest and the seizure of their paper. By three-thirty the warrant had not appeared.

With some curious mental or emotional twist, Comstock must have decided erotic writing couldn't hurt him who was smiting it, because he studied the *Weekly* again and found that copies were being sent through the mail. Whereupon he appealed to the Federal authorities.

At noon two deputy United States marshals went to 48 Broad Street with a warrant issued by Commissioner Osborn for Victoria C. Woodhull and Tennie C. Claflin. They were not in their office, but the officers found them on Broad Street, in a carriage with five hundred copies of the *Weekly*.

The officers arrested them and took them immediately to Commissioner Osborn. They summoned a lawyer.

Somehow the news spread, and crowds flocked to the United States Circuit Court, where the sisters sat next to the railing, in the centre of the room. They were dressed alike, in black, with purple bows, but

THE ARREST OF THE CLAFLIN SISTERS, NOVEMBER 2, 1872

Tennie C. was amused. Her eyes sparkled with excitement, she smiled when her counsel or the District Attorney said anything that struck her as funny. Victoria looked grave, and listened with intent and painful interest to everything.

General Davis, United States Assistant District Attorney, appeared for the prosecution and blurred Mr. Comstock's case by saying: ". . . Not only have the defendants, by circulating an obscene publication through the mails, committed an offense against the law, but they have been guilty of a most abominable and unjust charge against one of the purest and best citizens of this State, or in the United States, and they have, as far as possible, aggravated the offense by a malicious and gross libel upon the character of the gentleman, whose character is well worth while the Government of the United States to vindicate. I therefore . . . ask that bail be fixed in each case at ten thousand dollars."

Mr. Reymart, counsel for the defense, very properly reminded the court that his clients were charged with sending obscene literature through the mail, not with libel, and that "The idea of the Government vindicating or defending the character of a gentleman is entirely outside of this case."

Commissioner Osborn said, ". . . An example is needed and we propose to make one of these women." He fixed bail at eight thousand dollars each.

Whereupon, the famous eccentric, George Francis Train offered to pay it.

Meanwhile Luther Challis got out a warrant for them at Jefferson Market Court on the charge of libel, and Victoria and Tennie were advised not to give bail until all the suits developed, since they would be more comfortable in Ludlow Street than in what was called New York's "Black Hole of Calcutta", Jefferson Market Prison.

In Ludlow Street they found Warden Tracy, "a true-hearted gentleman of philanthropic impulses and devoted to the alleviation of the conditions of prison life" and his assistant, Mr. Gardner, "a person of refinement, large culture and wide research, and a gifted author and poet." Except for the fact of imprisonment, Victoria said she would not regard her stay as "wholly unpleasant." Their quarters were clean, and the food was adequate. And again Victoria was the talk of the town, though the talk was not flattering.

The *New York Times* said editorially that license never had been carried to such an extent as in "the free love journal of Woodhull & Claflin," and that "the female name" never had been "more disgraced and degraded than by these women."

Luther Challis had Stephen Pearl Andrews arrested for participation in the libel on him, as well as Colonel Blood, and William A. Smith, who did the press work on the paper, and William Denyse, who made electrotype plates of the type. Luther Challis stated at Jefferson Market Court that the sisters had tried to blackmail him. He said Miss Claflin wrote to him on March 29th, demanding two hundred dollars. He didn't answer the letter. She called on him and he refused to give the money. Immediately afterward he received a proof of the article subsequently published in the *Weekly*. He paid no attention to it and thought the matter was settled.

Tennie C. told a reporter from the *New York Ex-*

press that Mr. Challis' charge was untrue, and that he had been on "intimate terms" with her; she had written to ask him to help pay the expenses for their Steinway Hall lectures. She said Fisk and Hatch, Henry Clews, and other leading brokers had given them various sums. Moreover, she had some affectionate letters from Mr. Challis, and now that she had gone so far, she intended to tell the whole truth and let the public judge.

On Monday, November fourth, the corridors, even the stairs of the Federal Building were filled with bankers from Wall Street, merchants from Broadway, and bootblacks from everywhere. When the courtroom opened the crowd pressed so dangerously that women groaned and wailed, to get a glimpse of Victoria and Tennie C. during their examination before Commissioner Osborn.

General Davis stated that in the morning the Grand Jury had found bills of indictment against the prisoners, on which bench-warrants had been issued from the Circuit Court. General Davis suggested that this took the case out of the jurisdiction of the Commissioner.

Mr. William F. Howe was the sisters' counsel on this occasion, and he delivered an eloquent though apparently unnecessary oration, inasmuch as the Grand Jury had taken the case out of the jurisdiction of the Commissioner. But Mr. Howe's oration probably had a strategical purpose. He was a master of strategy as well as the king of tears. He could have brought tears to a jury trying Nero, Judas, or Lady Macbeth; and in those days the ability to bring tears to juries was priceless. Howe's partner, Abe Hummel, dealt with the law and the judges in his own way. And not only could Howe play the tremolo on any home, any mother and all orphans, he could talk to a jury until it was so tired that it grew doubtful. Then he told it what to do. And his clothes always made the opposing counsel seem drab and insignificant. Today Mr. Howe wore plaid pantaloons, a purple vest and a blue satin scarf, on which an immense diamond reflected the rainbow.

He said the ladies were victims of private malice from a source that did not dare come into court. They were in custody and this action of the Grand Jury deprived them of bail. He added shrewdly that he considered those indictments a mark of disrespect to the officer before whom the examination was supposed to proceed. And if the *Weekly* were obscene, then the Holy Bible, the works of Lord Byron and Shakespeare could not be sent through the mail. And not only was this a case of malicious persecution, it was a blow at the freedom of the press.

Victoria and Tennie C. were arrested under the bench-warrants and returned to Ludlow Street. Victoria was deeply moved. Tennie looked defiant.

Back in jail Tennie objected to a newspaper statement that she smoked bad cigars and used blasphemy. "If I was out of here," she told another reporter, "where I could deny such statements, I wouldn't mind so much, but as I am now I feel it very much."

The Challis Case was heard before Judge Fowler in Jefferson Market Court on November tenth.

Mr. Howe wore a Scotch plaid vest, a massive glittering watch guard and a diamond breast pin. George

Francis Train's curly gray locks were arranged in a "distractingly talented manner", and another lime-lighter, Count Joannes, appeared in brass decorations and a nut-brown wig. The courtroom was packed to suffocation. No wonder the *Herald* called it, "the sensational comedy of free love."

Colonel Blood said he was the agent of Woodhull, Claflin & Company, and as punishable as the principal, "if the agent of another man's malice or of a woman's slander."

Mr. Howe said the ladies expected to bear the responsibility which rightly should be theirs. He said Colonel Blood didn't have the ability to write the article, and should bear none of the penalty. "The prisoners admitted it was their production," said their counsel.

In fact Victoria had first related the Beecher-Tilton story on the platform in Boston. It is likely that she dictated it for publication to Colonel Blood, her usual amanuensis. The dialogue in which she admitted that she was an evangel and a Saviour showed her unmistakable touch.

Tennie C. swore that Blood had no connection with the *Weekly*. She swore that she wrote the Challis article and that she herself sent money to the printer to pay for his work on it.

Afterward Stephen Pearl Andrews said both articles were brought to him for correction. He rewrote bits of them, obviously the preamble to the Challis article.

Apparently the sisters wanted to exonerate Colonel Blood. To issue the *Weekly* from Ludlow Street, according to their plans, he had to be free. And maybe Victoria wanted him exonerated because she loved him.

Buck Claflin, with a peculiarly cheerful countenance, gave some damaging testimony. He said he had heard a conversation through the hall door about the proposed publication; Mr. Challis' name was mentioned, and Mr. Beecher's also. He didn't object to the exposure of Beecher, but he did object to the other matter. The night before the arrest he told his children they were going to get into trouble and that they had better keep out of the way until Monday and then face the music.

"Blood then told me to shut my venerable mouth. He said, 'We believe it, and we mean to publish it.'"

Tennie, who had been very calm, played with her gloves at this point, and her eyes blazed. Victoria had not tried to be composed during her father's testimony. She whispered first to her counsel and then to the Colonel, who sat next to her with little Zulu Maud.

Victoria came to the stand hurriedly, obviously excited. She said Colonel Blood had advised her not to publish the article; but that she had done it, and she was glad she had done it. She said she and her sister were the editors of the paper. Colonel Blood had no more to do with the *Weekly* than any other servant around the office. Sometimes he wrote articles for it, but not the one complained of. He received a nominal salary and none of the profits.

She said Luther Challis had visited them in Ludlow Street and that he had offered to pay them to deny the slander. She went on about his visits to her house last winter, and about the French Ball.

The District Attorney interrupted a sentence that "boded indecency." The *Herald* said the rest of her narrative was "far too indecent and obscene for publication."

On cross examination, Victoria said that Commodore Vanderbilt gave them the money to start their *Weekly,* and that the firm was composed of Tennie and herself. Colonel Blood took charge of the brokerage business. She said she did not write the alleged libel, she knew nothing of the proof sheet Mr. Challis said he had received. She admitted that she had talked to a Mr. Maxwell about the alleged libel before it was published.

Mr. Maxwell came to the stand.

"What are you?" asked the counsel.

"I live on the town," said handsome Mr. Maxwell.

He testified that he had heard Challis use the words in question and confirmed other parts of the article. Maxwell's connection with the case was confusing.

Mr. Challis was asked about some undergarments he had presented to Tennie C. Claflin. He denied them with dignity. He was asked if he ever had kissed Tennie C.

The question was excluded.

Mr. Challis denied that he had offered to stop the proceedings if the sisters would deny the slander.

Mrs. Laura Cuppy Smith was called to the stand. She said she had introduced herself to Victoria Woodhull after reading the Tilton biography. She was a woman and a mother, and her soul was in the new social movement.

She had gone to Murray Hill in February to see Mrs. Woodhull, and first she saw Miss Claflin in her room upstairs. Miss Claflin told her she was expecting Mr. Challis.

Mr. Challis came in and kissed Tennie, and told her she looked charming. When Mrs. Smith left the room, they were sitting down very familiarly, and as Tennie's mother passed through, Challis said, "Good evening, Mother."

The prisoners were taken back to jail. And Victoria sent a card to the *Herald*.

"Sick in body, sick in mind, sick at heart, I write these lines to ask if, because I am a woman, I am to have no justice, no fair play, no chance through the press to reach public opinion. How can anybody know for what I am accused, arrested, imprisoned, unless the public are allowed to see the alleged libel. If the paper is suppressed and I charged with crime, in what way can I substantiate the truth, when the judge before whom I only appear as witness, constitutes himself as plaintiff, prosecuting attorney, judge, jury and witness? When has it ever been known in this land of so-called religious freedom and civil liberty, that pulpit, press and people tremble before a cowardly public opinion? Is it not astonishing that all Christian law and civilization seem to be scared out of their senses at having two poor women locked up in jail? Suppose, Mr. Editor, that some enemies of yours should throw you into a cell for publishing the Challis article, suppress the *Herald,* arrest your printers, prosecute your publisher, shut up your business office, close all the avenues of press and lecture hall against your honorable defense? Would not every land ring with the outrage? 'Oh, liberty,' said Madam Roland, when the French capital was shaking the conscience of Europe, 'what things are done in thy name!' . . ."

Victoria C. Woodhull, Cell 11, Ludlow Street Jail."

Chapter Ten

WOODHULL WITCHERY

AN INDIGNANT friend spoke to Mr. Beecher about the "Woodhull Outrage."

Quietly, Beecher lifted his lionlike head. "My friend, I do not need any sympathy." He felt troubled for his friends because they were troubled, but his life in Plymouth Church was his defense. The majestic preacher could not bend to notice Mrs. Woodhull; but, when his indignant friend said the woman must be insane, Beecher smiled kindly. "I believe so too. At any rate I can only wish people had better minds."

"Of course, Mr. Beecher, the whole thing is a fraud from beginning to end."

With an indescribable motion of his head, Henry Ward Beecher said, "Entirely!"

It was a measure of Beecher's personality that his friend said that not only had he never realized the potency of that word "entirely," but never had Henry Ward Beecher appeared so grand.

When this conversation was printed, Susan B. Anthony wrote Beecher's sister Isabella that if the Lord ever did strike anyone dead for telling a lie, He would have struck then. Mrs. Stanton wrote Miss Anthony that if her testimony would save Victoria from prison she would give it. Elizabeth Cady Stanton did not "propose to shelter a man when a woman's liberty is at stake."

Isabella Beecher Hooker wrote to her brother Thomas that she did not understand Victoria but knew her to be pure and unselfish and "absolutely driven by some power foreign to herself to these strange utterances, which are always in behalf of freedom, purity—truth as she understands it. . . ."

In April Henry Ward had written Isabella that "you and I are nearer together than any of our family." Now she begged him to tell the whole truth. ". . . the one radical mistake you have made is in supposing that you are so much ahead of your time, and in daring to attempt to lead when you have anything to conceal." She prepared a paper advocating a social freedom with which he could divert public attention from personalities to philosophy. And thereafter Harriet Beecher Stowe sat in the front row at Plymouth Church in case Isabella should appear with it.

But the Reverend Thomas Beecher wrote her:

"I respect, as at present advised, Mrs. Woodhull, while I abhor her philosophy. She only carries out Henry's philosophy, against which I recorded my protest twenty years ago, and parted, (lovingly and achingly) from him. . . . In my judgment Henry is following his slippery doctrines of expediency, and in the cry of progress and nobleness of nature, has sacrificed clear, exact integrity. . . . Of the two, Woodhull is my hero, and Henry my coward. . . . I was not anti-slavery; I am not anti-family. . . .

". . . You cannot help Henry. You must be true to Woodhull. . . .

". . . Follow the truth, and when you need me cry out . . . I think you are all in the wrong. . . . But I honor and love them who suffer for conviction's sake. . . ."

All these letters were printed, as well as any conversation in which Beecher, Tilton or Victoria Woodhull was mentioned.

And when the pillars of Plymouth Church inexplicably blamed Theodore Tilton instead of Beecher for not denying the Woodhull story, that ready writer wrote an equivocal "Letter to a Complaining Friend," whom he asked to consider whether it was easy "to give the lie to the wicked story and thus end it forever!" The story, said Theodore, contained so many statements. It would be strange if some were not correct, and yet he doubted if any were. He alluded vaguely to the futility of denying twenty-four pages of illustration in the Police Gazette. His wife had "a Christian mandate of silence." Her heart was a "fountain of charity and quenches all resentments" lest others be injured. He was the chief victim of public displeasure and he would keep his answer "lest it shoot forth like a thunderbolt through other hearts."

When Luther Challis began a civil action against Victoria, Tennie, Blood and others, and the papers couldn't be served because the women still were in jail, the *Brooklyn Eagle* complained: ". . . The statute on which the proceeding independently and disinterestedly initiated by Mr. Comstock is based, reads larger than the astute mind of the Assistant Federal District Attorney at first suggested. . . . It shows that without having generally known it, the people of this country are living under a law more narrow and oppressive than any people with a written constitution ever lived under before. . . . We can discover no intention on the part of the authorities to try these women at all. The seeming disposition indefinitely to incarcerate them . . . is discernible. . . . If the lies and libels they print were true, then most certainly they ought to have been printed. . . . Being untrue it is a folly to persecute women who deserve prosecution the severest. . . ."

Victoria was cosmic as usual. In her name the right of free speech was evoked. All over the country newspapers protested against Federal interference in a private affair.

Said the *Hartford Times*, ". . . the United States Government is taking possession of the people and ruling them. The servants are becoming the masters of the people." The *Hartford Times* wanted to know why United States marshals instead of representatives of the State of New York, arrested Victoria Woodhull and Tennie C. Claflin.

Epithets alternated with protests.

The *Philadelphia Star* said neither Mrs. Woodhull nor Miss Claflin "could put the humblest decent man upon his purgation by anything she might allege. . . . I should render myself liable to persecution by Mr. Comstock if I were to describe the 'free life' of these women as it is notorious in downtown conversation, provable by unimpeachable evidence, if that were called for."

Stephen Pearl Andrews was nothing worse than "the distinguished free love philosopher," for even those who loathed his views respected his learning and his dignity. Apparently the case against him was dropped.

But when Victoria and Tennie C. were brought out of jail, after twenty-eight days, without a trial, an officer met them with another warrant sworn out by Luther Challis, so they stayed in Ludlow Street until they could get bail to cover both cases. Mr. Howe had procured a writ of habeas corpus for Colonel Blood.

On December fifth, 1872, Dr. Augustus Ruggles and Mr. Kiernan of Brooklyn gave bail for the sisters. They were rearrested in the court house on another charge, and bailed again.

A week later George Francis Train was arraigned for publishing an obscene newspaper which he called *The Train Ligue*. In the first number he repeated statements from the *Weekly* of November second, exaggerating them to make it a test case, but nothing happened. When he quoted sections from the Old Testament under sensational headlines, the Federal authorities refused to do anything, but Comstock got an indictment from the state courts. Train pleaded guilty to having in his possession an obscene paper made up of Bible quotations, and went to the Tombs.

Train did not believe in free love; he had disapproved of the sisters until they were sent to Ludlow Street. There he visited them constantly; he offered to pay their bail and wrote letters to the newspapers, defending them.

He was a knight-errant who loved the limelight, a handsome Communist with a golden touch. He owned lots in Omaha said to be worth thirty million dollars. He had built a fleet of sailing ships. He introduced street railways into Europe and organized the Marseilles Commune in France. He organized the Crédit Mobilier, but he had nothing to do with the scandals that tainted it.

Now he refused to give bail. He declared he was

guilty of Comstock's charge, the liberty of the press was at stake. For five months he stayed in the Tombs, on Murderers' Row, and twenty-two murderers formed a club and elected him president.

But his health was injured by his stay there. It was a loathsome place in those days, and Train advertised its horrors. The *Sun* investigated it, and eventually a municipal commission confirmed all his assertions.

Revived by the sisters' publicity, the *Weekly* resumed publication with the issue of December 28th, 1872.

Victoria wanted to speak in Boston on "Moral Cowardice & Moral Hypocrisy, or Four Weeks in Ludlow Street Jail", but Governor Claflin of Massachusetts feared she might "repeat the vile stories about Mr. Beecher or even attack some of us in Boston." He said, "She is no better than a panel thief or a common street walker, and I will see that she don't open her vile mouth in the city which was so recently honored by Mr. Beecher's presence."

The speech was delivered at Springfield, Massachusetts, and the *Springfield Republican* found Victoria's voice, "singularly pathetic" when she recited her wrongs and her intents. It marked the "rapid, eager, magnetic manner" with which she warned the Y.M.C.A., Plymouth Church and the Government that the social system would be torn down in the *Weekly*, unless the press lost all freedom, and that the plaintiffs would go from state to state, to "sow the seed of social revolution, which, springing up, shall sweep the despots like chaff before the fan from their thrones built upon the liberties of the people. Stop their press they may; but their tongues, never!"

This was printed in the *Weekly,* with sympathetic press comments, fervent letters from admiring friends as well as new followers won by the martyrdom in Ludlow Street. The *Weekly* started a series of laudatory biographies, too, featuring the lawyers who aided the sisters.

On January third, it was announced in New York that Victoria C. Woodhull and Tennie C. Claflin would tell "The Naked Truth," at Cooper Institute on January ninth.

Whereupon Anthony Comstock had a letter mailed from Greenwich, Connecticut, to Woodhull & Claflin, in which he enclosed money for copies of the issue of November second, and to which he signed the name of John Beardsley. When he received the *Weeklies* with a letter offering more copies of the suppressed edition at an advanced rate, he got an indictment from the United States grand jury, which charged the sisters with sending obscene literature through the mails.

Colonel Blood was arrested in Broad Street on the day of the lecture, and he sent a warning to Victoria and Tennie C.

Tennie C. hid under a big washtub, and Maggie the cook, put another tub on top of it and started the family laundry. When the police arrived, she unscrewed the ringer and flourished it. "Get out of here!" she cried.

Victoria went to Jersey City with her bondsmen, and stayed in Taylor's Hotel, until dark. Then, disguised in a borrowed hat and a heavy veil, she crossed the Twenty-third Street ferry.

Near Cooper Institute posters advertised Woodhull and "The Naked Truth." But United States marshals guarded the door and told people to go home. "There will be no lecture tonight."

Though it was cold and bitter, an eager crowd lingered around the Institute, shivering. Finally they went inside the hall, and waited, staring at the vacant platform, hoping something would happen. Some looked like a Bowery congregation, others like a scientific lecture audience. They waited an hour, and nothing happened. They began to shout and clap and stamp their feet.

An old lady, dressed in Quaker gray, passed up the middle aisle to a front seat. She wore an ancient coal-skuttle bonnet, heavily veiled, and she was such a funny old thing that many smiled; a few laughed outright.

Outside the marshals and a dozen policemen waited for Victoria Woodhull; as many policemen waited within.

Laura Cuppy Smith came on the stage and said, "The enemies of free speech have another order of arrest for Mrs. Woodhull. She cannot appear tonight, lest she be again thrust into an American bastile . . . though they may shut out Mrs. Woodhull, they shall not prevent the delivery of the lecture, for she has deputized me to read it to you . . . the custodians of the law guard the doors of the Institute, and neither Mrs. Woodhull nor Miss Claflin can, no matter how much they may desire it, appear upon this platform tonight."

That old Quaker lady tottered irresolutely up the

stairway of the platform and walked halfway across the stage, and the people laughed at such an incongruous sight. She disappeared behind a broad pillar.

Suddenly she darted out. Flinging off bonnet, veil, gray dress and old age, she stood there, Victoria Woodhull herself, defiant and irrepressible. Her disguise coiled at her feet, her hair in gorgeous disarray, she raised her arms aloft with a magnificent gesture of freedom.

The crowd went mad. Somebody shouted, "Comstock's euchred!" Applause pealed forth. They yelled with excitement, and stilled when Victoria began to speak.

At first her voice was choked with anger, but it rose like a song.

No policeman moved. The marshals forgot their writs.

For one hour and a half, she held that hall spellbound.

She rang all the tones of tragedy when she said she had been deprived of her heritage as an American citizen. All the furies stirred with her arraignment of the courts, the press and public opinion.

She said Comstock was Beecher's agent; Challis had started a vindictive persecution. The newspapers never printed her side of the case. Officers of the law seized their types, destroyed their business, purloined their private papers, and threw them into jail, without allowing them to communicate with the public. The people were outraged, when an individual was wronged by the law. A revised edition of the suppressed *Weekly* would be on sale at 48 Broad Street, because the United States had no case against them. For, since the Challis article had been reprinted by the *Herald* and other papers, they, too, were guilty of obscenity if it were obscene.

She said it was not a question of Beecher nor Tilton, nor Tilton's wife, nor of Noyes, nor Andrews, nor Brigham Young nor Woodhull; it was the question of a new gospel. The world always maltreated the annunciator of a new gospel.

She warned a district attorney who "discriminated against women," not to defy the stab of a steel pen.

She wondered whether some woman would be arrested for adultery for kissing her baby boy.

The crowd cheered and hushed to hear more.

She said every third person in the audience was a conscious rebel against a galling domestic tyranny. The others were unconsciously wretched.

"Repulsions, discontent and mutual torment, haunt the household everywhere. Brothels . . . crowd the streets . . . passional starvation, enforced by law and a factitious public opinion . . . sick and weary wives, and even husbands . . . overwrought, disgusted . . . in their utter incompetency to meet the legitimate demands of healthy natures coupled with them; ten thousand forms of domestic damnation and everybody crying, 'Peace! Peace!' when there is no peace. . . .

"Rising up out of our false notions of propriety and purity; coming to know that everything is proper which enhances happiness and injures no one; and that everything whatsoever is pure that is healthful and natural, . . . we shall . . . prepare . . . for the perfect and pure blessedness of the coming millenium of the absolute liberty of the human heart."

She whirled off the stage. Her audience stirred;

the policemen remembered they were policemen; the marshals remembered their writs.

They arrested Victoria and took her to Ludlow Street Jail; and with her went public sympathy, which usually goes with gallantry.

Leslie's Illustrated Newspaper said, "These people have been placed in a position to give them real consequence." A dangerous precedent had been established. *Leslie's* thought Mr. Beecher should have remained silent, if he didn't want to contradict the charge. Or he should have evoked the law of libel; instead, his friends had evoked the United States Government. It was generally believed that Beecher's friends were behind the persecution of the sisters, and persecution it was called.

Groups met to pass resolutions against it in Philadelphia, Cleveland, Providence, Worcester, St. Louis and elsewhere.

The *Weekly's* circulation leaped, and when the American News Company refused to handle it, people formed clubs for its distribution. So many sympathetic letters went to Victoria that she said in the *Weekly* that "the large, blue sorrowful eyes of her who has so faithfully stood by my side during these three eventful years," saddened her, because "she, equally with me, is not enshrined in the freedom-loving hearts of the country. I know that it has been mine to take the more prominent and forward positions that have brought me to public notice . . . but . . . I could not have accomplished even the little I have, had it not been for her precious assistance, for her unwavering support." Victoria asked people's hearts to throb for

Tennie, too, and for Colonel Blood, "without whom we had both of us fainted by the wayside. . . . Ours is a trinity that is indeed a necessity to the work in which we are engaged."

Victoria and Colonel Blood were brought from Cell 12 in Ludlow Street for another hearing before the Grand Jury on January tenth, and record crowds attended the show.

Mr. Purdy, for the prosecution, said Mrs. Woodhull came into court with unclean hands. Bail should be fixed to teach her that it was no light matter to violate the law of the United States as she had done.

Their bondsmen were rejected until Victoria pleaded her cause before Commissioner Davenport with such effect that he relented, and Mr. William H. King was permitted to pay bail for Victoria and Colonel Blood.

At the next hearing two days later, Tennie C. appeared, followed by two deputy marshals. She walked up to her sister, shook her hand warmly, bowed sweetly to the commissioner and all the reporters, and sat beside Victoria. There was a stir in the courtroom, because everybody thought Tennie C. was hiding in Jersey. She explained that she had stayed home to nurse a sick sister.

Mr. Howe, Mr. Jordan and Mr. Edward McKinley spoke for the defense. Mr. Howe showed that the five line sentence on which the obscenity charge was based, had come from the Holy Bible, Deuteronomy, chapter XXII. His partner, Mr. Hummel, brought volumes of Smollett into court. Mr. Jordan quoted Hudibras, and Mr. McKinley discoursed on Social Freedom.

Dr. Ruggles went Tennie C.'s surety for five thousand dollars, the triad left the courthouse, and drove hurriedly to their office in a cab.

Eleven days later, District Attorney Phelps granted bench-warrants for the arrest of Woodhull, Claflin and Blood, on a charge preferred by Luther Challis, of sending an alleged obscene article about him through the mails.

"What have we done now," Victoria wearily asked Sheriff Jarvis, who arrested the triad at their office in Broad Street, at four-thirty in the afternoon.

Somewhat confused, the sheriff said, "This is for libel." There were so many arrests and rearrests, it was hard to know which was for what.

But people knew malice when they saw it, and they saw it in an arrest made too late in the afternoon to get bail and have it recognized. When Victoria, Tennie and the Colonel got to the District Attorney's office he had gone home, and the under-sheriff had to lock them up in the Tombs.

Rain soaked through the walls of that Egyptian mausoleum on Centre Street, walls already covered with mold. Sometimes waterpipes overflowed, and their effusions seeped through the cells. The cells were five feet by eight, and sometimes they had three or four occupants. When doors were opened to get a circulation of air, the prisoners inhaled putrid vapors. The windows and skylights never were opened; prisoners got neither fresh air nor exercise.

Victoria, Tennie and the Colonel were arraigned to plead at the Court of General Sessions the next day, and Judge Sutherland fixed one thousand dollars bail for each sister, and two thousand dollars for the Colonel. Mr. Howe reminded the court that Boss Tweed, who was charged with looting the city was under fifty-one thousand dollars surety, while sixty thousand dollars was demanded for his clients for an alleged misdemeanor. Victoria and Tennie C. were allowed to go in the custody of former bondsmen, but in default of bail, the Colonel went back to the Tombs. And there he stayed for awhile.

On February third, an open letter from General Benjamin Butler to Victoria Woodhull, was published in the *New York Sun:*

"I shall not be able to find time from my public duties to take part in the trial of your case. . . . I cannot believe that in . . . the prosecution of yourself and sister for sending obscene literature through the mails, in the Courts of the United States, there is the slightest need of my services or my counsel, I feel as certain as I can of any question, upon the construction of the statute, that the action of the United States Prosecuting Attorney was based wholly upon a misconstruction and misconception of that statute. . . . The statute was meant to cover, and does cover, sending that class of lithographs, prints, engravings, licentious books and other matters which are published by bad men for the purpose of the corruption of youth, through the United States mail. . . . To test it, suppose on your trial the indictment should set out the words which you are alleged to have sent, and then the District Attorney should send a copy of that indictment through the mail to his assistant, and the words should be held to be obsence writing, then he would have transmitted through the mails the same obscene writing which you had and would be liable to a like condemnation.

" . . . If I were your counsel I should advise you to make

no further defense but mere matter of law. . . . I do not believe that a legal wrong can be done you in this behalf before any learned and intelligent judge. . . .

Benjamin F. Butler."

On the same day came the long awaited decision from Commissioner Davenport. He said such a case was never contemplated, when the statute was passed, under which the proceedings were started. Ordinarily he would at once "release the accused." But in view of the importance of the questions involved, "the anxiety of the prisoners, as well as the community, for a definite settlement of the whole matter, I am disposed to, and shall hold the prisoners to await the action of the Grand Jury, to the end that a judicial determination by the Circuit Court of the United States may be had, and the rights, both of the prisoners and the public, be finally ascertained," said Commissioner Davenport.

Victoria went on a lecture tour, and told "The Naked Truth" to enormous audiences, wherever she could get a hall. She was the woman of the hour, piquant and prurient according to the press. But she never was coarse; many were amazed at her refinement and earnestness. Many who went to condemn were captivated by her oratory and her personality.

Between arrests, the *Weekly* came out. Undaunted, in every number it printed articles called, "Beecher, Tilton and Bowen," rehashing some phase of the affair. In May, 1873, it reprinted "The Beecher-Tilton Scandal Case," from the issue of November second, and Mr. Beecher didn't even say "Entirely."

VICTORIA C. WOODHULL
(From a photograph taken by Sarony in 1873)

In the meantime, Bowen had been attacking and defending the great preacher, alternately. The story involving Beecher with Bowen's first wife had been printed, and nobody had denied it conclusively. Neither Mrs. Stanton nor Miss Anthony had denied their share in Victoria's exposé.

The public knew that the District Attorney had said that Victoria, Tennie C. and Colonel Blood had libelled a gentleman whose character "is well worth the while the Government of the United States to vindicate." But the public was beginning to doubt whether the United States could vindicate Mr. Beecher's character, though they no longer could doubt that some of its minions were making an effort, obliquely, through Luther Challis' wish for revenge, and Comstock's fear of the devil's disciples.

Some Americans wanted to save the country from graver dangers than the devil's disciples; Americans just as zealous as Comstock were stirred to action by any crisis that seemed to threaten the idealistic foundations of the Republic. They thought it an outrage for the United States Government to try to vindicate any private citizen; they thought it a disaster for the machinery of the State to be distorted to persecute two young women and a Missouri colonel.

This feeling culminated in Edward H. G. Clark of the *Troy Whig* and the *Troy Daily Press*. He said, "Through these two women, American law has been outraged, the rights of the press assailed, freedom of speech endangered and the functions of republican government usurped, to cloak the reputation of one or two prominent individuals."

Then this young journalist, who had been "raised

Number I. NEW YORK, ALBANY AND TROY, MAY, 1873. Price Ten Cents.

THE REPUBLIC THREATENED!!

THE BEECHER-TILTON SCANDAL

AND THE

BEECHER-BOWEN-COMSTOCK CONSPIRACY.

THE SEAL BROKEN AT LAST.

Woodhull's "Lies" and Theodore Tilton's "True Story."

THE ACCOUNT HORRIBLE AT BEST.

NO "OBSCENITY," BUT GOD'S TRUTH.

The Sexual Ethics of Plymouth Church—A New Revelation—The Brooklyn Saints Torture Saint Paul into a Free-Lover.

The THUNDERBOLT Shatters a Bad Crowd and Ploughs up the Whole Ground.

AGAINST THE

WHOLE PEOPLE OF THE UNITED STATES!

In no other terms will I ever consent to describe that bastard New York monstrosity, begotten of lust, fear and guilt,—the arrest of Woodhull and Claflin for "PUBLISHING OBSCENE LITERATURE."

If I had myself been situated like Theodore Tilton on the day of that arrest, and the darlings of my household had been so cruelly belied as his "true story" claims of his own, I don't know but I could have gone into Broad Street and cut the throats of Woodhull, Claflin and Blood, with as little compunction as I would shoot a mad dog. But that would have been a business and a risk confined to three or four persons. It would not have been a NATIONAL FRAUD, ENDANGERING EVERY GREAT PRINCIPLE AT THE BOTTOM OF HUMAN LIBERTY. The special friends, however, of Henry Ward Beecher—the skulkers of Plymouth Church and the Young Men's Christian Association—preferred to dishonor the laws of their country and the freedom of its people by a gigantic performance of bigotry and chicane. In the shadow of their false pretenses, the Woodhull slanders, however atrocious, have grown comparatively dim and insignificant. The question of the MERE RAKE, WHOM THE MORALIST MIGHT PITY AND FORGIVE, sinks in the question of the CONSPIRATOR AND TRAITOR, WHOM THE PATRIOT MUST HATE.

A law of the United States, passed June 8th, 1872, makes a very proper provision in aid of public morals by branding the transmission of obscene literature through the mails as a misdemeanor. The Act is this:

"No obscene book, pamphlet, picture, print, or other publication of a vulgar or indecent character, or any letter

and as hell, also, is said to be paved with the same materials, I have never doubted their presence in the man. God seems to have made him partly a fool, in order that the fellow could do a good work as long as he could be kept from getting above his business. The dirty wretches, who corrupt young minds by feeding them on licentious books need some little man, by nature a spy and hypocrite, to check their villainous trade. A full-grown, honest soul could neither sell the books nor dodge and lie to catch those who do. In such a dilemma the earth has a Comstock.

Mr. Comstock declares that, in prosecuting Woodhull and Claflin, he has never moved in collusion with Mr. Beecher. In spite of the habit of tongue necessary to his vocation, he probably tells the truth: Mr. Beecher has acted, from the first, through his friends. But one of the affidavits on which the arrest of the two women was procured, was made by one Taliesin William Rees, a clerk in the office of the *Independent*; and that Mr. Henry C. Bowen, the proprietor of that journal, might be trusted to act for Mr. Beecher, (when he could *save himself* by the same industry,) will be quite evident by-and-by to the "gentle reader" of the THUNDERBOLT. Is it not known that the scheme was planned in Mr. Bowen's office—spies being thence dispatched to Woodhull and Claflin to buy papers, and order them sent to certain persons by post? On receipt of the papers, Mr. A. J. Comstock made his complaint before Commissioner Osborn, and the women were arrested. They were in a carriage at the time, and claim to have been hunting up the officials who had come for them.

As the charge against them was

A FRAUD, BORN OF A PLOT,

and as they, if no one else, had brains enough to know

on Garrison's knee," published a special paper to "defy conspirators, beat free speech, and rouse a nation." Playing on Tilton's phrase in the "Letter to a Complaining Friend" he called it *The Thunderbolt,* and in it he printed a "True Story" of the Beecher-Tilton affair, which Theodore Tilton had prepared to read to his friends. Clark had made his own investigations and his own additions, and *The Thunderbolt* was much harder on Beecher than *Woodhull & Claflin's Weekly* ever was. It was not friendly to Tilton, either, but when Tilton, vacillating like Bowen between Beecher's salvation and his ruin, carried *The Thunderbolt* through the streets of Brooklyn when people were going home from church, they thought he was back of it. This was most unlikely. Clark called Tilton a "wretch," and he was not one of Victoria's followers.

"She ought to be hanged," said he, "and then have a monument erected to her memory at the foot of the gallows." He said she was a rapt idealist, regarded as a liar and a quack. "At one time she sinks every vestige of egotism in the absorbed expression of ideas; and at another she would steal the genius of a friend to aid her in 'putting on airs.' . . . she loves notoriety more than any other being on earth; yet she loves her notions of duty more than notoriety. . . . It is probable that she never wrote unaided and alone any of her 'great speeches' or her stirring editorials. . . . Yet she is the inspiration, the vitality and the mouthpiece of her clan and cause. . . . *Woodhull & Claflin's Weekly* has voices from the 'seventh heaven' and the gabblings of a frog-pond . . . yet the amazing journal is crowded with thought, and with needed information that can be got nowhere else."

Mr. Clark loathed free love and said so. He was neither a radical nor a celebrated eccentric like Train whom nobody took seriously. And he was ready to prove his assertions in court.

Nobody took him there. He was not arrested for obscenity nor libel. When Colonel Mix reprinted most of the *Thunderbolt* in *The Chicago Times,* and charged Henry Ward Beecher with an offense more serious than adultery, Colonel Mix wasn't arrested either.

The foundations of the Republic were safe.

Stimulated by Victoria's notoriety "The Victoria Leagues" of the Equal Rights Party issued "campaign documents" in which the party's platform was set forth, a platform that called for a new constitution for the United States; a national referendum for important legislation; universal suffrage and minority representation in the government; government ownership of mineral resources and public utilities; reformation of criminals instead of capital punishment; government employment for the unemployed; fiat money; graduated taxation to prevent the accumulation of fortunes; the abolition of duties on imports; the abolition of war through international arbitration; and an ultimate of universal government for all governments.

Spiritualist societies rallied to Victoria.

Woodhull & Claflin's Weekly reported the annual convention of the National Woman's Suffrage Association, but Victoria was not invited to attend it. "The Woodhull Memorial" was praised, but Victoria was not mentioned. Too self-righteous to realize that her own performance at the Steinway Hall convention was their justification, Victoria was deeply hurt.

There was a lanky young visionary named Joseph Treat whom she had befriended, a radical lecturer, whose wife was a distinguished botanist and entomologist. Treat filled the papers with letters about "Valiant Victoria"; he had visited her constantly in Ludlow Street, and was loyal now. But the influence of clothes on the minds of contemporaries who create images for posterity is so profound that Treat survives as a comic figure because he wore a white linen duster, summer and winter, with a hot brick in his pocket when it was cold. He was a poor substitute for Tilton and Beecher in Victoria's mind.

Laura Cuppy Smith stayed with her one sleepless night while the Colonel was in the Tombs. She took food to Ludlow Street when Victoria was there, and defended her on platforms all over the country. Mrs. Smith was the daughter of a British naval officer, a serious romantic, who left her family at fourteen and came to America. When financial difficulties drove her first husband to suicide, she went into the lecture field. She was an ardent Spiritualist, and the *San Francisco Chronicle* pronounced her "the acknowledged leading champion of Radicalism on the Pacific Coast." But just as she championed Victoria when other friends vanished, she plunged into labor agitations in San Francisco, and later in Pittsburgh she participated in the famous "sand-lot" meetings. When E. H. Heywood was imprisoned for mailing "Cupid's Yokes", she secured his pardon from the President. She dashed into every social storm and bore the brunt of it, too sincere, too faithful and too impractical to win fame or fortune.

And Victoria's old scars ached for famous people like Miss Anthony and Mrs. Stanton.

But Victoria was a dangerous associate.

Afterward she told about coming uptown in a Broadway stage with several business men and a well-dressed woman. Without noticing her particularly, Victoria sat beside her. Whereupon the woman put her fan to her face and whispered behind it, "For Heaven's sake, Mrs. Woodhull, don't recognize me here. It would ruin my business."

Then Victoria remembered her as the keeper of a famous assignation house on whom she had called on an errand of inquiry.

Some of the woman's customers must have been in the stage; if they knew she knew Victoria Woodhull, they would not revisit her house for fear of exposure.

"I am ostracized by those whom the world calls prostitutes almost as fearfully as I am by those whom I call the real prostitutes. Sometimes I doubt if I belong anywhere," said Victoria, miserably.

On June second the Challis libel case was called in the Oyer and Terminer Court before Judge Davis, who must have had a bad memory because Mr. Howe had to remind him that he had instituted the obscenity proceedings against the defendants while he was District Attorney. Then Judge Davis saw the impropriety of trying persons he had prosecuted, and the case was shifted to Judge Barrett's court.

When Mr. Howe told Judge Barrett that the case

had been called without allowing enough time for him to get affidavits from witnesses beyond the jurisdiction of the court, the case was postponed until Tuesday, after some argument.

On Tuesday affidavits were produced from Laura Cuppy Smith and from Mollie de Ford at whose house a part of the alleged action took place. Then Mr. Brooke, of the defendants' counsel, said he also was counsel for the man Maxwell who was under indictment for perjury, based on his testimony against Mr. Challis. Mr. Brooke said he had been trying for three months to get Mr. Maxwell's case tried, since the truth or falsity of Mr. Maxwell's testimony had a direct bearing on this libel case. Whereupon the District Attorney tactlessly said he "had reasons satisfactory to him for not trying the case."

Judge Barret said that while he had no control over the District Attorney, he would suggest the propriety of trying the Maxwell case before this one, and granted a two weeks' postponement to Victoria, Tennie C. and Colonel Blood.

The Colonel could stand the strain. He was not a worrier; he was a philosopher and a fighter, and he didn't care about anybody's opinion but his own. Tennie C. was more robust physically than Victoria. She, too, was worn out from the sojourns in jail and her work as business manager of the lecture tours, but she didn't feel responsible for the rest of the family as Victoria did and public sympathy didn't mean as much to her.

The New York papers gave small space to the trials

which were too monotonous to be interesting, and those who flayed the courts often flayed the sisters, too. Victoria winced at every criticism. There was so much unfairness, so much bungling, that she feared a conviction. Some of her bondsmen who were getting impatient for their money might abandon the triad. That would mean more jail, and jail had exhausted Victoria. Then she had had to go on a long lecture tour to make money. She had had to travel in overheated cars and make connections in icy stations at any hour of the day or night, and she never knew where she would be a triumph or a by-word; she had had to charm and scheme to get a hall to speak in, and win a hostile audience when she got it.

Worn and worried, harrowed and humiliated, she was such a marvellous engine for self-preservation that she could escape from the world when it was unbearable.

One sultry afternoon in June, she called at the office of the *New York Star,* and begged them to insert her "card" of protest against the injustice of the courts. Certain that she was being "railroaded" to Sing Sing, she was worked up to a pitch of intensity.

At five o'clock she left her office in a rainstorm, and on the way home she told Tennie C. she felt sick, but Tennie C. thought it was only the strain and the heat.

She took a cup of tea for supper; and while Colonel Blood was helping her upstairs, she fell prostrate. Restoratives were useless. Two doctors said she was dead. According to the looking-glass, the feather and other tests she was not breathing.

Wild with grief, Tennie C. telegraphed her sweetheart on the *New York Sun,* and the news went forth.

But in a half hour blood began to ooze from Victoria's lips; the doctors said she had ruptured a blood vessel in her lungs, which might save her life. Her hands and feet were put in hot water; mustard plasters were applied to her body. All night, Tennie C. and the Colonel sat beside her, dumb with anxiety. The Colonel's philosophy failed him now; he was almost frantic.

The next day she was still too ill to know that the papers were full of her again, the papers that she seemed to live for, throughout her long parade.

The *Graphic* said, "Her influence over people of intelligence and refinement, women as well as men, amounting in some instances to fascination, and in spite of theories and actions they condemned, is a phenomenon which has yet to be satisfactorily explained."

The Pittsburgh Leader ungraciously suggested that her illness might be an attempt on the part of the "obscene sisters" to get public sympathy; but if true, and if she died, "the world will be rid of one of the most remarkable, albeit terrible and dangerous women, who ever lived in it."

Brick Pomeroy's *Democrat,* as usual, was eloquent:

"At the door of death! . . . Mental anxiety, overwork and the unnatural excitement of weeks in prison or at the bar of incompetent courts, have combined against her vitality, and one of the bravest, if not the most discreet, women of the world is prostrate. . . .

"No more libels on the Biblical bulls and boars of Brooklyn! No more dragging the tomcats of Puritanism by their tails from rooms made sacred to lust by standing a Bible before the door to retard the step of the man whose wife was being debauched within. No more pointing to pillows of satin on beds of slush, wherein reposed the self-anointed Lord, for the wicked Woodhull is dying. . . ."

Chapter Eleven

"THE SCARE-CROWS OF SEXUAL FREEDOM"

BUT in a few days Victoria was sitting up in bed, free from pain. Nature had given her a respite from trouble, as well as public sympathy, which rarely is withheld from anyone who fights death, the common enemy.

It had given her a new friend, too, in George Ellery, whose daughter, Cornelia Böcklin, had been a reader of the *Weekly* and one of Victoria's devotees. She lived out West, and once she took care of Zulu Maud while Victoria was on a lecture tour. Now she wrote her father to do what he could for her.

George Ellery was a wealthy New York merchant; and as her friend, he was present when Bowen and the venerable H. B. Claflin, who was one of the mainstays of Plymouth Church, came with a shorthand reporter and others to see if she had any documentary proof against Henry Ward Beecher.

Utica Brooker started this curious meeting with a war-whoop, but she was eliminated, and Victoria came in, looking haggard from her illness. She gave them a free love lecture and said, "Didn't I know Theodore Tilton! I stayed with him at his house days and nights. I know Henry Ward Beecher! I have stayed with him at his house days and nights, and gentlemen when I say I stayed with them, I mean no myth." Then she said she would produce the evidence "on one condition. My case is set down for trial for next week, and I will reserve it until after that, but if you will get that trial out of the way, I will produce it. . . ." She showed them Beecher's signature on two letters.

Later Beecher told Bowen that one was a refusal to preside at Steinway Hall and the other a refusal to contribute to the Suffrage cause.

But Victoria told a reporter from the *Brooklyn Eagle* that anyone of sense "would have known that after several months of intimacy with Mr. Beecher, being with him frequently and alone, that our correspondence was not one of mere platonic affection." Whereupon Beecher wrote to the *Eagle* that Mrs. Woodhull or anybody had his cordial consent to publish his letters. He added that "the stories and rumors which have for some time past been circulated about me, are grossly untrue, and I stamp them in general and in particular as utterly false."

The current rumor was that Beecher had bought his written indiscretions, but it never was proved.

On June twenty-sixth, the jury was chosen for the obscenity trial before Judge Blatchford. The stuffy court-room was packed with spectators, and Victoria, tired and pale, took off her bonnet and fanned herself; Tennie C. and the Colonel were imperturbable.

Mr. Brooke, for the defense, stated that the laws passed in 1865 and 1872 bore on an indecent "book, pamphlet, print or other publication," and inasmuch as *Woodhull & Claflin's Weekly* was neither a book nor a pamphlet, "other publication" was too vague a phrase on which to base an indictment. He cited the opinion of General Butler, who was a member of the committee which drafted the statute, that it did not apply to newspapers.

Judge Blatchford criticized the acts of 1865 and 1872, and said that since the act of 1873 added the word "paper" the inference must be that the previous acts did not include it. As the act of 1873 was passed after the beginning of the prosecution, Judge Blatchford said the prosecution could not be maintained. Inasmuch as the defendants were entitled to a verdict, he instructed the jury that no testimony had been presented.

The jury rendered a verdict of "Not guilty."

Victoria presented a petition before the Senate Committee on claims, for damages suffered from the suppression of the *Weekly*, and nothing happened but publicity.

Susan B. Anthony convinced an election board that she had a right to vote under the Fourteenth Amendment,—according to the "Woodhull Memorial,"—and was indicted for illegal voting. She was tried, found guilty and fined one hundred dollars, but she said, "Resistance to tyranny is obedience to God. I shall never pay one penny of this unjust claim." And nobody ever tried to make her pay it.

Victoria wrote the Free Love Convention at Ravenna, Ohio, that the noble work of defying the law that compels legal prostitution would bring present contumely, but "it shall work a crown of future glory that shall make you blessed."

From the scope and drama of her public life, Victoria constantly was jerked by some melodrama in her private life, and whether it was farcial or tragic, it always was out of the rut of human experience and Victoria always confided in the press.

When her family stated that she and Colonel Blood had assaulted Utica Brooker, she wrote to the *Sun:*

"Mrs. Brooker in a drunken or insane rage, attacked Mrs. Miles, her sister, with a heavy chair; for which, and her subsequent acts, Mrs. Miles had her arrested for disorderly conduct. It was, however, at my special solicitation that Mrs. Miles did not appear against Mrs. Brooker. It was expressly understood that she should not return to the house further to molest us, but no sooner was she released than she did return, and at once began her insane and disorderly conduct. Her complaint is purely malicious, and by her own avowal was made to affect the public against me."

A week later the *New York Herald* reported "The strange death of Mrs. Brooker," but stranger was the whisper that she had been poisoned, and strangest was the source, within Victoria's own family, a source from which anything might come to prejudice the world against her. When Victoria and Tennie C. insisted on an autopsy, Tennie C. wanted to watch it. That was not permitted. The autopsy showed that Utica had died of Bright's Disease. She had been drinking excessively for fifteen years, and when she could get nothing better, she drank bay rum.

Victoria neither ate nor slept for several days. A friend said, "The agony in her sweet, sad face is enough to wring tears from a stone." It came from grievances as well as grief. "Do you wonder, brother," said she, "that I should feel desperately in earnest to reform the evils of our social life when I remember what I have suffered in my own family? Opposed and misunderstood by my parents and sisters, compelled to bear an idiotic child by a drunken husband. O, my God! and the world thinks me only ambitious of notoriety!"

This was printed in *Woodhull & Claflin's Weekly*, with Utica's obituary, which was a little bewildering. ". . . perfection itself in form and almost in feature, in intellect a giantess, in moral sense a heroine, and in affection a very Venus," she lacked concentration, and yet "she was ambitious to excel in some great thing." "What she needed most was a master mate . . . she yearned for love . . ." but, "she cursed those who would have labored to set her, and all other women like her, free." She was married twice, "and while either of those to whom she was married would have made any ordinary woman happy, in marriage as the world goes, to her they were restraints that at the same time both curbed and nettled her proud spirit and kept her constantly on fire." "All this led her to narcotics and stimulants," concluded the *Weekly*, she was "cut off at thirty-one by marriage."

That Victoria Woodhull was a puppet for whom Colonel Blood pulled the strings and through whom Stephen Pearl Andrews ventriloquized was the accusation of her enemies in the 'seventies, and the intimation of her friends in the 'eighties. But Laura Cuppy Smith had opportunities to learn and the intelligence to recognize an independent devotion to the cause of social freedom that Victoria expressed fervently in conversation, as well as in extemporaneous bits on the platform.

Victoria's association with Mrs. Hooker and Mrs. Stanton was cordial but formal. Laura Cuppy Smith probably was the only intimate woman friend Victoria ever had, outside her own family.

Mrs. Smith shared some of Victoria's traits. She, too, was lovely to look at, and she had personal charm. She, too, was a gifted orator. But unlike Victoria she was not a demagogue. She wasn't a terrible siren either. She was a romantic aristocrat with the spirit of democracy. Whenever she made money, she gave it away. She was a radical without a following, because she fought injustice anywhere. She didn't specialize like Miss Anthony and Mrs. Stanton. But she was as honest as they were, and too real a fanatic to have proclaimed any puppet as "The Redeemer, and virtue and respectability as the two thieves on the cross," which was her characterization of Victoria at the Spiritualists' Camp Meeting at Vineland, New Jersey, a meeting the *New York Herald* called "The Witches' Sabbath."

Though Vineland was ninety-seven miles from New York, the *Mercury,* the *World* and the *Herald* sent reporters there to hear "the great gun" Victoria Woodhull "who made the most outrageous address ever yet delivered by her," according to the *Herald.* It was called "The Scare-crows of Sexual Freedom."

She said the safe-guards thrown around the family had made it "a community of little hot hells," it was monstrous to compel people to live together; a prostitute could refuse to cohabit, but a wife couldn't. And "what does it matter whether the child or anyone, knows who is its father?" She laughed at so much pretended solicitude for the children when the city streets were full of homeless, half-starved, untaught little ones.

She referred to the scarecrow of "License," and said that anybody had a right to be promiscuous who wanted to. "What is it to you whether I live upon fish or flesh," the only sexual crime was "sexual intercourse obtained by force."

"I would rather be the labor slave of a master, with his whip cracking continually about my ears than the forced sexual slave of any man a single hour. . . . They say I have come to break up the family; I say amen to that with all my heart."

She told the story of a friend whose husband's "brutal approaches, when first married, made sexual reciprocity impossible for her. He knew but one thing, selfish gratification, and was oblivious to everything else. . . ."

". . . In a perfected sexuality shall continuous life be found. So also shall life not come to an end when its springs shall not cease to send forth the vitalized waters of life, that earth's otherwise weary children may drink and live. . . . Then shall they, who have in ages past, cast off their mortal coils be able to come again and resume them at will; and thus also shall a spiritualized humanity be able at will to throw off and take on its material clothing, and the two worlds shall be once more and forever united.

"Such to me, my brothers and sisters, is the sublime mission of Spiritualism, to be outwrought through the sexual emancipation of woman, and her return to self-ownership, and to individualized existence. . . ."

Dramatically, with Colonel Blood by her side, Victoria declared, "This is my lover; but when I cease to love him, I will leave him, though I trust that will never be."

The convention passed resolutions to further the cause of social freedom.

Victoria gave the "Scarecrow" speech at the Spiritualist meeting at Silver Lake, Massachusetts. And Laura Cuppy Smith wrote to the *Weekly* about a curious phenomenon. In one of Victoria's photographs, the bearded face of a man appeared, with one arm outstretched towards Victoria, a wreath or a crown in his hand, as if in the act of coronation. Another correspondent reported the same vision.

But when Victoria, Tennie C. and Colonel Blood went to Chicago in September for the tenth annual convention of the American Association of Spiritualists, Mr. S. S. Jones denounced Victoria and her free love doctrines in his *Religio-Philosophical Journal*. The Colonel never felt any animosity towards anyone, he was aloof from the hates of men, but he never hesitated to punish Victoria's enemies. With a friend as witness, he went to Mr. Jones, (who didn't know him) and engaged several rooms in Mr. Jones' building. The Colonel said he wanted to house women there for purposes of prostitution, and Mr. Jones made no objection. Whereupon the Colonel swore out a complaint against him, and swore it out on a Saturday, so that Mr. Jones would be locked up over Sunday. Of course the Colonel did not use the rooms.

During the convention, storms raged around Victoria, but the Colonel sat in the front of the platform, facing the crowd with a smile. He was imperturbable when the delegates presented a protest against the "degradation of the society" to the uses of President Victoria's political aspirations. A Mrs. Mills opposed the Woodhull program, but when she started to speak Victoria, Tennie C. and Colonel Blood glued their eyes upon her. She moved uncomfortably and said, "I can't talk with these in the way." She took a dental plate out of her mouth and laid it on the table in front of the chairman, and everybody laughed; nor did they stop laughing while she spoke. And still the triad glued their eyes on her. She finished her speech and retired to the back of the platform. But as she had forgotten her teeth, the chairman picked them up and handed them to her, and people guffawed. She was not very effective. Many thought Victoria, Tennie C. and the Colonel had combined their will power to disconcert her.

Afterward Victoria grabbed her by both hands and began talking rapidly. "Why, my dear woman," she said, "when they put those handcuffs on my wrists when I was arrested, I said, 'You had better take those things off for you will only make my voice more powerful!' "

None of the accounts of the arrests had mentioned handcuffs, and a surprised by-stander said, "Why, Mrs. Woodhull, did they put handcuffs on you?"

She went on talking to Mrs. Mills.

The young man repeated the question more forcibly. Victoria paused, put her head down a little, frowned and went on talking, in her inimitable manner. But so strong had been her will against the questioner, that he moved off, his desire for an answer lost.

That evening a speaker said he had heard Mrs. Woodhull tell Mrs. Hardy, "If Colonel Blood should love you, I could love you the better because I love him." The gentleman said he couldn't follow her, and suggested that she "come out and divulge the whole thing . . . in connection with uncovering individuals from Butler down." She was going to tell you, he suggested, "that she, not for love or lust, but for power to carry on this glorious work, prostituted herself sexually to do it. . . ."

There were loud cries for "Woodhull!" Ghastly pale, she came forward and asked what the gentleman was trying to get at.

". . . A man questioning my virtue! Have I any right as a woman to answer him? . . .

"I hurl the intention back in your face, sir, and stand boldly before you and this Convention," said Victoria, "and declare that I never had sexual intercourse with any man of whom I am ashamed to stand side by side before the world with the act. I am not ashamed of any act of my life. At the time it was the best I knew. Nor am I ashamed of any desire that has been gratified, nor of any passion alluded to. Every one of them are a part of my own soul's life, for which thank God, I am not accountable to you. . . .

". . . When I came out of prison I came out a beggar. I appealed to the Spiritualists, to the reformers of the country, to send in their money that I might send you my paper. But did you do it? No; you left me to starve in the streets. . . . I knew my paper had to live or I should assuredly be sent to Sing Sing. . . . I went to your bankers, presidents of railroads, gamblers, prostitutes, and got the money that has sent you the paper you have been reading, and I do not think you are the worse for handling it. I used whatever influence I had to get the money and that's my own business and none of yours; and if I devoted my body to my work and my soul to God, that is my business and not yours.

". . . The spirits . . . have entrusted me with a mission, and I have done and shall do everything and anything that is necessary to accomplish it . . . whatever that has been or may be I am not, nor shall be ashamed to proclaim it to the world, standing side by side with my lover, who stands by me now, as he has stood for nine years, manfully holding up my hands . . . when deserted by everybody else. . . .

". . . Are there any of you who would have come forward and put your bodies in the gap? . . . If you will not, don't put me before you as needing to confess anything that in your self-sanctified spirits you may conceive to be prostitution . . . and if I want sexual intercourse with one hundred men I shall have it. . . . And this sexual intercourse business may as well be discussed now, and discussed until you are so familiar with your sexual organs that a reference to them will no longer make the blush mount to your face any more than a reference to any other part of your body. . . ."

So she told them about "The Elixir of Life."

". . . Take this as coming from the wisest and best of spirits," said she ". . . to whom for six years I have yielded a willing and appreciative obedience, I am commanded to declare unto you that in the despised problem of sexuality lies the key that shall serve to open the doors of materiality."

She said that nothing was so "destructive as that intercourse carried on habitually without regard to perfect and reciprocal consummation. . . . I need not explain to any woman the effects of unconsummated intercourse. . . . But every man needs to have it thundered in his ears . . . that the other party demands a return for all that he receives, demands that he shall not be enriched at her expense, demands that he shall not, either from ignorance or selfish desire, carry her impulse forward only to cast it backward with its mission unfulfilled to prostrate the impelling power and breed nervous debility or irritability and sexual demoralization. . . . This involves a whole science and a fine art, hardly yet broached to human thought, now criminally repressed and defeated by the prejudices of mankind. . . . Repressions by law and pretended public opinion, . . . are resulting in a growing disgust sexually between the sexes. . . .

"When sexual science is introduced into the schools, as assuredly it will be, sexual ills that now beset the young will vanish."

With an overwhelming majority the Convention voted to support the Woodhull program: social freedom, in all its phases. Delegate after delegate announced his intention to vote for Victoria, in spite of his instructions to the contrary. She was triumphantly re-elected president of the Association.

While she was in Chicago, a shy young spiritualist happened to walk down the street with her. He took her arm because the pavement was rough. That evening at his boarding house, this retiring youth surprised himself no less than his fellow boarders, by holding the floor for over an hour, talking with an eloquence he never had before or since. He had no personal attachment to Victoria, but he was convinced that the contact with her had "magnetized" him. And who can prove that he was wrong?

When a Republican candidate for the Massachusetts legislature said, "There were no nobler women than Victoria Woodhull," it was used as campaign material against him. But his friends convinced the convention that he was the son of an orthodox minister and that he neither drank beer nor even cider, so he got the nomination.

The Equal Rights Party had expired. Victoria wasn't even on the presidential ticket, but she told a San Francisco audience that such corruption had re-elected Grant that, "If Jesus Christ had been running against this man, he'd have been defeated." Which was greeted with hisses and cheers. When she said it was better for a woman to "bear twelve healthy children by twelve different men than twelve such children as we have now by one man," groups left Platt's hall. But *The Republican* of Galesburg, Illinois, said Victoria Woodhull's advice was a "profitable lesson" for mothers; *The Times* of Dubuque, Iowa, editorially found her "fervid, earnest eloquence" entrancing; and the *Dubuque Herald* said she "has created more stir, more sensation in our city than any man who ever trod the dust of its streets."

She was a country-wide sensation. Husbands forbade their wives to hear the brazen creature and heard her on the sly; wives snatched at husbands as they passed her on the streets; she was the glamorous scarlet woman for adolescents everywhere. There were other reform lecturers, but she had a Gargantuan reputation for wickedness, irresistible to a generation brought up to fight needs and fears with discipline. Who could measure the influence of her beauty and charm on men and women who associated her with sex, and sex with ugliness and shame? Who could measure her influence on the larger aspects of feminism? She dramatized womanhood on every platform and in every newspaper of her time.

The lectures were a family affair. Tennie C. was the advance agent, and with what a Western paper called "her faculty of walking right into the affections of the sterner sex," she bargained for halls and advertising. One editor confessed that "so fresh, so plump, so charming, so entertaining in his lonely office" was she, that he knocked down his advertising to a ruinous rate. Colonel Blood opened the meetings with the announcement that Victoria's printed speeches were for sale, and little Zulu Maud read a poem before Victoria stepped on the stage, in a black dress with a rose at her throat.

Then their earnings had to be spent on the Challis libel case, which started on March fourth, 1874.

An unfriendly judge allowed the plaintiff's counsel to cross-examine Victoria about her social theories.

He asked whether she believed a woman should leave her husband and live with another man, if prompted by such a desire.

Said Victoria, under oath, "If her will takes her away from a man, she surely ought to go." And "I hold that any man or woman, whether married or unmarried, who consorts for anything but love, is a prostitute."

"And has a right to break it off at will?"

"I hold there is nothing to break but hate; when they hate each other it is already broken."

The judge interpolated moral lectures, while the examination went into Victoria's divorce from Canning Woodhull, her relations with Colonel Blood; into Tennie C.'s past and the Ottawa indictments; into anything, however irrelevant to Luther Challis, that might prejudice the jury; with the encouragement and cooperation of the court.

But there was no testimony to convince the jury, the press or the public that the stories about Challis were untrue. His counsel tactlessly dared the jury to decide for the defendants; the attitude of the court would have aroused anybody's sense of fair play; whereas Mr. Charles Brooke's brilliant defense was a masterpiece of psychological appeal.

The jury debated all night and brought in a verdict of "not guilty."

George Ellery flung his hat in the air and shouted, "Hurrah!" Victoria and Tennie C. burst into tears. Roxanna clasped her hands and thanked the jury. Colonel Blood sat immovable; and Judge Sutherland said, "It is the most outrageous verdict ever recorded; it is shameful and infamous, and I am ashamed of the jury who rendered such a verdict."

Victoria went back into the lecture field and prospered in the reflected ingloriousness of the Beecher-Tilton affair, which glittered in the limelight now; thanks to all the busy-bodies who wouldn't leave it in the darkness, preferred by those most concerned. At a church meeting in 1873, Tilton asked Beecher if he ever had slandered him, and Beecher said he had no charges to make against Mr. Tilton. However, other Congregational pastors criticized Plymouth Church for dropping Tilton's name without an investigation, and they held an ecclesiastical council; which only caused more talk. The moderator was Dr. Leonard Bacon, and when he began to call Tilton a "dog and a knave", in print and on the patform, Tilton wrote Bacon the facts, and published the letter, since his reputation was his livelihood. Then Henry Ward Beecher appointed six members of Plymouth Church to investigate Tilton's charges.

Elizabeth Tilton left home and husband to vindicate her lover, who told the world she had "thrust her affections on him unsought", and vehemently denied their consummation. He spared nobody. He even tried to blacken Moulton's name. He said he had only met Victoria Woodhull three times, formally, because his sister Isabella regarded her as "Joan of Arc would a vision of the Virgin Mary." Beecher had to have his little joke. But he said that Tilton's "association with the Woodhull was fatal to him," and accused Tilton of blackmail, forgery, insanity and immorality, until Tilton's old popularity turned to jibes and jeers to his material damage. Finally he sued Henry Ward Beecher in the courts for alienation of his wife's affections.

The trial began in January, 1875, and ended in July with a disagreement of the jury. During the one hundred and twelve days that it ran, the papers reeked with it. They issued special supplements and pamphlets. Cartoons and doggerel took it across the seven seas. But Elizabeth Cady Stanton pointed out three beneficial effects. "It has knocked a blow at the priesthood . . ." said she. ". . . Men will not forget . . . that in all the associations of men with women, better a strong, self-poised woman than the weakling who is today domineered by this man's magnetism and tomorrow by that; confesses here, retracts there, and re-confesses and re-retracts," which was Elizabeth Tilton's muddled way. And, "For once . . . fellowship has been given to a woman the same as to a man in the same circumstances." For Plymouth Church upheld Mrs. Tilton to uphold Beecher. Theodore himself said she was blameless.

Victoria Woodhull was the scarlet woman of the trial, the red herring whose name was mentioned as often as Elizabeth Tilton's, in an effort to prove that Tilton's adulteries had driven his wife from home. But neither side ever dared to put her on the witness stand.

On behalf of the plaintiff, Stephen Pearl Andrews testified that Mrs. Woodhull's house was a center for the "radical advanced minds, on the basis of science and progressive reform . . it resembled the salon of Madame Roland during the first French Revolution." He said Victoria was "quite as distinguished a personage—(as Madame Roland) of a different type." Theodore Tilton was interested in the ideas agitated in the house, "but always with a vein of strong dissent on his part, which led to a great deal of discussion." Andrews swore that the recital of the Beecher-Tilton scandal "contained in the article (in the *Weekly* for November 2nd, 1872), remained as it came to me (for correction); the introductory part and the close, the literary cast and the philosophic cast of the paper, show my marks, perhaps."

Tilton told the court he had done favors for Mrs. Woodhull to silence her, to protect his wife and Beecher, but said he, "I wish distinctly to say to the jury that my relationship with Mrs. Woodhull was a foolish one and a wrong one as the event has justified, and I do not ask any man to defend me for it, but to blame me for it; but I say here before God that Mr. Beecher is as much responsible for my connection with Mrs. Woodhull as I am myself. . . ."

Then Victoria wrote to the *Herald:* ". . . No matter how inconsiderately (Tilton) has treated himself —not me—in regard to his relations with me, I forgive him heartily all his intended harm, now that the defense are making use of those relations to crush him in this case, and do what I can to relieve him from the effect of this testimony upon the public, not having the pleasure of denying it in a better way upon the stand. . . ."

One day she was subpœnaed by the defense, and when she walked into the court-room in a blue silk promenade suit with a tea rose at her throat, her black chip hat covered with a navy-blue veil, Mrs. Henry Ward Beecher saw her for the first time. She closed her mouth firmly and gazed at "The Woodhull", then her lips curled and her eyes glittered. Tilton was surprised to see Victoria; they looked steadfastly at each other for nearly a moment, and Victoria's face flushed slowly but vividly.

Mr. Shearman stated that she possessed letters which she declined to produce without instructions from the court. "Mrs. Woodhull, we call upon you for those letters of Mr. Tilton," said he, and added that she wanted to address the court.

She bowed to Judge Neilson and said that when she was arrested for publishing the scandal, her office and home were ransacked and she had no important papers left. The letters she brought were "entirely creditable to myself as well as the gentleman that wrote them." Others, she had reason to believe, "were in the hands of the defense, as well as of the prosecution."

Mr. Shearman read the letters. "These won't—do, Mrs. Woodhull," he told her angrily in Mr. Beecher's consultation room.

"Very well, sir, I am not to be the judge of that. They may not do for Mr. Beecher, but you were anxious to have them," said Victoria coolly.

And when he asked her what she and Beecher talked about when they were alone together for two hours, according to her story, her reply was, "We didn't talk about the weather all that time."

No wonder she had to tell her story in the *Herald!*

There she said the testimony of her negro servants, Lucy Ann Giles and James Woodley, was introduced "to leave the effect upon the jury that Mr. Tilton and I occupied the same bed those two nights." The beds were occupied by other members of the family, but said she, ". . . He frequently went up the stairs with me to the roof of the house to enjoy the starlight and cool breeze of pleasant summer evenings."

Apparently she wanted the public to know the means as well as the end.

After Theodore's testimony, Victoria prepared an article called "Whom the Gods would Destroy. To Theodore Tilton." Though "Circumstances modified the temper of the writer and prevented its publication," a proof copy was kept. "As Mrs. Woodhull is not apt to be called by either side, her testimony will tell loudest of all," said the New York *Herald,* which published it.

It not only was a paean of pride, and a scourge for disloyal lovers, it was a relief in contrast to the Brooklyn buncombe. The *New York Sun* voiced a general admiration for her "audacity . . . in following her premises so logically."

Referring to Tilton's "shameless departure from truth . . . to shield himself from the odium which he has conjured up in his own mind as existing on account of his relationship with me," she wondered if "he imagines that I shall remain silent under these new imputations as I have done thus far under others he has cast on me."

He said he left her when she wrote the "Tit for Tat" article. She said, "At this really last interview, Mr. Tilton knows well enough that there was no display of attitudes on his part. He had learned their inutility with me long before. He knew well enough that this interview was intended by him to be one of the most affectionate we ever had. He knew well enough that I warned him against apostasy to the movement to which he had given his allegiance. . . . But the dazzling phantom of a secretaryship under Mr. Greeley was more than his devotion to his pledges could withstand. . . .

". . . Mr. Tilton's real downfall dates from the time the Greeley movement collapsed, and not when his intimacy with me began. By his bold course during this intimacy he had won the admiration of the radical element of the whole country. He had forfeited all claim upon the conservative element long before he knew me. By his apostasy to the radical movement . . . he . . . was left standing almost alone ready to be ground to death between the upper and nether stones of radicalism and conservatism.

". . . I shall consider . . . his condition during the period of his relationship with me—shall show how he was complimented on all sides for the piquancy and brilliancy of his editorials, and how a very dear friend and competent critic withal, then absent in Europe, wrote that his articles sparkled in every line like rare old wine, which was to be accounted for only upon the theory that he was newly and madly in love, for nothing else could have inspired him to write so grandly.

". . . That he now regards his action as having been 'foolish and wrong' I have no reason to disbelieve. . . . But the attempt to make Mr. Beecher equally responsible . . . a little schoolboy's snivelling, —'He made me do it; if it hadn't been for him I shouldn't have done it' . . . ought to make him a laughing stock. I have said before that I believed that Mr. Tilton would make quite a man if he should live to grow up. . . .

Victoria C. Woodhull."

The next day she told the readers of the *Herald* that this had been printed without her knowledge and consent, but she saw the hand of God in it.

She said she had gone West to escape the mire and muck of the trial, but when Tilton held her up to the "public gaze as . . . an intriguing, vulgar and untruthful woman, I dropped my engagements and hastily returned to New York, my heart bleeding at every pore with indignity and outrage. . . . Under this feeling I . . . poured out the indignant truth that was boiling in my breast, wrung, as it were from my soul by direst cruelty. . . .

"But on the verge of its publication . . . I remembered . . . how, when they had cast me into prison and turned the whole world so much against me that not a man could be found who would come forward to turn back the iron bolts and set me free; how in the grated cell, before our iron bed, upon that stone floor, my darling sister and my angel mother kneeled with me . . . and how, as we prayed our cell was lighted up with spirit-light and the power of Heaven overshadowed us, while a still small voice whispered comfort to our troubled souls, assuring us that help would come. . . . I remembered all this and also how wondrously it had been verified; and then with the proofs of the article in my hands, I went before the throne of grace and asked that Jesus . . . come and show me the right. And He did come and He said:—'Stay thy hand, my child. All these things are committed to my charge. In the fulness of time all hidden things shall be revealed and you shall be justified where now you stand condemned. Wait!' "

This letter not only suggested a new attitude towards Roxanna Claflin, who was the Colonel's enemy; it was the first suggestion of Victoria's own great change. She always had visions when her world was out of joint.

But poor Tilton was bound for Coventry. His old friend, Mrs. Stanton, rebuked him in the *Newark Call:*

"Theodore Tilton need not have shirked an acknowledgment of his association with Mrs. Woodhull. Victoria Woodhull's acquaintance would be refining to any man. . . . She has a beautiful face! the ideal of spirituality. Victoria Woodhull has done a work for woman that none of us could have done. She has faced and dared men to call her the names that make women shudder, while she chucked principle, like medicine down their throats. . . . And when with a meteor's dash she sank into a dismal swamp, we could not lift her out the mire. . . . Theodore Tilton was ashamed to acknowledge Victoria Woodhull; but in the annals of emancipation the name of which he was ashamed will have its own high place as a deliverer. . . . I have worked thirty years for woman suffrage, and now I feel that suffrage is but the vestibule of woman's emancipation. . . ."

Chapter Twelve

MR. BENJAMIN R. TUCKER'S STORY

VICTORIA WOODHULL'S dramatic life, her beauty, and her association with celebrities made her the most vivid person in her time, who preached what she practised. But many others were just as consistent and just as zealous. It was a sociological era, an era of hope for any reform, because everybody had seen abolitionists who had stepped down from the stand dripping with rotten eggs, step into history. Everybody had seen the triumph of a cause; no wonder causes flourished and avowels of faith were rife.

A Spiritualist lecturer named Moses Hull wrote the *Weekly* in August, 1873, that people who travelled for a change of air or scenery, "might need a change of sexual relations more than either." He had "died daily" in monogamy. After he "humbly and prayerfully yielded to the diviner impulses" he "found peace, happiness and intellectual growth." His wife Elvira announced that he was a "better husband, a better man for it . . . where there is free untrammeled, spontaneous love, its expression in the way most suited to the lovers must be beneficial both to them and society." Readers of the *Weekly* whose ideal of liberty was license, cried "Promiscuity!" and were shocked. Moses Hull's lecture engagements were cancelled. Then he started a paper of his own called *The Crucible,* in which others confessed similar experiences. Said one, "We are man and wife without the aid or sanction of the church; but came together as two drops of water, blending perfectly,

Yours progressively, Angeline Brown."

When Victoria, Tennie C. and the Colonel went on lecture tours, the Colonel's brother George Blood and R. W. Hume, an old land reformer, edited the *Weekly*. Stephen Pearl Andrews didn't write for it any more. Inasmuch as Colonel Blood believed in fiat money and Victoria believed in the sovereignty of woman, while Andrews believed in "free money" based on different standards and on the "sovereignty of the 'Pantarch' ", they couldn't agree, but Andrews never quarrelled.

Victoria's friends and husbands never turned against her; but when she fell from the pedestal on which her adorers put her, they growled according to their natures.

Joseph Treat was the most pitiful of these because he was the most futile. He said Victoria "stood to me as one sacred and holy, and the very room in which I sat and wrote was transfigured every time you entered it, and the very sound of your voice heard through open doors, thrilled every fiber of my being, though we were nothing to each other, and both knew we never could be."

Something happened. Then Joseph Treat had to expose Victoria, as he had been "exposing" Commodore Vanderbilt, A. T. Stewart and Jay Gould in hare-brained lectures for years. But this time, Victoria said, "Having been warmed into life and into the power to do harm by me, he takes advantage of the knowledge he has obtained in the guise of a friend to send his envenomed shafts where he thinks they can do injury and create prejudice that will damage the interests of freedom. . . ." Which was puzzling, since in the pamphlet he published in 1874 called "Beecher, Tilton, Woodhull, the Creations of Society" there seemed to be no knowledge he could have "obtained in the guise of a friend"; it was so vile.

In fact the Treat pamphlet was a romantic caricature, too obviously malicious to throw any light on Victoria's personality; whereas another man who was disillusioned tells a story that illuminates her, because it just as obviously is told without malice; it is told from the perspective of half a century, with the detachment of a philosopher, though Victoria had attacked her old friends who were his friends, though she assailed her old cause, which was his cause.

It never would have been told, however, and we should never have learned how free love worked, when it worked, if Victoria had not assailed that cause; for in an age of sociological battle, men worshipped causes and ideas as they worship motors now and science. And like Victor Hugo's "Enjolras" in *"Les Miserables"* Mr. Benjamin R. Tucker's first love always has been the revolution. He tells his story now, not to avenge it, but to pierce the mists Victoria created by her apostasy in 1876 and later.

Mr. Tucker is a distinguished publicist, who, since 1908, when his New York publishing business, including his periodical, *Liberty,* was wiped out by fire, has lived in retirement in Europe; in France till 1926 and subsequently in Monaco.

The first number of *Liberty* announced that "This

BENJAMIN R. TUCKER WHEN TWENTY-THREE YEARS OLD

journal will be edited to suit its editor, not its readers. He hopes that what suits him will suit them; but, if not, it will make no difference." He might have added: "As soon as it suits them it will cease to appear." For Mr. Tucker says, "I find my great happiness in my knowledge of the truth and my ability to state it clearly. As soon as everybody knows it and can state it as clearly as I, my occupation will be gone, and I shall be uncomfortable. Incidentally, I hope to convince others, but that is secondary as far as my personal enjoyment is concerned."

In the 'eighties and 'nineties, *Liberty* expressed the doctrines of "Individualistic Anarchism," on which Josiah Warren's colony, "Modern Times," had been based in the 'thirties. At "Modern Times," property resulted solely from individual industry and free exchange. Sexual freedom was only incidental to what Warren called individual sovereignty. Other exponents of similar views were Proudhon in France, John Stuart Mill and Lysander Spooner.

Tucker said anarchism means absence of rule instead of absence of order, and that "Anarchists are simply unterrified Jeffersonian Democrats," as opposed to violence, as they are to socialism or capitalism. He described it further as "the doctrine that all the affairs of men should be managed by individuals or voluntary associations, and that the State should be abolished."

But Mr. Tucker's own words must tell his story, for reasons that will be manifest to its readers.

"This revelation is prompted by no spirit of revenge, since I freely declare that I have never suffered the least wrong, personally, at the hands of Mrs.

that this Revelation is prompted by no spirit of revenge, since I freely declare ~~that~~ I have never suffered the least wrong, personally, at the hands of Mrs. Woodhull. I justify myself simply by the fact that she, by her apostasy, and even more by her brazen disclaimer of her ~~American career~~ free-love advocacy in America as a species of mirage, not even corresponding to ~~no~~ reality, has forfeited the respect of every libertarian and made herself a fair target for critical exposure. And, as will appear in the course of this narrative, the present is not my first shot at that target. I opened fire during Mrs. Woodhull's life. ¶ Just one more preliminary word. In order to throw light on Mrs. Woodhull's personality, which is the immediate purpose of this revelation, it will be necessary to dwell upon my own personality to a disagreeable extent.

FACSIMILE OF MANUSCRIPT IN WHICH MR. BENJAMIN R. TUCKER TELLS HIS STORY OF VICTORIA WOODHULL

Woodhull," says Mr. Tucker. "I justify myself simply by the fact that she, by her apostasy, and even more by her brazen disclaimer of her free love advocacy in America as a species of mirage not even corresponding to reality, has forfeited the respect of every libertarian and made herself a fair target for critical exposure. And, as will appear in the course of this narrative, the present is not my first shot at that target. I opened fire during Mrs. Woodhull's life.

"Just one more preliminary word. In order to throw light on Mrs. Woodhull's personality, which is the immediate purpose of this revelation, it will be necessary to dwell upon my own personality to a disagreeable extent.

"Born in 1854, in the town of Dartmouth, Massachusetts, adjoining the city of New Bedford, of Quaker and old Colonial stock; bred in New Bedford from the age of seven; sitting steadily under the very radical preaching of Rev. William J. Potter, at the Unitarian Church in that city; clever at school, but less interested in my studies than in my outside reading; a daily devourer of the *New York Tribune* from the age of twelve until Horace Greeley's death; a student of Darwin, Spencer, Buckle, Mill, Huxley and Tyndall from the age of fourteen; an absorbed listener every winter to lectures delivered before the New Bedford Lyceum by Wendell Phillips, William Lloyd Garrison, George William Curtis, Anna Dickinson, Ralph Waldo Emerson and many others; living in a community noted for the important part that it played in the long struggle for the abolition of slavery; and gifted with a thoughtful mind and a voracious appetite for the intellectual nourishment thus abundantly afforded,—I naturally took a decided stand on all religious, scientific, political and social questions, and cherished a choice collection of chaotic and contradictory convictions, which did not begin to clear until I reached the age of eighteen, when a lucky combination of influences transformed me into the consistent anarchist that I have remained unto this day. In the meantime I had been an atheist, a materialist, an evolutionist, a prohibitionist, a free trader, a champion of the legal eight-hour day, a woman suffragist, an enemy of marriage, and a believer in sexual freedom. My anarchism dissipated some of my old beliefs and confirmed others. In the latter class was my Free Love faith.

"Thus it was that in 1872 I was ready to follow and admire the career of Victoria Woodhull, which had attracted my attention a year or two earlier (partly through my acquaintance with Theodore Tilton's editorial work), when she was conducting her campaign for the Presidency, a feature of her activity which I was never able to view as otherwise than silly. Little did I dream, however, that I was destined to enjoy the high privilege of her intimate acquaintance. If my memory does not betray me, I first set eyes upon her charming face in the winter of 1872, when, if I am right, she stepped, unattended, upon the platform of the old Boston Music Hall to deliver to an audience of three thousand people, in part friendly, in part hostile, her great lecture on 'The Principles of Social Freedom', the previous delivery of which in Steinway Hall, New York, had made her famous in the eyes of some, infamous in those of others. I was then living in Boston, a student in my second year at the Massachusetts Institute of Technology. I went to the lecture, accompanied by two boy friends of mine. We occupied seats well to the front. When the lecturer, not defiantly, but with quiet resolution, proclaimed her right to take a new lover every day, should she so desire, we joined vigorously in the waves of applause that for long moments vied with storms of hisses for the mastery. Without a tremor, apparently, Mrs. Woodhull awaited the cessation of the battle, and then resumed her discourse. That evening established her in my mind as a modest, determined, and courageous woman, preëminently fitted for leadership in a great cause. All the more, then, to me, she stood fixed on her pedestal, I at her feet, a clod of common clay.

"Some months later (I should say, in the late spring or early autumn of 1872) I saw her and her sister Tennessee, for a moment only, in the office of Woodhull, Claflin & Co., Brokers, 48 Broad Street, New York. I went there with Ezra H. Heywood and another gentleman whom I do not now recall. Mr. Heywood was the principal figure in the American Labor Reform League and New England Labor Reform League, the one holding annual conventions in New York, the other semi-annual conventions in Boston, and it was he who had put me in the path that led me to Anarchism. One of these conventions was the occasion of our visit to New York, and Mr. Heywood took advantage of it to make Mrs. Woodhull's acquaintance, asking me to accompany him. The two sisters received us, and a short conversation ensued, but we were not seated. I believe that I was introduced, but I remained in the background, saying nothing. Probably I made no impression on Mrs. Woodhull whatever. Incidentally I may state here my conviction that the brokerage business, in which, according to rumor, the sisters had been established by Commodore Vanderbilt, was nothing more than a façade, put forward to persuade the public that women, no less than men, may be competent financiers. I do not deny the proposition, nor do I question the native faculties of the two sisters, but certain it is that they knew nothing of brokerage, and that any transactions in that line effected under their names must have been conducted by some competent employee.

"In December, 1872, Mrs. Woodhull desired to lecture again in Boston, but could obtain no hall. Her recent exposure of Henry Ward Beecher had brought such a storm upon her head that the mayor of Boston and the governor of Massachusetts used all their powers to prevent her from getting a hearing. Even Parker Memorial Hall, built in honor of Theodore Parker by the society over which he once presided, was closed against her, causing Rev. Octavius B. Frothingham, always to the fore when freedom was in danger, to rebuke the society roundly in a Sunday morning address before it, to which I chanced to be a listener. His criticism was received first with hisses, then with applause. He stood his ground, declaring quietly: 'Hiss if you will; I have nothing to retract.'

"In this critical situation the matter was taken up by the New England Labor Reform League. Mr. Heywood and Col. Wm. B. Greene, the president of the League, determined that free speech should be upheld in Boston. Accordingly Tremont Temple (then, next to the Music Hall, the largest hall in Boston) was engaged for a League convention to be held late in February, 1873. Later the League issued its announcements, through which it became known that Mrs. Woodhull had been invited to participate. Learning of this, the owners of the hall cancelled the contract, and, being threatened with a suit for damages, paid a considerable sum to the League to avoid court proceedings. The League then secured several smaller halls for a convention lasting three days. The authorities threatened all sorts of interference, but the convention was held nevertheless. . . . It met Sunday morning, February 23, Mrs. Woodhull being present. The night before, resolutions had been drafted in denunciation of the action of the authorities and the owners of halls, and a speech in support of the resolutions had been prepared by Col. Greene, who was to preside. I was asked to offer the resolutions and to deliver the speech, which I accordingly did. The speech was in no way extraordinary, but, coming from a boy not yet nineteen, it excited much comment, and won many encomiums. These caused me much embarrassment, but I could not tell the truth. I had to play the hypocrite, resolving simply never again to be guilty of such a fraud,—a resolve to which I have adhered. I was far from realizing at that moment that Victoria Woodhull's career was one long fraud of just that sort. Did she suspect me? Probably not. At any rate she complimented me, though during the three days' convention but few words were exchanged between us. In all, she addressed the convention four times, including two set lectures, and the authorities were powerless to intervene. Her final address was given on Tuesday evening, February 25, but she was obliged to cut it short in order to catch the night train for New York. Hurrying from the hall, she left a wrap behind. Mr. Heywood asked me to make a rush to the station to restore it to her. Accompanied by William B. Wright, one of the boy friends who heard the Music Hall lecture in my company, I started, and we reached the station just as the train was about to pull out. There was a single sleeper, and I boarded it at a venture. As I ran along the corridor, Mrs. Woodhull stepped from her compartment, accepted the wrap with thanks, and then, suddenly and to my intense astonishment, she put her face up to mine and kissed me squarely on the mouth. The train was already moving. I ran to the door and leaped off, a much-excited and wondering youth. Some days passed before my excitement wore off. But I heard nothing more, and concluded I had received simply a kiss of gratitude.

"A part of the summer of 1873 I passed at my old home in New Bedford. During that time Mrs. Woodhull was seized with a severe illness, which barely escaped being fatal. In fact, at one time a report of her death was flashed over the wires. I read it with deepest grief and consternation, mourning less the loss of a friend than the loss of a leader. . . .

"During this summer of 1873 it was arranged between my parents and myself that, instead of finishing my course at the Institute of Technology (which did not interest me), I should, in completion of my education, pass a few months in Boston for the lecture season, a few months in New York (with which city I was not yet very familiar), and, finally, from six months to a year in Europe. Accordingly the autumn found me in Boston. In October Mrs. Woodhull's husband, Col. James H. Blood, whom I had never seen, came to the city. I do not remember whether we met by appointment or by accident. At all events our first interview took place in the reading-room of the Parker House, a place which I frequented. He told me that he had come to Boston to arrange a lecture tour for Mrs. Woodhull in various New England cities, such as Salem, Lynn and Lawrence, and that her subject would be finance. He detailed his plans at some length, and then (whether from sudden impulse or in pursuance of a previously-formed design, I know not) asked me to join him in the management of the tour. I was not very enthusiastic over the project: first, because on nearly all subjects save love and marriage I was in fundamental disagreement with the teachings of *Woodhull & Claflin's Weekly*, and second, because I doubted the possibility of drawing, on so dry a subject as finance, audiences large enough to make the tour profitable. Nevertheless I desired to help in the almost hopeless struggle for sexual freedom, and therefore accepted the invitation, at the same time warning Col. Blood that the business was new to me and that I could promise only to do my best. The first lecture was scheduled for Salem on Tuesday evening, October 28th, and I started for that city about a week in advance. I engaged the largest hall, arranged for the printing and placing of the posters, paid at the newspaper offices for advertisements to be inserted at specified dates, and returned to Boston. Probably some local journal announced the news in advance of the advertising. At any rate the municipal authorities got wind of the affair and hastened to declare that the lecture would be prohibited. When I reappeared at Salem on Friday, October 24, I found, to my astonishment, that the use of the hall had been withdrawn, and that the unusually philanthropic newspapers had omitted the advertisements, thinking thereby to save me money, and had announced instead that the lecture would not be given. Without stopping to thank them for their kindness, I ran to the office of the mayor, General Cogswell, an eminent lawyer of generous girth and imposing presence, who either had been, or later became, a rather prominent member of Congress. I asked him why the city government had forbidden the lecture. He vouchsafed no further information than that the good people of Salem could not be permitted to listen to Mrs. Woodhull's pernicious teachings on love and marriage. I reminded him that, since the subject of the lecture was finance, the objection was malapropos, in reply to which he intimated that the subject was a shield under cover of which the objectionable doctrines would be promulgated. Seeing that he was beyond the reach of reason, I took the next train for Boston that I might consult Col. Blood. He gave me a copy of the lecture in the form of printed proof-sheets, and Saturday morning I reappeared in General Cogswell's office (my bashfulness did not extend to fear of mayors), flung the proof-sheets on his desk, and announced to him that there was the lecture to be delivered, that Mrs. Woodhull certainly was entitled to deliver it, and that, should her right be denied, a suit against the city for damages would be brought straightway. And in the same breath I reminded him of what had occurred in the Tremont Temple case at Boston. He looked at me apparently with some surprise, wondering, I fancy, what the cheeky kid would say or do next. When he had recovered, he answered: 'Very well; the aldermen are to meet here this afternoon, and you may call at three o'clock for your answer.' You may be sure that I was on time. He handed me the proof-sheets, saying: 'We have looked the lecture over; it's a mess of nonsense (I did not tell him that I agreed with him), but we suppose that the woman has a right to utter it if she wants to, and so the prohibition has been rescinded.' 'Well,' I replied, 'it's pretty late in the day, and irreparable damage has already been done, but I suppose that I must accept the situation.' I hastened to the newspaper offices, re-ordered the insertion of the advertisements (though they could not appear until Monday afternoon, some twenty-four hours prior to the lecture) and eagerly took the Boston train, Col. Blood having promised me that Mrs. Woodhull's arrival was looked for on that day. I was living in a furnished room on Bowdoin Street. On my arrival my landlady, who up to that time had been blissfully unaware that she was harboring so disreputable a person, haltingly informed me that a certain Mrs. Woodhull had called that afternoon in a carriage, and, not finding me, had left word that she was at the Parker House. My dinner that evening was dispatched with greater speed than usual. After it, I started for the hotel, not knowing, but rather hoping, that my 'ruin' was near at hand, and much concerned as to how one ought to behave when faced with the impending disaster. . . .

"It is fitting at this point to state just how virtuous I was at the age of nineteen, and why. As already indicated, my mental activity during my 'teens was enormous. It entirely absorbed my physical energy. Athletic sports did not attract me. Marbles during my early 'teens, billiards (occasionally bowling) during the later, and now and then a game of cards,—these were my only amusements. Luckily I had an iron constitution and perfect digestion, and these preserved my health. But my manner was rather that of a weakling. I was bashful, shy, timid, ill at ease, in a degree exceptional. I had to be driven to dances, parties, and every sort of social diversion. Anything that exercised my mind attracted me; almost any other form of exercise I found repellent. Toward girls I felt a special indifference. I would walk around the block to avoid meeting one. And, so far as I know, no girl had thc slightest use for me. I had read much on sexual problems and sexual physiology. On these subjects I was more than usually well-informed. But my sexual instincts had not been awakened. And so it was that at the age of nineteen I was still virgin.

"Many persons will imagine that, in telling the story of the next four or five days of my life, I am striving to damage Mrs. Woodhull's character. Far from it! I am willing to inflict *deserved* injury on her, but, in this particular affair, she deserves, not injury, but honor. It was a part of her doctrine, as it is a part of mine, that, in cases of sexual attraction, the initiative may be taken as properly by the woman as by the man, and that, when she takes it, she should do so frankly, modestly, and unmistakably, rather than by arts and wiles and coquetry. It is decidedly to Mrs. Woodhull's credit that, in this at least, she was faithful to her creed.

"On reaching the hotel I was ushered into Col.

Blood's room, where I found Mrs. Woodhull also, as well as two callers, one of them being Mrs. Hardy, then a well-known Spiritualist medium, and the other a woman, unknown to me, who had come in Mrs. Hardy's company. As I entered, Mrs. Woodhull came forward, her face wreathed with cordial smiles, and her two hands, both outstretched, clasped mine and shook them warmly. The callers remained some time longer, during which I told the news that I had brought from Salem. About a quarter before ten they rose to go. Mrs. Hardy lived about a mile away, and Mrs. Woodhull asked Col. Blood to escort the ladies to their homes. I noticed that, though he was always courteous and kindly, he did not seem over-anxious to comply. Probably he was tired. The event showed, however, that he was not disturbed as to what might happen in his absence. At any rate, he went. Before they were twenty feet from the door, Mrs. Woodhull turned the key, and hung a wrap upon the knob to cover the key-hole. Then, always in a quiet, earnest, charming manner, she marched straight to the chair in which I was seated, leaned over and kissed me, remarking then: 'I've been wanting to do that so long!' Then, with a grace all her own, she gently swung herself around, and placed herself upon my knee, I behaving always like a puzzled brute. In that attitude we talked for some minutes. Then she arose, and I went to another chair near a table in the centre of the room. Presently she returned to my knee. A few moments later she took another chair and sat in it by my side. The conversation continued, and I made some reference to the Beecher-Tilton exposure. In that connection she remarked very quietly that she herself had

had sexual relations both with Tilton and with Beecher. As to Tilton I did not need the information. No person, possessed of insight, can read Tilton's biography of Victoria Woodhull without perceiving that it is the work of a man madly in love, who, for the moment at any rate, has lost all sense of proportion. As to Beecher, I was more surprised. But I believe that she told the truth. Let me say right here that I could easily have learned much more than I ever did ascertain about Mrs. Woodhull's past, had I been disposed to be inquisitive. But I have always been averse to asking questions that could by any possibility be deemed intrusive.

"When Col. Blood returned, he asked her if she did not feel the need of another meal after her day's journey. 'Oh, no', she answered, with a meaning smile, 'we have just had refreshment that you know not of.' But we really had had no other refreshment than that just described.

"I said 'good-night,' promising to return the following morning. Accordingly the next day, Sunday, found me at their room at ten o'clock. Col. Blood was not there. Mrs. Woodhull lay on a lounge, and I took a chair beside her. After some conversation, she said: 'Do you know, I should dearly love to sleep with you?' Thereupon any man a thousandth part less stupid than myself would have thown his arms around her neck and smothered her with kisses. But I simply remarked that were her desire to be gratified, it would be my first experience in that line. She looked at me with amazement. 'How can that be?' she asked. And I explained, much as I have already explained in this narrative. Col. Blood soon came in, and we talked of the Salem affair. I went away for luncheon, and was to come back in the afternoon. When I arrived, about three o'clock, Col. Blood was writing at a table in one corner of the room. Mrs. Woodhull lay on a lounge in the opposite corner. She complained of a slight headache, and asked me to sit at the head of the lounge and place my hand on her forehead. I did so. After a time, as I was stroking her forehead, Col. Blood rose, gathered up his papers, and said: 'I must go down to the reading-room to finish my work. There's altogether too much magnetism about here for me.' Believing his excuse to be genuine, I asked, 'Is it possible that you feel this, way over there?' 'Well, I should say I do,' he answered. And down stairs he went. After that, affairs moved rather more rapidly. Mrs. Woodhull was still obliged to make all the advances; I, as before, was slow and hesitating, because of my lack of *savoir faire*. But, despite all obstacles, within an hour my 'ruin' was complete, and I, nevertheless, a proud and happy youth. 'What will Col. Blood think of this?' I finally had the courage to ask. 'Oh, that will be all right,' she replied, 'and, besides, he cannot deny that it's largely his own fault. Why, only the other day he wrote to me of you in glowing terms, declaring, "I know very well what *I* would do, were he a girl."'

"As I rose to go, she said, 'Be sure to come back this evening; and, as you pass out, please step into the reading-room and speak to Col. Blood, in order that he may know that you are no longer with me.' I did as told, and was received by the Colonel in a most natural and hospitable manner, after which I departed, walking on air. In the evening I was there again.

Communicating with the room was a large bath-room. Toward ten o'clock Col. Blood, without saying a word, pulled the lounge into the bath-room, shut himself up there, and went to bed, leaving the sleeping-room, to Mrs. Woodhull and myself. At one o'clock in the morning I left the hotel, in order that Col. Blood might not be obliged to pass the entire night so uncomfortably.

"On Monday I went again to Salem to assure myself that no further difficulties had arisen. On Tuesday we all went to Salem for the lecture. There were not more than a hundred people in the hall, and scarcely a woman among them. The lecture fell flat, as I expected. The receipts were insufficient to pay for the hall. Consequently the tour was abandoned, although six cities had been scheduled. The list may be found in *Woodhull & Claflin's Weekly* of November 8, 1873, that paper having had the strange habit of dating its issue a fortnight later than the day of its actual appearance. I think that no mention of the failure of the tour was ever made in its columns.

"Mrs. Woodhull and Col. Blood remained in Boston about a week. I think that it must have been on Sunday, November 2, that we all went to a Spiritualist camp-meeting at Silver Lake, where Mrs. Woodhull delivered an address. Several group photographs were taken there. In one of them Mrs. Woodhull and Col. Blood were the central figures, with myself, her boy lover, seated between them, but slightly in their rear. There were about twenty persons in the group —all Spiritualists, save myself.

"I told Mrs. Woodhull, on her departure for New

SPIRITUALIST CAMP MEETING IN 1873 AT SILVER LAKE GROVE, PLYMPTON, MASS.
(Victoria Woodhull in center foreground; Benjamin R. Tucker between Victoria and Colonel Blood)

York, that she would see me there early in 1874. Some days later I sent her the first love-letter of my life. She did not answer it; but, instead, I received a friendly letter from Col. Blood. Her failure to answer me mystified me at first, but later I attributed it to unfamiliarity with the art of penmanship,—a matter to which I will refer again. Naturally I did not attempt to continue the correspondence.

"I am unable to fix the date of my arrival in New York. Probably it was in February. At any rate I made my first appearance at the office of the *Weekly,* 111 Nassau Street, one winter day, at noon, in the midst of a very severe snow-storm. There were two persons in the single room of which the office consisted,—Tennie, seated at a desk, and Zulu, sitting opposite her. Both were in street costume and busily engaged in doing nothing at all. I stepped up to Tennie's desk and asked her if Mrs. Woodhull was to be seen. She answered that her sister was just returning from a Western lecture tour, and was expected to arrive, together with Col. Blood, that evening. I told her that I had come from Boston, and that my name was Tucker, 'What! is this Bennie Tucker?' I allowed that she was a good guesser. 'Why!' she exclaimed, 'Vicky just thinks the world of you! She'll be awful glad to see you. But isn't this weather terrible? Just look at this!' And up went her skirts to a point midway between knee and waist (remember that this little scene occurred fifty-three years ago), revealing drenched stockings and underwear. I am unable to say what would have happened next, had not the door opened at this juncture, permitting the entrance of Col. Blood's older brother, George, leading Byron, the idiot. George Blood did not resemble his brother in personal appearance. He was short, frail, and blond, wearing a full and long beard. He always seemed to have full powers in the Colonel's absence, and was uncommonly efficient, energetic, and industrious, and, above all, devoted absolutely to the interests of his brother, the devotion extending to the entire care of Byron. . . . He was an expert accountant, and his hand-writing was beautiful. As to the cause and the doctrines, I never saw him exhibit either sympathy or antipathy, but certainly he could not have been a bigot. I never knew where he and Byron slept or ate, but his task was far from enviable. . . . I do not know how the boy came to be named Byron, but he certainly looked like Lord Byron gone daffy. All visitors to the office saw him. Presumably there was no other place in which he could stay. . . .

"After the entrance of George Blood and Byron, Tennie proposed that she and Zulu and I should go out to luncheon. Accordingly we did so. . . .

"I was to go away and return the next morning to meet Victoria. But before leaving I made the acquaintance of Johnnie Green and Jim McDermott. The former was Tennie's sweetheart and city editor of the *New York Sun*. A tall, handsome, smooth-faced chap, of about thirty, with an olive complexion that made him look like a Portuguese, and 'all gone' on Tennie. McDermott was his chum, a free-lance reporter, and a frequent visitor at 111 Nassau.

"The next day, I met Victoria and the Colonel, and I may add at once that for five or six months ensuing very few days passed when I was not in the company of some member or members of the family from ten in the morning until ten or later in the evening, meal hours generally excepted,—either at the office, or on the streets, or at their apartment. The Western lecture tour had been shortened in order that the trio might prepare for the approaching trial of the criminal libel suit against them instigated by Luther C. Challis, a rich Wall Street broker, an exposure of whose profligate life had been made in the same number of the *Weekly* that ventilated the Beecher-Tilton scandal. That trial lasted ten days, in the month of March, and I was in the court-room every moment of the time, except when doing some little errand in the service of the defence. There it was that I first came under the observation of Anthony Comstock, who was an important witness in the case, and with whom I had a dramatic encounter three or four years later in the vestry of Park Street Church in Boston. But, as Kipling would say, that's another story. The trio, having been surrendered, I believe, by their bondsmen at the opening of the trial, were obliged to pass two nights in the Tombs, after which, I think their bonds were renewed. I remember that on the first of these nights, after seeing the prison gates close upon them, Johnnie Green and myself escorted Zulu to the apartment, if my memory serves me, of . . . Mrs. Margaret Miles. . . . In the Challis trial the defence was conducted in magnificent style by Charley Brooke, a dashing young Irish lawyer, who, after making a reputation in Philadelphia, had transferred his practice to New York under the wing of Tammany Hall. At his up-town residence he had an office for evening consultations, and twice during the trial I accompanied Victoria thither, waiting for her in the parlor while he outlined with her the programme for the following day. The trial ended in a triumphant acquittal, much to the disgust of the judge, who, however, had to content himself with a violent expression of his displeasure, as in the State of New York in criminal libel cases, the jury is judge of the law as well as of the facts, as it ought to be in all cases. One of the jurors in the Challis trial was Col. Wm. C. Church, editor of *The Galaxy* and of *The Army and Navy Journal.* Sometime after the trial, when Victoria, Tennie, the Colonel and myself were walking in a street near City Hall Park, we met Col. Church, and Victoria seized the opportunity to stop him and express her thanks. He answered that the jury had simply done its duty, but, he advised her to be more careful in the future in dealing with such matters.

"After the trial the sisters rented an entire floor, furnished, in a house on the East Side, where they lived, as well as Zulu, Colonel Blood, and Roxanna Claflin (Victoria's mother). I am unable to give the exact situation, though I was there for hours—nearly every day. I think that it was on the south side of Eighteenth St., between Union Square and Third Avenue. It was my habit to visit the office in Nassau St. in the forenoon, go to luncheon independently, return in the afternoon, start up-town with Victoria and possibly other members of the family about three o'clock, remain in their apartment until dinner-time, and return again for the evening until about ten o'clock. They lived in a condition of Bohemian disorder. When the hotter weather came on, some one usually took a large pitcher from the wash-stand and went over to Third Avenue to have it filled with beer. Many a time have I 'rushed the growler' for the family. Callers at both office and house were much fewer than in former days, for the old friends, one by one, were deserting. It was difficult for me to understand how the paper was gotten out. Undoubtedly George Blood edited much of the 'copy' and superintended the 'make-up'. Colonel Blood did a good deal of the writing. An old land reformer, Professor Robert E. Hume, a stout and mild-mannered Scotchman, apparently wrote most of the editorials on economic subjects. He spent hours in the office every day, and doubtless was on a salary. But to outward appearance that was all. Though Victoria doubtless was consulted regularly as to the conduct and policy of the paper, I do not remember seeing Victoria or Tennie do a single thing toward its issuance. Not once did I ever see Victoria have a pen or a pencil in her hand. Never did she read a book or give more than a cursory glance at the contents of a newspaper. I was told (I forgot by whom) that she could manage to write her own name with difficulty. Her book entitled "The Origin, Tendencies, and Principles of Government" has as frontispiece an engraved likeness of herself, with a signature under it that looks almost like copperplate. In my opinion the signature is not genuine. Tennie could scrawl a page or two, but on serious subjects nothing in the least worthy of attention. The writings put forth over her name teem with the names of historical personages about whom, had you questioned her, she could not have given you the smallest particle of information. It can be said with truth of Victoria that she clearly understood the Free Love position, and that she had a gift of extemporaneous speech that enabled her to defend it with eloquence and effect. But that was all. Neither sister had the least capacity for authorship. Of course, I speak only of their life in the United States. What they learned in England I do not know, but I do not believe that they could have attained more than a very superficial culture. On the other hand, both knew perfectly what they were about. They were not deceived, or overmastered, or hypnotized, or utilized as unwilling tools. Any claim to the contrary is the most impudent pretence. The various documents that were written for them but that have appeared over their own names were accepted by them voluntarily and even enthusiastically and with full knowledge of their significance; and the responsibility which they thus assumed cannot be evaded. Every person familiar with the thought and style of Stephen Pearl Andrews is morally sure that he wrote the lecture on 'The Principles of Social Freedom', and every person who was intimately acquainted with Victoria C. Woodhull in the early 'seventies is equally sure that, when she uttered that lecture, she was in ardent sympathy with every word of it. She has seen fit to deny it, but I am determined that her denial shall not stand.

"One afternoon, when I was walking up town with Victoria from the office, she said to me suddenly, 'Tennie is going to love you this afternoon.' I looked at her wonderingly. 'But,' I said, 'I don't care to have her.' 'Oh, don't say that,' she answered; 'nobody can love me who doesn't love Tennie.' Not liking to be impaled upon either horn of so perplexing a dilemma, I resolved to make at least a temporary escape. As we were nearing the apartment, I found an excuse for leaving her, and did not go back. The next day, when I saw her, no reference was made to the matter. Nor did she ever broach the subject again. Tennie herself, however, gave me numerous hints and opportunities. For instance, she once asked me to take off her shoes and put on her slippers. Seeing her motive, I became confused, and tried to put the right slipper on the left foot. She laughed at my stupidity, and at the same time seemed a little vexed. On another occasion, when I was going out for the beer, she accompanied me. On the way she managed to suggest, though I forgot in what way, the possibility that some night we might sleep together. 'Are you in earnest about that?' I asked. 'Why, yes, Bennie, of course. Do you think that I wouldn't do a little thing like that for you?' Months later we were staying at the Grand Hotel in Paris. Victoria and the Colonel had one room. Tennie and her mother and Zulu had the room adjoining. My own room was about a hundred feet away. Probably the others felt a little crowded. At any rate Tennie entered my room one afternoon, and, looking about, remarked: 'Why, Bennie, your bed is plenty big enough for two, isn't it?' I allowed the accuracy of her estimate, but refused to take the hint. . . .

"However unpleasant and disappointing may be the truth about Victoria and Tennie, it is equally true that for years they were victims of the most abominable liars. Blackmailers beset them continually, some of these belonging to their own family. One day Victoria handed me a post-card that had just been received, threatening terrible things unless certain demands were met. It purported to come from a certain address far up Third Avenue, but of course bore no signature. She asked me to visit the neighborhood, and see what I could find out. I found, at the number given, a tenement house with a shop on the ground floor. At the right of the shop was an entrance to the stairways leading to the upper floors. For some time I stood on the opposite side of the street, surveying the premises. I had just determined to venture into the shop and make some inquiries regarding the tenants, when down the stairs and through the side entrance came that frightful old scoundrel Buckman Claflin, Victoria's father. Having seen him once or twice, I instantly recognized his face. Among the many people passing I do not think that he saw mine. At any rate I had no need of further information, and so hurried back to 111 Nassau. When my report had been made, the matter was dismissed. They were accustomed to trouble from that source.

"Dr. Joseph Treat was perhaps a miscreant of another sort. He had been an active and stanch supporter of Victoria and her policies. What caused him to become a vigorous opponent I do not know. Blackmail may not have entered his head. In any case he was a reckless slanderer. . . .

"Victoria and Tennie were fond of money, but not miserly. They spent freely when they had the means. On several occasions I was the guest of the family at Delmonico dinners, and was entertained lavishly. This hospitality was never returned in kind, largely because I had not the means. I am absolutely sure that Victoria's love for me was thoroughly sincere and disinterested. She had little or nothing to gain by it. I was too unsophisticated to offer her a fruit or a flower or a jewel or a scarf, and she never gave me the slightest hint that such testimonials were expected of a lover. She received from me nothing but affectionate admiration and steadfast devotion, and with that she seemed to be content. Of the Claflin tribe, save Victoria and Tennie, Tilton wrote, 'Being daughters of the horse-leech, they cry "give" '. To me Victoria's cry was always 'receive'. Bitterly do I regret that her conduct to others compels me to ingratitude.

"After the Challis trial our life was not varied or outwardly exciting, yet the months passed swiftly. The summer was approaching, when I was to sail for Europe. . . .

"I had engaged passage on an English steamer, had paid my fare, and was to sail late in June or early in July. Suddenly Victoria exclaimed: 'Why shouldn't we all go to Europe on a short vacation?' And the proposal received immediate consideration. Tennie, who was always chosen for such errands, perhaps because of the abundance of her assurance, visited the various steamship offices to ask reduced rates for the trip as journalists, and finally succeeded in engaging passage on the steamer *Lafayette,* of the French line, for the entire party, myself included, at half the regular fare. I, in turn, was able to cancel the passage that I had engaged previously. We sailed, I believe, shortly after the middle of July. My father came from New Bedford to see us off, and perhaps a bit nervous as to the outcome, nevertheless confided his rather wayward son to the care of his elder companions. We had four cabins,—two outside and two inside. The former were occupied, one by the Colonel and Victoria, the other by Tennie and her mother.

Of the latter Zulu had one and I the other. I remember vividly only a single incident of the ocean voyage. On no other occasion, during my acquaintance with Victoria, did I ever see her in a state of angry excitement. One night, after I had gone to bed, Tennie came into my cabin holding a bottle of whiskey, which she was endeavoring to open. Just then Victoria happened along, and, at the sight of Tennie thus engaged, went into a panic. She begged and implored and threatened and wrung her hands, in the hope of inducing Tennie to desist. But all in vain. Evidently it was not the first time that Victoria had seen Tennie with a bottle of whiskey, and scenes of the past remained vivid in her memory. Her fears, however, were not realized, for Tennie, after opening the bottle, contented herself with a small glassful.

"On reaching Havre we took a carriage for a drive in the city and suburbs, and in the afternoon started by train for Paris, where we put up at the Grand Hotel. . . .

"The stay at the Grand Hotel lasted a fortnight The sight-seeing gave rise to some differences of opinion. At times the sisters preferred to go in one way, I in another. Old lady Roxanna, whom I detested, but who had taken a shine to me apparently, said one day: 'I'd much rather go along with you, Bennie, 'cause you like to stop and see; but, you see, the gals, they alluz wud travel on the fast line.'

"In that summer of 1874 the ravages resulting from the struggle between the Paris Commune and the besieging army of Versailles were still very much in evidence. Ruins were visible on every hand. One afternoon, when all of us were taking a carriage-drive through the Paris streets, Victoria began to condemn in round terms the incendiarism traceable to the Commune. As this seemed to me strange language on the lips of one who not many months before had marched in New York behind the red flag in honor of the Paris Commune, I remarked that the Commune had given Paris a very good administration, that much of the destruction was due to the besiegers, and that none of the incendiarism was comparable in gravity to the wholesale massacre conducted by the Versaillists during the Bloody Week. Seeing that Victoria had made a bad break, Col. Blood spoke up, confirming my attitude, and Victoria said no more. This incident indicated, not that Victoria acted in obedience to superiors, but that she was in the habit of espousing causes without examining their merits. The Free Love cause was the single one that she understood. There she was at home.

"It may be added here that Victoria was very nervous during her stay in Paris, as reports had reached her ear that the Paris police had been warned of her journey by the New York authorities, and that the whole party was under observation. This may have been true, but I was never able to detect the slightest evidence of it.

"At the end of their fortnight's stay my travelling companions re-embarked for New York, and I continued my tour. During the ensuing months I had abundant opportunity for reflection, which led me slowly to a realization of the fact that, however, worthy the ends that the Claflin sisters claimed to be pursuing, the means to which they resorted were unjustifiable and even disgraceful; and, in consequence,

I resolved to break away. When I landed at New York toward the beginning of 1875, I was somewhat relieved at finding them absent from the city, so that I was able to go directly to New Bedford without seeing them. When I discovered that they were filling their paper with Biblical interpretations as nauseating as they were silly, my disgust deepened. And so it was that our acquaintance ended with the same absence of ceremony that attended its beginning. My sweetheart's ignorance of penmanship, which had made things awkward for me at the outset, had its compensations at the end. . . .

"I desire to bear testimony that I always found Col. Blood to be an honest, whole-souled, openhearted, open-handed, generous gentleman. I acknowledge, however, that his participation in an agitation in which pretence and humbug frequently figured puzzles me. It must be regarded, I think, as one of those incomprehensible complexes occasionally encountered in human nature.

". . . Victoria was never very gay, but almost always cheerful and charming. . . . Her natural preference was for Jekyll, but under pressure, she fell back on Hyde; at least so I think now. . . . She would have been glorious, if she hadn't been infamous. . . .

Benjamin R. Tucker."

Chapter Thirteen

APOSTASY

WHEN Theodore Tilton called Victoria Woodhull the Joan of Arc of the woman's movement, it was not such a wild exaggeration. Victoria Woodhull fought the folkways that oppressed her sex, as audaciously, as courageously as the Maid of Orleans fought the enemies of France. Like her, Victoria heard voices from the otherwhere, and had the strange power which often is their source, or their effect. She, too, stirred the imaginations of men. She was an absurd extremist, but extremists are useful. No doubt, she was unscrupulous under stress; she was a fraud and a pretense, and yet she might have been the historical symbol for man's release from fundamental fears and artificial shames. She might have dramatised the sex hygiene that Havelock Ellis founded on scientific realism; that Sigmund Freud popularized with scientific eroticism. She was on the way to sociological significance when she took the turning that led to fortune instead of fame; a turning that made her an interesting phenomenon instead of a heroine of history. And probably she took it because of sickness and poverty.

There is some evidence that she had a feminine ailment, amenable to surgery, and aggravated by neglect, which could have produced enough anemia to sap any woman's fortitude, as well as her interest in sex, after a period of morbid stimulation. And anemia not only would intensify the discomforts of poverty, it would intensify the dread of the extremities of poverty, which haunts anyone who has suffered them.

Victoria had neither the time nor the money for surgery during 1875 and 1876, and while this is only an hypothesis, it would help to explain her "new departure", as well as the apostasy that followed it, an apostasy thorough enough to have been physically profound.

The new departure was preceded by announcements in the *Weekly* that one lecture tour after another had been abandoned on account of Victoria's health; and by repeated appeals, "to the generosity of the friends of true reform not to withhold any pecuniary aid that they can consistently extend us in this crisis"; and by "An Open Letter" to Commodore Vanderbilt, signed, "Affectionately yours, Victoria C. Woodhull and Tennie C. Claflin." It reminded the Commodore that his name and his check had opened the financial world to them, and that he had helped them to start the paper which "has caused the world to think as it had never before been made to think, and which has started one revolution, at least, that will last until the shams and hypocrites shall be dethroned. . . ." They asked him to be a "Patron Saint", to endow their work for "the personal sovereignty of woman", to make her "queen in the domain of the affections, where too long she has been subject only." This was a royalty Victoria stressed in those days of her extremest feminism.

But the Commodore had grown conservative. An old man now, he no longer was the bear of the market. And he didn't speculate with his body or his mind any more When he was sick he sent for Dr. Linsley, a medical man, instead of magnetic healers. A clergyman looked after his spiritual needs; he was through with clairvoyant seances. And his name had become an obsession. To perpetuate it, he gave a million dollars to endow Vanderbilt University, instead of the sovereignty of woman.

So Victoria turned to the otherwhere. Josephine had been her constant companion until she went into public life, she said; there Demosthenes instructed and guided her, and Napoleon gave her strength. But, "another tall, elegantly formed spirit, of gallant bearing" whom she knew to be Alexander the Great of Macedon appeared to her now and told her, "Your body shall never know corruption", which must have been comforting. She said those spirit-guides by whom she was controlled, were members of a "spirit congress, whose head and centre is a name more revered and widely known in the Christian world than any other," and then according to her last Tilton letter in the *Herald,* Christ himself came and spoke to her.

The editorial page of the *Weekly* had been headed by a quotation from John Stuart Mill: "The diseases of society can, no more than corporeal maladies, be prevented or cured without being spoken about in plain language." Quotations from Christ and Paul took its place. "The truth shall make you free" and "If a man keepeth my saying he shall never see death."

In the issue dated April tenth, the *Weekly* announced that the day of the Seventh Angel had come; the seals would be removed from the Book to reveal the hidden mysteries. People in Christian countries had rejected the Bible when science proved that it could not be a literal record of facts. If read symbolically, it would be a "light and an aid," instead of a "darkness and a hindrance," said the *Weekly*. Adam and Eve were universal man and universal woman; their fall was "brought about by improper physical habits" from which mankind still was suffering.

The *Weekly* purposed to interpret the Book of Revelations, "indeed, a book of symbols". And then began a series of elaborately symbolical articles and speeches based on a new interpretation of the Bible which indicated that the Garden of Eden was located in the body of woman and that perfected sexuality was the secret of eternal life.

Hitherto Victoria Woodhull's sexuality had been intense and extreme, but it had been purified by absolute realism. It had been an amateurish approach to the salutary science of Havelock Ellis. But as it veered now into symbolism, it seemed morbid, and morbid it probably was.

No doubt Colonel Blood wrote the Biblical articles. He had a clinical style which made them like metaphysical charts. But the Biblical lectures sounded as if Victoria had dictated them with "spirit-help", and as if she gradually were reverting to the ecstatic revivalism of her early Methodist training, as her physical condition produced an inordinate sexual stimulation which became violent during the interval when she was whipping herself to emotions she no longer wanted, before the time when desire stopped altogether.

She went on a lecture tour through the South and Southwest to support herself and her family. She defied the sick fatigue of overstrain which is so much worse than pain because it is inescapable. She dragged herself from town to town and stepped onto platforms, as erect as a queen, with a morocco bound testament in her hand, and a white rose at her throat. She wore her hair long now, knotted in the "club" style of the day. Her black silk dress had a demi-train, and she threw a lace veil over her shoulders.

With texts from the Bible and a sibylline air, she introduced "The Hidden Mystery". "As I contemplate its wondrous meaning, I . . . stand appalled before the fearful responsibility that it has pleased God to impose upon me. . . ."

She hurried into rhapsody, her worn face lighted, until she was beautiful again. She declared the Bible was an everlasting magnet because it held the secret of eternal life. A unity of sentiment and purpose linked the beginning to the end. "The tree of life, in the midst of the Garden of Eden is the culminating fact of the figurative creation", and of "the revelations to John on Patmos. The tree of life, the leaves of which were for the healing of the nations, together with a pure river of the water of life, proceeding out of the throne of God, stands the important feature of the new heaven and the new earth, which is to be, when man shall drink of the water of this river properly and die no more."

The *Weekly* told its readers that a missionary had come back from South Africa with news of a "pre-Adamic" tribe, who "have never eaten of the forbidden fruit of the knowledge of good and evil." They ate fruit, shrubs and herbs, and had neither disease nor crime. They lived to old age, and "rather go to sleep than die." Their differences were adjusted by the oldest man of the tribe, but women controlled the relations of the sexes, which began "when the sexual instinct first makes its appearance in the girl, and lasts till near death, and the women never menstruate." Because, "The amative desire begins to show itself in the female two or three years before the appearance of the monthly waste, and this appearance is caused by the non-appropriation of the life-force in the natural way." This "pre-Adamic" tribe propagated slowly, inasmuch as healthy women "bear the fewest children" and "the best." There was no restriction "between the sexes save the determining power of the female, and yet commerce does not obtain to one-half the extent that it does among the enlightened races;" because "the instinct has its natural expression before it gathers into a furious passion to rule instead of to subserve its subjects."

This was elaborately indicated in Victoria's speech called "The Key to the Hidden Mystery," with a mysterious reference to methods by which pregnancy could be "Governed by causative and not preventive will power." ". . . But I would not have it inferred that the true relations will tend to detract from either the happiness that is now realized by the heart or the enjoyments that are experienced by the senses. No!" said Victoria emphatically, "these will, on the contrary be increased beyond computation." She urged her audiences to "Remember the words of Malachi, 'Bring your tithes into the storehouse'. . . . Not waste them on the way thither. . . . Search the Scriptures. They point out the way to eternal life. I have given you the key. The holy temple is the human body, is the male and female perfectly united and joined together in Christ; or as he showed the way and the key to unlock the temple so that it's now hidden glories may be realized, are the tree and the river of life, blending their fruits and waters to become the healing of the nations, that is all the ills to which the flesh has made us heirs. . . ."

The *Watertown Despatch* said the purpose of this "Queen of the Rostrum" seemed "to be based upon a deep-seated religious enthusiasm."

But Mr. George Macdonald of *The Truth Seeker* which always has been a free-thought weekly, thought the lecture should have been given at one of those places that frequently were raided by the police.

Victoria began her speech called "The Garden of Eden" with an apostrophe to "thou land of pleasure and delight . . . where man fell and where woman was degraded. . . . Shall they now quench their thirst from the waters of the beautiful river Euphrates?" She explained why Bible commentators never had been able to locate Eden geographically, and after she examined the meaning of the names of its boundaries according to the languages in which they were originally written she concluded that "its four rivers, which have their source in the extension of the mouth, are the Pison, the blood; the Gihon, the bowels; the Hiddekel, the urinary organs, and the Euphrates, the reproductive functions. . . . Suppose . . . it should . . . turn out . . . that the long-lost Garden of Eden is the human body. . . ."

Then came such detailed eroticism at such length that it was dull to read, though Victoria probably made it stirring when she spoke. She ended it volcanically. "Welcome! Thrice Welcome!! Thou messenger of God! . . . Thou rebuilt Temple of God!!! In thy magnificent splendors we fain would worship the great High Priest and King, and pour out our souls in holiest praise and song. . . . Art thou the realization of that for which the gentle Jesus suffered, died and lived again. . . . When we catch glimpses of thy perfections, do we indeed see them through the door by which he entered once into the holiest place, and is set down forever at the right hand of God, to invite us all to seats beside him! Shall we enter through the gates into the Holy City, by 'The straight and narrow way' and find eternal life in the sunshine of thy everlasting glories, O, enchanting Garden! . . ."

This speech could be interpreted in terms of modern dream symbolism to express wishes, fears or exhibitionalism, according to the whim of the interpreter. It could be explained by Victoria's physical concentration on her body at the time. It could be explained in a dozen ways by as many schools of psychology, and all the explanations would be neat; none would be certain.

The *Albany Evening Post* was content to note her "Earnestness," and considered "her faith in her errors . . . so great that she becomes a power at once dangerous and fascinating." *The Age* of Houston, Texas, "rarely ever beheld an assemblage of any kind so completely under the influence of a speaker. Men and ladies were to be seen brushing the tears from their eyes as the pathos of this strange woman went home to their hearts, linking them together in that chain of common sympathy whose weird spell no individual present could successfully resist, if they would. . . ."

The *Weekly* needed a new faction, and so did Victoria. The left wing reformers were beginning to split. When Victoria flayed promiscuity and declared monogamy to be the highest ideal, (however unconventionally it was reached), the *Weekly's* radical adherents went over to the *Crucible,* which never wavered. Conservative Spiritualists read *The Banner of Light,* the most important Spiritualist paper, which came out squarely against free love, or any scheme for the regeneration of society, and advocated concentration on phenomena from the otherwhere.

Whereupon the *Weekly* printed a series of articles to expose the fraudulent materializations, cabinet manifestations, and paraffine hands that eventually brought Spiritualism into bad repute; and Victoria resigned from the presidency of the National Association. She said she could not participate in any organization that "ignores the most vital of all questions, and to reach which, I have advocated woman's social emancipation; for until children are born and bred properly there can be only slight improvement in the race. . . . I also desire to make it further unnecessary for anybody to travel over the country opprobriously, unjustly and untruthfully denouncing the cause of social freedom, and putting contumely and disgrace upon a divine thing, by reason of their personal dislike of me. . . ."

Victoria had endured too much dislike and opprobrium. Now that she had no more physical buoyancy, she had to have admiration. It was a tonic she craved.

In Homer, when her first audience got tired of Hell she talked about Indians. Now she talked about purity, and marriage and motherhood.

She began to skim her printed speeches, to insert bits with an ingenious shift of emphasis. "When the sex is disenthralled, there will be no need for prisons and gallows," said she, "the offspring of free mothers and fathers shall revel in moral and intellectual grandeur," when "a race of gods and goddessess" is reared.

The *Courier* of Greenville, Ohio, found her lecture "overflowing with the love of a mother's heart, appealing to fathers, mothers, sons and daughters for a purer morality, and closer interchange of thought, a commingling as it were in spirit, so that impure thoughts and desires cannot enter the holy temple of home."

In Dallas, Texas, she urged man to be pure. The mothers of the earth must "cultivate the acquaintance of their children, to make them their confidants, and to teach them from childhood their true origin and the dangers that await them in society." "And this is the great social question," said the *Dallas Statesman,* "about which, through ignorance she has been anathematized. She would lift mankind into a higher sphere, out of which there would come a noble freedom of love, which would purify the races of the earth; and thus she defines her theory of free-lovism."

In fact Victoria had to be saintly or silent. Her reputation was so widespread that she couldn't get a hall to speak in, unless she promised not to deliver an "immoral speech." Men complained that she "shouldn't be allowed in" their state, she "ought to be suppressed," and illogically went to hear her. Then after the lecture, one of these declared with tears in his eyes, "My God, this is the woman whom we have been decrying! I never heard such an effort as this.

ROXANNA HUMMEL CLAFLIN PHOTOGRAPHED IN SAN FRANCISCO, CALIFORNIA, IN 1874, WHEN VICTORIA WAS SPEAKING THERE

I will give five dollars to have it repeated Sunday night, and twenty-five if my darling daughter could listen to it every Sunday evening for a year. My lips shall never utter anything but deep regard for her again."

Said the *Atlanta Herald:* "The sacredness of motherhood was a prominent idea in the lecture. . . . No one could hear the appeal for purity in connection with that holy name and tie without an obeisance of reverence, perhaps a memory of tears."

Roxanna Claflin went with Victoria on this tour when motherhood was stressed. Roxanna hated Colonel Blood because "he kept her daughters from riding around in their own carriages." She hated social freedom because it was unprofitable. She told reporters who called her silvered hair "courtly," that her daughters had noble blood in their veins. "Her eyes flashed fire when speaking of them." No doubt she influenced Victoria and hastened her apostasy. She was a powerful old creature, and at that time all Victoria's energy was fighting for her energy. She had none left for people nor for principles. Instead she had to lean on somebody, and Roxanna had an eager shoulder and a strong one.

Colonel Blood stayed home to edit the *Weekly,* which reported every phase of Victoria's apostasy, through newspaper accounts of her lectures. The Colonel probably thought it was a coup. He announced in the *Weekly* that reform had various steps. Victoria Woodhull had attacked the huge trees and burned them.

". . . We won with the battle ax; now we win with the plow. Harsh means are no longer required . . .

and if they were used they would destroy the tender blades of freedom that begin to show above the crusts of law and custom. . . ."

Tennie C. was no support for a sick tiger; she was only too glad to crawl into the new lair, where it was comfortable. She announced that "intellectuality of women" was her fundamental principle, and very appropriately recited Charles Mackay's, "Death of Tom Paine" as an introduction to Victoria's lectures.

But when the *Republican* of Salem, Ohio, said "Freelovism had no advocacy in Mrs. Woodhull's Salem speech," Sada Bailey wrote the *Weekly,*

". . . I deem this a wholesale libel on her. . .

"Some of her hearers think she has changed her opinions. . . .

"I reply that Victoria will not refute any declaration she ever made upon 'Free Love.' But why have they concluded that she repudiates that which to them is unpalatable truth? . . . Victoria has been condemned so severely for declaring unwelcome truths, that her yearning heart would burst ere long did she not soften some of her expressions to which she has resorted to command the public attention, and plead for the love of the people; and I rejoice with my whole heart that she is receiving it, for she deserves it from everybody. . . ."

But Victoria told the people of Kokomo, Indiana, that "My free love, is the free love of God to the world. I have been traduced, vilified, misrepresented and imprisoned for maintaining the right." She "offered her bleeding heart in love to a world that has hated her and tried to crush her." The *Kokomo Dis-*

patch said, "She talks as a mother who knows the joys and sorrows of maternity, as a woman who has suffered much for her principles, as a representative of her sex who is boldly breasting public opinion for the promulgation of a great social reformation. She made many friends in Kokomo and removed a false prejudice that had long been entertained against her."

The *Washington Gazette* said more: "Not the least remarkable of the revolutions wrought in the sentiments, feelings, and conduct of the people of this country, and in the tone of the public press, is that which has taken place in respect of Mrs. Victoria Woodhull. . . .

"Mrs. Woodhull . . . is today admitted to be engaged in a great and noble work. . . ."

On June 10, 1876, the *Weekly* printed a letter from Victoria, addressed to the "Boston Investigator." As of old, Victoria told all to the press:

"Mr. Editor:

" . . . I believe in the sanctity of marriage, and it is because I so believe that I have pled so earnestly . . . for woman's complete emancipation from legal thralldom. . . . When our daughters are no longer prepared for the marriage mart simply as commodities to be sold at the highest price; when we exact the same purity of man that he requires of woman; when woman, in her matronly dignity and Godlike purity shall, by her intellectual power, crush the demon lust, then sorrow and desolation and misery and vice, will be banished from the face of the earth. . . .

" . . . Your remarks would lead one to believe that I do not believe in the marriage relation. . . . It is I who believe in the institution as a divine provision, but law alone cannot make it divine. There must be honesty, purity, intelligence, goodness.

. . . Nor do I believe in the loose system of divorces now so much in vogue. . . . To me this business is as reprehensible as the promiscuousness that runs riot in the land. . . ."

With that number dated June tenth, 1876, *Woodhull & Claflin's Weekly* ceased publication.

How its readers must have howled when they read it! Most of them had heard Victoria's last radical speech called "Tried as By Fire." On platforms throughout the country she had said:

"I am conducting a campaign against marriage, with the view of revolutionizing the present theory and practise . . .

". . . The marriage law is the most damnable social evil bill—the most consummate outrage on women that was ever conceived. Those who are called prostitutes, . . . are free women sexually, when compared to the slavery of the poor wife."

The Victoria Woodhull who declaimed "Tried as By Fire" in 1874, was different from the Victoria Woodhull who proclaimed the sanctity of marriage in 1876, only in her reaction to sex and social freedom. That reaction had changed profoundly, for she was too great an orator, too real a reformer at both times ever to perform a lip-act for expediency.

Great orators convince themselves through convincing others; and inasmuch as their gift springs from a passionate impulse to reveal, to be effective the revelation must be a sincere one, however momentary. Reformers always want the world to know what they think, because they are so constituted as to be uncomfortable if they are silent about their philosophy; and they are so constituted as to be able to atone for any inadequacy, by persuading others to be as they are.

Victoria Woodhull was as fervent in her apostasy as she had been in her radicalism.

She wasn't robust enough for sex or social freedom now. Conventional marriage meant protection, her greatest need. Colonel Blood was devoted, but he wasn't protective. He didn't know how to make money, and Victoria wasn't well enough to make any more. No wonder she told a reporter from the *Cincinnati Enquirer* that she was "sick in mind, sick in body, and sick in heart."

The favorite saying of her old age was that "Only fools and the dead never change their minds." Maybe she just changed hers. She had seen others practise what she preached and prosper, because they didn't preach it. While she was crucified on the altars of consistency, Henry Ward Beecher was crowned on a throne of deceit. The "Brooklyn Sensation" had played a big part in her life; maybe the end of it influenced her now.

Tilton was of no economic interest to anybody but himself and his family; and when he got into a mess few helped him. Finally he left the country and went to Paris, where he wrote minor poetry and played chess until he died, the victim of his own weakness as well as Beecher's strength.

Victoria Woodhull insisted on her virtue just as sturdily, just as vividly, as Beecher did. Like him, she convinced a public, though not a jury, that she had been maligned. Like him, she claimed to be the victim of a plot. She was as dramatic as Beecher ever was, but Beecher had scrip-holders to pull him up, while she only had a malady to drag her down.

But she made Colonel Blood swear out a warrant against Joseph Treat for "publishing an obscene libel" against her, though his pamphlet was two years old, and she called attention to it, but the gesture might have been a comfort. Treat swore that every word of it was true; he had published it in the interest of morality. Which sounded like Victoria's own obscenity defense. Treat's bail was paid by James C. Jones, and three days later he lectured on man's inhumanity to man at the Harry Hills Theatre. The suit never was brought to trial and bail was discharged on June 27, 1879.

It is possible that Victoria's morocco bound Testament helped to change her attitude towards social freedom; it may have been the association that brought back early fears of a God who sent one to hell-fire for scarlet sins. The lecture she gave at Cooper Union in May, 1876, certainly suggested a period of tainted penitence, as well as some justification for the rumor that she had become a Catholic, which was current among her old friends.

It was preceded by young Zulu Maud's recitation of "Portia's Plea for Mercy," from the "Merchant of Venice." Then Victoria read the third chapter of Genesis as she walked majestically to the centre of the stage, where a statue of the Virgin Mary stood on a pedestal. She selected the verses in which God promised woman that her seed should crush the head of the serpent for her text, and said that the redemption from the ills of humanity must come from woman. Woman should be the teacher of her family and the confessor of her child; and in order to do all this, she must imitate the purity of the Virgin. Whereupon Victoria pressed her hand to her forehead, swept back her luxuriant hair, lifted her head with flushed face and shining eyes, and turning dramatically to the image of Mary, she gathered the power of a hurricane into her silver voice and pled for purity. If everyone were pure, men no longer would be hanged for murder, for murder would cease to exist. Intelligent mothers could bring forth virtuous children, through whom vice would vanish from the world; they would crush the head of the serpent.

Meanwhile, the first Mrs. Blood had moved from St. Louis to Brooklyn. She was sick and poor, and, when she got in touch with the Colonel through George Blood, the Colonel helped her as much as he could, which was less than Victoria had done for Canning Woodhull under similar circumstances.

For years Roxanna Claflin had been trying to get Blood out of her family. He kept them "from riding around in their own carriages." Now she told Victoria that he was robbing her to support the first Mrs. Blood. Victoria was not in an altruistic mood just then, and Roxanna worked on her mind until Victoria told the Colonel to leave the house forever.

She brought an action in the Supreme Court of Kings County for an absolute divorce, on the ground of adultery. A witness, whom Colonel Blood had never seen, swore that he had accompanied him to a house of prostitution, though men as attractive as Colonel Blood rarely need to visit prostitutes. But that gallant soldier didn't deny a story, which sounded better than the truth, to a public that might have remembered Victoria's kindness to Canning Woodhull.

The *New York Times* and the *Brooklyn Eagle* of September 18, 1876, announced that Judge Dykman had signed a decree, giving Mrs. Woodhull the right to marry again, and denying that privilege to Colonel Blood.

The *Daily Graphic* said, "The High Priestess of free love gets a divorce for infidelity. Look out here, or the religion of unselfishness will tumble down."

Two weeks later Victoria lectured at the Boston Theatre: "People call me a free lover," she said. "The first time I ever heard the words 'free love' mentioned was at a Methodist Church. The minister was holding one of those protracted meetings, and telling everybody to come forward to the mourners' bench where the love of God was free to all. Then for the first time the idea that this was true, struck me to fruition. God is love and love is God. Who dares to tell me tonight that the love of God is not as free to me as it is to you? On the one side is pure undefiled love; on the other is abominable forced lust. I appealed for the former, and my appeal has closed the halls of Boston to me for four years. Your abominable lust I abhor, and God's intelligent love I adore."

When Victoria couldn't lecture any more, she sent a private card to subscribers and friends of the *Weekly*, urging "the widow to send her mite," and others "their dollars—their fives, tens, twenties, their fifties, hundreds, thousands" to her. She asked them to circulate the card "privately among friends of the cause." She didn't say what cause. In her extremity she was like a beggar with a tin cup, a sick beggar, who had to beg or starve; she was more pitiful than base.

But Hull's *Crucible* very properly told its readers that "Mrs. Woodhull has taken herself out of the field of Reform—she is not a reformer, let her go to her own, the church and the Christian Association for support. . . . We greatly prefer not to meddle with the business of other people, but reformers are poor and many of them will be deluded into sending Mrs. Woodhull money . . . she has a right to turn against reform, but she has no right to demand that reformers shall support her in her Jesuitical course. . . ."

When *Woodhull & Claflin's Weekly* stopped publication, radicals wrote to *The Crucible,* and asked why it stopped and why Victoria divorced Colonel Blood. Her old followers were more upset by her change than the public ever was. She was excitedly discussed in *The Crucible.*

Finally it printed a letter from Robert Hume, who had been associate editor of the *Weekly* for nearly two years:

"When Mrs. Woodhull wrote the letter published in the *New York Herald* in which she stated that Jesus had appeared to her in Ludlow prison, I resigned . . . because I could not defend the Woman's Movement on the doctrine of Moses and Paul, and base social reforms on the teachings of the Bible.

"I never doubted the truthfulness of Mrs. Woodhull's statement to the effect that she saw what appeared to her to be the Great Nazarene, any more than I doubt that Methodists often see the eidolon of Jesus in their camp meetings. . . . Religion is a terrible stimulant. . . . It is the alcohol of the soul.

"Mrs. Woodhull always appeared to me highly spiritual and imaginative; consequently a capital subject for the visitations of Demosthenes, Alexander of Macedon, Bonaparte and Jesus. I am not imaginative and consequently accepted the verity of such interviews as apocryphal. . . .

" . . . The statement that Mrs. Woodhull has accepted the Catholic faith is, however, news to me. Still I do not consider it improbable; for she has too much good sense to accept any of the thousand and one phases of Protestantism. If it be true, I dare venture to prophesy that the next canonization that will occur in the Catholic Church will be that of 'St. Victoria!'"

Chapter Fourteen

THE CUCKOO

ROXANNA CLAFLIN went into the Catholic Church and she was influencing Victoria then; Catholicism would have been a vent for Victoria's symbolical solemnity as well as an anodyne for her penitential pangs. But those pangs must have been short; Victoria was so self-righteous. Whatever she did was right, because she did it. And while purgatory was more cheerful than hell-fire, sanctification surpassed either; and it, too, was a haunt from her past. Victoria Woodhull did not become a Catholic. Instead she went reverently, though rather slowly, into respectability, on capital acquired through the agency of Commodore Vanderbilt's will.

When the Commodore died in January, 1877, and left about nine-tenths of his fortune to his son William, the other children contested the will on the grounds of undue influence while the testator was mentally incompetent. In an effort to prove this the plaintiffs brought out his connection with Woodhull and Claflin, as well as his faith in magnetic healers and Spiritualism. Enough fraudulent phenomena had been exposed to discredit Spiritualism; a prominent official had been ousted from the New York schools because of his belief in it that same year. A conservative jury might discredit the Commodore for trading through the "lady brokers", or for financing their sensational paper, but the defendant certainly was lost, if Tennie C. and Victoria went on the witness stand with Demosthenes, Napoleon, Josephine, and Alexander of Macedon, and any dramatic revelations that might occur to either. And the will involved about a hundred millions of dollars.

It was generally believed that Victoria and Tennie C. were paid to go to England and stay there during the trial. They went to England at that time with no other visible means of support and every motive to leave America, where Victoria was, "sick in body, sick in mind, and sick in heart."

If she hadn't confided in the press for so many years, if every newspaper library were not equipped with an envelope full of her sensational clippings, with time and persistence and all her old strength, she might have built a future in America on those denials of her past, so short is the public memory when assailed with energy. But her old reputation was too wide-spread; it was too vivid; print made it indelible. In America she probably would have been crushed, as she said Theodore Tilton was, "between the upper and nether stones of radicalism and conservatism."

She was through with "social freedom." There is not the faintest evidence that she ever wandered from the most conventional paths of sexual rectitude after she left America in 1877. She always practised what she preached, while she was preaching it.

She rested awhile in England. She had the time and the money for surgery too. Then, in December, 1877, Victoria "Woodhall" delivered her "sparkling lecture, The Human Body, the Temple of God," at St. James Hall, London. Posters advertising "the great American orator" were placed in shop-windows with a religious legend printed beneath Victoria's charming face.

Unwilling to renounce all her old celebrity, she must have thought that if she changed her mind, her locality and one vowel in her name, she would change its nature. "Woodhall" was a futile gesture she never repeated, but it was years before she learned that the newspapers would let her past alone only when she let them alone. When she was silent, they were silent; but whenever she went into public life and after publicity, some journalist would look her up in the library of his paper and find an envelope full of copy that he would have to use if he were a real journalist. For real journalists, or any writers who are story-tellers, are so constituted as to be uncomfortable until they tell the stories they know. That is their nature as well as their livelihood, and there is no malice in it. Victoria's legends were so vivid, so dramatic, so full of every human appeal that any writer who found them would suffer if silent.

And why should they have suffered for a woman who not only had not spared others that wanted privacy more than she did, but who had confided in the press of her own free will, time after time! Victoria Woodhull had put herself intimately, gratuitously, sensationally and indelibly into the public prints, and she had to pay the penalties of piquancy.

Now the English papers which had American correspondents reviewed some of her past, but the crowds who went to St. James Hall to be shocked were disappointed.

For Victoria carefully picked the purity out of her old lectures, and talked about a mother's duty and "stirpiculture" (which was the word for eugenics, in those days). No longer was the human body God's temple of delight; it was His instrument for the virtuous production of healthful humanity. But Victoria had something yet to learn about the extremes of mid-Victorian propriety. When she said mothers ought to tell their children "all they know," one English journalist said, "No man would dare discuss such subjects as Mrs. Woodhull is ready to discuss anywhere," but "her half-nervous style of utterance, her little womanly ways, so out of keeping with the matter of her lecture, pleased the audience."

She certainly pleased John Biddulph Martin, the younger son of Robert Martin of Overbury Court, and a partner of Martin's Bank, one of the oldest banking concerns in Lombard Street. According to the romantic tradition, he said, "I was charmed with her high intellect and fascinated by her manner, and I left the lecture hall that night with the determination that, if Mrs. Woodhull would marry me, I would certainly make her my wife."

Victoria needed ease and protection; John Biddulph Martin could give her both; and next to the presidency of the United States, he was the ultimate answer to the old contempt. Not only was he a man of wealth, he was a man with an established position in England; he was at least a minor angel in the current heaven of all those American snobs who had snubbed "The Woodhull."

Moreover, John Biddulph Martin was a man of considerable culture and charm. He had taken classical honours at Oxford, as well as athletic trophies. He was a famous runner. He was three years younger than Victoria, a tall, slender, full-bearded Englishman with fine eyes and a gentle manner, "typical of the best in the upper middle class," said one of his friends, and another dubbed him, "the last man on earth to have chosen a wife who would shock his family and amaze his friends."

It is unlikely that Victoria herself ever shocked his family. She had too much intuition to shock anyone she wanted to please, and her lovely face and charming personality were always disarming. But it is unlikely that the Martins would have welcomed any American; Anglo-American marriages were not popular in England then. Divorce was anathema and Victoria had been twice divorced. She certainly had advocated free love; it was generally believed that she had practised it. And now the Vanderbilt will case was dragging her as well as her sister into the papers again.

No wonder the Martins opposed the marriage so actively that it was six years before it took place.

Victoria had associated vindication with newspaper publicity ever since it made her first fame, and now she appealed to an American newspaper correspondent. "All between him and me is what those papers have said of me," she said. (She had a way of using pronouns for names.) Then she dropped on her knees, so fervently, so gracefully that, as in a good melodrama, her histrionics took him out of the everyday world where a spectator might have felt awkward. "Help me . . ." she begged, "I love him better than life. He is my all, my everything. . . . Stop those slanders in the American newspapers. Place me right with the world . . . and my loved one will come back to my arms."

Whereupon a sketch in the *London Traveler* announced that she was a "martyr woman," the victim of a conspiracy between church and state, who had been dragged from the rostrum to the dungeon. "Three times did she stray to the river, but the mighty impulse of a million prayers ascending to the angels stayed her footsteps." Extortion and blackmail absorbed every cent she made; she had had to open halls with keys of gold, because she had said that a woman should require the same chastity of man that he requires of her, because she was appointed to "the solution of the great mystery which the Bible itself declares to be sealed up within its pages." Hers was a "drama of pathos"; and "the malice of enemies together with her opinions on the social question, have combined to give her a reputation of sin, but no slanders have been heaped on any human soul with greater injustice. A more unsoiled woman does not walk the earth. She carries in her very face the fair legend of a character kept pure by the sacred fire within," otherwise, "she would long since have been sunk beneath the forces that have sought to crush her."

Then she began lecturing again, on "Woman," and on "The Garden of Eden," which still were allegorical. Victoria still promised that "when men and women shall beget children in love, purity and health, and in accordance with natural, not artificial laws, then 'there shall be no more death, neither sorrow nor crying, neither any more pain.' " She still asked what was the interpretation "of the reappearance of Christ to

(From a supplement of the *American Traveler,* London, England, September 6, 1879)

John," saying, "I am the root and offspring of David," and " 'there shall be no more curse' but 'whosoever will, let him take the waters of life freely.' "

Her answer left the waters of life in Eden, but how they had changed! "There are . . . four rivers, or periods of allegorical import," she said. "The period of incubation or changing; the birth of civilization, the growth of intelligence; and the millennium. The period of incubation was the early efforts at lawmaking; civilization was thence made complete, or born in the honest spiritual sentiment of Jesus Christ; spirituality has since Him become the foundation of a wide confederation of nations; and the millennium will appear in the unity of this growth, under the bond of a universal sentiment, if not absolutely under the personal reign of a King of Kings and Lord of Lords."

And anybody who heard that Victoria C. Woodhull had delivered a shocking lecture called "The Garden of Eden" could get this one, printed in a pamphlet with a preface by Charles Steuart Welles, who had married one of her nieces, and who must have been her current amanuensis. According to the pamphlet, this lecture was "delivered by Mrs. V. C. Woodhull in conjunction with her sister, Miss Tennessee C. Claflin, throughout the United States, Canada and Great Britain."

In 1880, Victoria wrote to the *London Court Journal* to complain of the abuse she had received in the English press. Regardless of the restraints that bind the scrupulous, she flouted anything that interfered with her, including her past. She declared that her name:

"has been most unrighteously associated with what is known by the name of Free Love. No viler aspersion was ever uttered. No greater outrage could be inflicted on a woman. No deeper wrong could be done to the innocent. And here, sir, it behooves me to mention the manner in which my name first got mixed up in connection with a small section of the American community called Free Lovists, for whom, ever since I became acquainted with their principles, I have entertained the profoundest abhorrence. For several years I was the ostensible editor of a New York journal, the main object of which was the elevation of woman, politically, morally, and religiously. I did my best to conduct the paper and to keep it true to the purposes with which it set out. It happened, however, that I could not always read, and select the contributions sent me for insertion therein. My lecturing engagements in distant parts of the States, sometimes extending over one hundred nights, prevented such rigid supervision, or, indeed, any supervision at all. Still I had not the slightest apprehension that any matter should find its way into the columns of my journal calculated to lower its tone or taint its character. But so it was. Articles favoring free love appeared without my knowledge or sanction, which startled the readers of my hitherto spotless print. . . . I became inculpated as though I was morally responsible for utterance and doctrines which I loathe and abhor from the depths of my inmost being. I now openly avow, with all the earnestness of righteous indignation, that during no part of my life did I favor free love even tacitly. With the feelings that should actuate every sanctified wife and mother of a family, I regarded it with loathing when once I got a slight idea of its character and the deep infamy to which it led. And such is my state of feeling at the present time. I only wish that this honest, unreserved declaration, which through your kindness, I am enabled to make, would exonerate me from any degree of responsibility in the matter, silence serpent tongues, and clear my reputation from the slur which ignorant, unthoughtful, or vindictive persons have cast upon it, reckless of the result. In further justification of my innocence it is my intention to republish my journal in London at once. Therein full particulars shall be given of the manner in which articles got into *Woodhull & Claflin's Weekly* bearing my signature. Those articles I utterly repudiate, more especially the one known as "The Beecher Article," the writers of which acknowledged the authorship of the same at the Beecher trial under oath.

"I remain, sir, yours faithfully,

"Victoria C. Woodhull,

"8 Gilston Road, West Brompton, December 29, 1880."

Nobody acknowledged the authorship of "The Beecher Article" under oath at the Beecher trial, according to the verbatim report of the testimony. Stephen Pearl Andrews only said that he had corrected some of the English, and that "the introductory part and the close . . . showed his marks perhaps." And Victoria related the substance of it on the platform in Boston, months before it was printed.

But she had the effrontery, or the desperation, to send a proof-sheet of this letter, with a request to print it, to the leading papers in America, where thousands had heard her proclaim her right to change her lover as often as she chose.

At that time Benjamin R. Tucker was exchange reader on the *Boston Globe,* and when he received one of those proof-sheets, he printed it, with a headline: "As Big A Lie As Was Ever Told," and sent it to Victoria, with a postcard saying that it would show her what he thought of her.

One cold evening, some months later, he walked into the *Globe* editorial rooms to do his customary work. Says Mr. Tucker:

"As I was going through the night editor's room to my own, I saw, through the open door-way of the managing editor's room, a woman sitting alone. Her position revealed her profile, and I saw at once that it was Victoria. She looked in my direction, but evidently failed to recognize me. At that time I wore a heavy, black beard, which disguised me in her eyes, for she had known me only as a beardless boy. Moreover, I was wrapped in a heavy overcoat. I knew at once why she was there. Not caring to have a scene, I walked to my desk, took something from a drawer, and walked directly out again. Returning two hours later, I learned from B. P. Palmer, the managing editor, that he had seen Victoria; that she had exhibited the copy of the *Globe* which I had sent her, as well as my post-card; that she had claimed that I was the owner of the paper (which was false), and that the card was evidence of malice; that she had threatened to bring suit for libel unless the charge of lying was retracted at once; that after much talk she had become calmer; and that finally she had left on being assured that the *Globe* of the following morning would contain a paragraph announcing her arrival in America with the intention of renewing her campaign for the presidency of the United States. The paragraph appeared as promised, but contained no withdrawal of the charge of falsehood of which she had complained nor any reference to it. I told Mr. Palmer that I was familiar with the facts, and that he need not fear any libel suit would be brought. Victoria had left with him some papers concerning herself, for which she was to call the next day. At noon of the next day I was sitting in the room, through which I had passed the night before, helping out at the news desk in the absence of one of the regular force. Looking up from my work, I saw, not Victoria, but Tennie, peering in through the doorway. After a moment's hesitation, she entered and walked through to Mr. Palmer's room, passing within two feet of me and evidently not realizing my presence. She got the papers which Victoria had left and went away. Mr. Palmer then came from his room, and, standing beside the desks of the news editors while filling his pipe, remarked with a sly chuckle that his visitor had had something to say about "Bennie" Tucker. Of course the boys had a great laugh, in which I joined, but I countered by saying that I supposed she had as good a right to call me Bennie as I had to call her Tennie. The sisters remained in Boston several days, during which time I caught a glimpse of them in the Parker House dining-room and another as they were passing down School Street. Those were the last times that I ever saw them. The *Globe* heard no more of the libel suit, and I heard no more of the presidential campaign.

"Whether it was a few months before or after this visit that Col. Blood appeared in Boston I do not remember. At any rate he came to see me, and, not being in good circumstances, shared my room for a time. He made no bitter remarks about Victoria; he even spoke rather warmly, in the presence of myself and another friend, of the perfect relationship which they so long enjoyed. Nevertheless, when I showed him in the *Globe* file the article of which Victoria had complained, he looked at the heading and then at me, remarking with a smile: 'That shot went home, for *she* knows that *you* KNOW.' "

In her naïve past, Victoria may actually have hoped for the presidency; but now it became a device, the only device she could think of, which might impress the Martins with her importance and assure them of her respectability.

Back in London she issued a manifesto to the English newspapers:

"Victoria C. Woodhull, the nominated president of the United States at the next election of 1884. She sends out this call that the people of all Europe, America, and all the world may rally round her standard and support her in her right to represent and to work for the people of America, and by becoming their president, prove the fact, for the first time in history, that they chose as their president, not of necessity a man, but the best person to represent, govern and maintain their rights.

"This call goes out from England issued by Victoria C. Woodhull, supported by English capitalists.

"Victoria C. Woodhull came to England some years ago broken down in health and spirits, but by Divine aid, rest and loving friends she has recovered, and is again ready, with all her wonted devotion to her country and to the cause of all humanity, to take this work upon herself and gives unreservedly all her strength, enthusiasm and all the wealth she has accumulated in England, to the result of this election.

"Upon receipt of this call, let every city, town and village in all Europe, and in every state and territory in America, by public announcement, summon their meetings, pass resolutions, appoint delegates, take minutes of such meetings, and send the same to the secretary of this call, to be put in form and to be used as campaign documents.

"All chosen delegates will be provided with free return tickets by steamer from Philadelphia or New York or Boston, and during their attendance of three days in convention, will have all expenses paid for them by Victoria C. Woodhull.

"All friends who wish to attend said convention can, by application to the secretary, receive tickets by steamer at excursion fare.

"The meetings for the nomination will be held at St. James Hall, Piccadilly, London.

"Address for all particulars and tickets to attend the convention to H. T. Belmont, Secretary, 32 Thistle Grove, S. Kensington, London, England."

Appended to the proof-sheet of this remarkable document was a long extract from a eulogy of Victoria C. Woodhull, to which Victor Hugo's name was signed, with the statement that it was reprinted from his paper, the Rappel of Paris, dated "October 1880." In fact, Victoria Woodhull was not mentioned in the Rappel of any day in 1880, nor was she mentioned in Hugo's collected prose works at the Bibliothèque Nationale, which includes his speeches and political writings; nor in any bibliography of Hugo's work.

While Elizabeth Cady Stanton was visiting her daughter in London, a woman called who wouldn't give her name; and Mrs. Stanton went into the drawing-room to find a heavily veiled figure swathed in black, who threw back her veils dramatically to reveal Victoria Woodhull. She asked Mrs. Stanton to go with her to Mr. Martin's solicitors and swear that she never had heard anything against her character. Mrs. Stanton said she couldn't do that, but she would be glad to say that she admired and honored Mrs. Woodhull. Which was not enough; so they did not call on Mr. Martin's solicitors.

One copy of *Woodhull & Claflin's Journal* was issued in London, dated January 29, 1881, in which Victoria appealed to "the whole press of the world to aid us in unearthing those vile traducers who wanton with our good name, which, though nothing to them, is to us our all, dearer than life itself. . . .

"If anyone living can point to any corrupt or unwomanly action of our life, now is the time for him to disclose what he has to say. Then we could proceed criminally against the parties, as our object is to right our reputation and not to recover damages by taking civil process." Evidently someone brought the Treat pamphlet to London, for *Woodhull & Claflin's Journal* said that "her husband, from whom Mrs. Woodhull had obtained a divorce, has recently been sending around letters, wherein he stoutly protests against the imputations which were once cast on his former wife's honor. . . . As an act of reparation, such a course may be justifiable. But how comes it that at the time when a malicious, obscene and scurrilous pamphlet was hawked about the streets of New York . . . he remained a silent spectator? . . .

"Upon what principle did he refrain from taking legal action against Treat, the vile mendacious vendor and reputed author of such an outrageous publication? An outcast from society endeavours to make his living at the expense of a woman's reputation and the injured lady herself has to go before a Grand Jury and obtain an indictment against the miscreant, whom the court for the Trial of Criminal Offenses finally acquits on the ground of insanity and the police destroyed his stock-in-trade. . . . It is not improbable that . . . he . . . who should have been his wife's protector, may yet be proven to have been not only the author, but the person who actually furnished the money for the obnoxious publication. . . ."

Such a fountain of lies glittered with a splendor all its own!

Colonel Blood had written to the *Cincinnati Enquirer* to protest against the rumor that Victoria was not the author of her lectures or her books. "I have always found my wife capable of putting her thoughts on paper or before the public on the rostrum much more brilliantly than either myself or anybody else could do it for her," said he with more gallantry than truth. He had written to *The American Socialist* to protest against the rumor that extravagance had ruined the *Weekly*.

But he couldn't have taken legal action against Treat when the pamphlet appeared, because he and the sisters were busy with the Challis trials. Two years later, he obtained the indictment, Victoria didn't. Moreover, Treat was not "an outcast from society." He was a lecturer, his wife was a distinguished botanist; and he was not acquitted on the ground of insanity, because his case never was brought to trial. And the police of New York City do not go about destroying pamphlets which have not even been suppressed. Every public library that collects Woodhulliana has a copy of Treat's effusion on its shelves. Moreover, it was printed in 1874, when Victoria and the Colonel were devoted to each other. What would have been his motive for attacking her, if he had been the sort of person who could have done so?

Now he, who had taught Victoria that the end justified the means, wrote to London for a life subscription to *Woodhull & Claflin's Journal*.

Physically robust again, Victoria at length grew shrill in her defense, so shrill that we can imagine a period of despair and desperation, in which she tried to sell her virtue to herself as vehemently as to the Martins; and we can imagine such a period complicated by moments when she wondered whether the sale was worth the price, for it may be significant that John Biddulph Martin left no mark on posterity except that he was "typical." Perhaps he was typically complacent, too, and stodgy and smug; perhaps he seemed tame after Colonel Blood.

Anyhow, the wails she uttered in an obscure English paper called *The Cuckoo* with singular appropriateness, must have been the crop of inner turmoil, if not the harvest of a vicious shrew, which is unlikely, for too many people had seen in her the beauty and dignity that flowers from real sweetness at the core.

Nevertheless, in *The Cuckoo* for April 14, 1881, she said:

"About twenty-five years ago, a moral leprosy broke out in New York City. A free love club was founded, the direct objects of which were for a time hidden from the public. Citizens of both sexes were eligible as candidates. By and by it was discovered that members of this strange organization repudiated the marriage tie—in fact were the most pronounced opponents of morality. To such lengths did they carry their vile practices that the civil authorities were induced to interrupt their nightly orgies. A raid was made by the police and certain persons were carried off to prison. A 'new sensation' was created in America, and the daily journals gave due space to much of the evidence given against the prisoners in public court. This publicity broke up the club. It did not, however, sweep away the contagious impurity from the land.

"The high priest of Free-Lovism entertained advanced views upon wedlock.

"Taking mean advantage of Mrs. Woodhull's long absence from New York City, he had opportunities for airing his monstrous doctrines and uttering his blasphemous sentiments. But the new apostle who came to perfect society and regarded his mission as inspired propounded views so shocking that the community and even the authorities interfered.

"Mrs. Woodhull, who started her journal in 1870, was made the scapegoat for others' evil doings. She was arrested and imprisoned as ostensible conductor of the print in which it was attempted to pollute the fountain of public morality. Nor are we surprised at this issue, seeing that one contributor, Stephen Pearl Andrews—the high priest of debauchery—actually had the audacity and unblushing effrontery to affix Mrs. Woodhull's signature to his filthy effusions. But, it will be asked, why did Mrs. Woodhull keep silent? The answer is simple and satisfactory. She acted thus to exculpate her husband Colonel Blood, who was the responsible editor and who was threatened with lynching by an exasperated public. When the whirlwind of public astonishment and reprobation reached her—the scapegoat of others' enormities—her hands were tied, for personal feelings restrained her. She shielded him who should have been as a right arm between her and the outer world. She bore many reproofs—a silent, living target pierced with innumerable darts. From that day to this have the tares sown by the enemy with furrows prepared for heavenly seed been growing up.

"Great pressure was brought on Mrs. Woodhull that she might disclose the name of the writer of the 'Beecher Article'. While in prison she was visited by leading people of Plymouth Church. They made her the tempting offer of a hundred thousand and immediate freedom if she would speak. Her reply was, 'no, we came here by no fault of ours and shall not depart hence till our character is vindicated.'"

Victoria's next lament appeared a week later, somewhat ironically entitled, "Truth Crushed to Earth."

"Looking with sorrowing eyes upon decaying nations, upon the fairest and noblest borne helplessly around in the maelstrom of human passion, I, ten years since, established a journal whose aspiration was the emancipation of women, the leading of her out from the bondage of many-centuried wrongs into the celestial lovelight of true womanhood," said she in one of those striking phrases that inevitably spring from people who express the force of their emotions in words, which may or may not defy their own meaning. Such phrases only proved Victoria's authorship of similar expressions in her old speeches. Certainly, neither Stephen Pearl Andrews nor Colonel Blood wrote this jeremiad, and it had none of the marks of their learning, which had splashed Victoria's era of social freedom. This was sheer melodramatic fantasy or a lyric cry of distress. It went on:

"The development of circumstances demands that the silence which I have long imposed on myself should be broken. . . .

"Stephen Pearl Andrews! I impeach thee before the judgment bar. Pure hearts, which might have communed with their Maker in the spiritual Sinai, hast thou by infernal wiles tempted to bow down before the idol of the flesh. With daring hand thou art filling up the measure of human wickedness. Arch-blasphemer!

"Many are willing to build tabernacles on the Mount

of Transfiguration, how few to carry the torch into the dark valley whence resounds the cry for help. But none liveth to himself, none dieth to himself. All ye who love humanity, aid me in rescueing sons and daughters of men from him who would trample all that is etheral, beautiful, incorruptible and immortal into a pestilential mire of sensual grossness. . . . Because I have unearthed the dust-eating serpent coiled in the death-mould of the flesh, and laid bare its material hideousness, unrelentingly have I been assailed. Victoria C. Woodhull."

Friends of Stephen Pearl Andrews and Colonel Blood, who saw this, laughed at it. But there were people who were familiar with the facts, though personally detached from them, who were irritated at the sight of such a tale in print. One wrote to *The Cuckoo,* that her "barefaced mendacity has never been exceeded. . . . Would it be believed that even Mrs. Woodhull would have the effrontery to deny that she ever had sympathy for or was in any way connected with the doctrine of free love? . . . How do her free love worshippers and quondam lovers in America relish this repudiation by their former high-priestess? . . ."

Whereupon "A correspondent" informed the readers of *The Cuckoo* that Mrs. Woodhull was preparing an autobiography to show how her speeches became "polluted and perverted." Furthermore this "Correspondent" insisted that,

"It is well known that from the moment Mrs. Woodhull knew Colonel Blood he adopted towards her a course of deception and treachery. After she had returned from a long Southern lecture tour, his conduct was so flagrant that she felt forced to apply for a divorce. Whilst this was pending in 1876, and she still his legal wife, he, under terrible pressure, essayed to defend her for the first time. The nature of this pressure was that if he did not perform so tardy an act of justice his whole history would be made public.

"But Blood's vindication was of little advantage to his wife. It came too late. Had it followed when she was first attacked she would not now be under the necessity of clearing her character from foul aspersions."

Which was another reference to the Treat pamphlet, such a scurrilous attack and such a malicious one that it was a stout red herring to drag across the trail of public scandal. But it wasn't enough. Here again the accusations against Colonel Blood were reprinted, verbatim from *Woodhull & Claflin's Journal.* Nor was that enough. Victoria had picked a villain for her melodrama, but she had to make him a monster. She made Colonel Blood play the part in *The Cuckoo* that Canning Woodhull had played in the Tilton biography.

It ended with a horrible suggestion:

"It will be known to many of her friends that some years ago Mrs. Woodhull was in precarious health, failing day by day, many persons expecting her death. She has since discovered that she was near being the victim of slow poison.

"Mrs. Woodhull was treated by an eminent American physician as a pronounced slow-poisoning case. In London also she has undergone similar treatment for at least two years. . . ."

And like Canning Woodhull, Colonel Blood played his part in silence. Surely no ordinary woman could inspire such devotion.

A few days after the break with Victoria a friend called at the office of the *Weekly* and found the Colonel almost prostrated. Tennie C. and Victoria had accused him of taking funds from the *Weekly* and apparently that turned the screws on his despair. In fact the seat of his trousers were so worn that he went out at night for air and exercise because he was ashamed to be seen on the streets; he had no money for new ones. But he uttered no word of resentment; the worst he ever said of Victoria Woodhull was that "the grandest woman in the world went back on me."

It was George Blood who gave him a bed to sleep in. George Blood was an expert book-keeper and when Victoria threw him out of the *Weekly,* for carrying messages from the first Mrs. Blood, he got a government clerkship on Governor's Island. The Colonel found some sort of a position there, but he didn't keep it.

Unwilling to accept a world in which there was no Victoria, he floundered into one thing and out of another, like a man in a dream. He ran a bakery shop in New York, a refreshment booth at Coney Island, a travelling show with exhibitions of hypnotism and other acts.

Finally, in 1878, he went to Auburn, Maine, and walked into the office of the *Greenback Labor Chronicle,* and said, "Well, I'm here."

The *Chronicle* was chiefly owned by the Fogg brothers when Colonel Blood joined the staff. He helped to edit the paper, and was an invaluable aid to the Foggs. He actually could recite reams of the Congressional Record, and yet he thought clearly and read constantly. He wrote well, always on political and economic subjects, his personal slant gone with Victoria.

He was a familiar figure in Auburn, and an impressive one. He wore a black cutaway coat, well-made of good material, usually worn threadbare. And yet he looked immaculate. His full beard was trimmed to chin-whiskers now, and he had a ministerial solemnity. A strict vegetarian, he ate two cups of raw wheat a day like a horse. But when he came into a room, "everyone knew he had arrived." He was irresistible to women, and he did not try to resist them.

It was said that one of the printers at the *Chronicle* broke with his wife an account of the Colonel. It was known that he spent every week-end in Portland with a woman. There were many women in his life. He talked plainly to anyone about sex matters, and openly associated with Moses Hull, and Leo Miller and the Stricklands, and all the free love crowd. His worst enemy never could accuse him of going back on a friend. And it is a curious fact that in that New England village where his "carnal practices" were known and deplored, he was known as "a man with a bleeding heart," as "a love-sick man who neither drank nor smoked," who "would have been a great man if 'The Woodhull' hadn't left him."

He rarely spoke of her, but sometimes his pent-up longings would accumulate until he had to mention her name. A few words seemed to relieve him; and, though they might be words of regret, they never were words of reproach.

In Auburn they said he planned and schemed to win her back.

One Monday morning he told the Foggs that a son

of Captain Jackson of Portland, wanted a job in the printing shop. The boy was employed, and later his mother appeared. She was remarkably beautiful. She needed to "take no back seat for Mrs. Woodhull," said Auburn, and they said it because she was the accepted reason for Jim Blood's trips to Portland.

Eventually the Colonel wanted to move the *Chronicle* to New York. He said, "I am in love with New York City, and always was; guess I always shall be." But in the fall of 1879, Frank Fogg ran for Congress and his defeat ruined the *Chronicle* which had backed him with all its strength.

The Colonel stayed in Portland awhile, and then he drifted. He considered himself a healer, and sometimes supported himself by what he called "Spiritual Healing." He practised hypnotism, too, and preached the free love doctrines. Whenever he was in need, George Blood helped him. And the Colonel wrote a friend: "I used always to be successful, but success has deserted me now."

As loyal to his causes as to his friends, somehow he managed to get to the Greenback Convention at Chicago in 1880. He wanted Ben Butler to be their presidential candidate; but, when Butler refused to answer any telegrams from the convention, Blood worked for Chase.

And then Victoria came to America in 1881, and the Colonel met her on the street in New York. She neither spoke nor made any sign of recognition. Blood turned pale, and faltered. That vital old soldier, with five bullet holes in his body, had to lean on another man's arm.

About four years later, Colonel Blood made a strange marriage. He married the mother of the Fogg brothers who had owned the *Chronicle*. And within six months he departed for Africa on a gold expedition. Some said he married Mrs. Nathan Fogg to finance this expedition, for she and George Blood bought his outfit. Others thought it was arranged to secure his pension in case he never returned. But stranger still was his choice of a companion. The Colonel sailed for the Gold Coast of Africa, with Captain Jackson; and Auburn buzzed with the sensation, for everybody understood that Jackson's wife had been the Colonel's mistress!

Jackson had been trading out of Portland and along the coast of Africa for years, and it is possible that he first heard of the gold mine. Anyway at Acra, which was no port for a big vessel then, he landed the Colonel in a small boat and went further down the coast with the machinery.

The Colonel went ahead to the mine, a hundred miles inland; and, when Captain Jackson got there, the natives told him that Blood had died of the "African fever." He was already buried.

The little that could be learned about the Colonel's illness had to be interpreted from the "Akim," through the "Bassa" and "Fantee" dialects, into bad English. The petty king of the tribe said he had taken care of Blood and that Blood was sick for nine days and did not think he was going to die. But the black woman who did his work said he was sick only two days, and that he begged the king to send him by litter to the coast and that the king refused. She said "Acquah" gave Blood some black medicine and that Blood couldn't swallow after he had taken it. And Blood did write to George Blood about a "difficulty in his throat," which kept him from swallowing. They agreed that he died on December 29, 1885.

This was what Frank Fogg heard when he went to Acra after the Colonel's body, which he brought back to Brooklyn for burial. He brought back a small vial of gold also, for the Colonel actually had struck riches.

Of course it was whispered in Auburn that Jackson took Blood to Africa to have him killed by the natives. Which was unlikely. George Blood certainly was devoted to the Colonel and he was intelligent; apparently he had no suspicion of Jackson, for he spoke of him with enthusiasm. Jackson was a graduate of Bowdoin College and while the long poem he wrote beginning

"Through jungles wild and strange wild flowers,
Twisted vines surround thy grave,"

was no credit to his alma mater, it was an improbable tribute to a victim.

But none who knew the Colonel in Auburn ever doubted that every step in the expedition had been a step to win Victoria Woodhull back. What if she were married to another with the Midas touch she craved! No marriage tie could bind the Colonel; he was a free lover to the end.

Chapter Fifteen

THE SIEGE OF LONDON

ACCORDING to their contemporaries, Henry James immortalized the Woodhull-Martin affair in "The Siege of London." And while identifications of fact with fiction usually are far-fetched, this one dove-tails so perfectly that one wonders whether such identifications wouldn't add to the enjoyment of other James novels, since without them, one often is so baffled by portentous hints of knowledge which the author fails to share.

"The Siege of London" tells the story of an American adventuress who forced herself into an honorable English family. It seems more than a coincidence that James' heroine, like Victoria Woodhull, not only had an "indescribable beauty," but "her complexion had the bloom of a white flower . . . her profile . . . was as pure and fine as the outline of a cameo." Like Victoria also, she "picked up ideas and took a hint from every circumstance," and "she had become a great critic and handled many of the productions of the age with a bold, free touch." Which was Victoria to the life. And Victoria, as well as James' Nancy Headway, was approached by the discreet as if she were "some glossy, graceful animal which had an occasional trick of biting." Victoria became "suddenly vehement," too, and she, too, had a way of designating "him only by a sort of conjugal pronoun. She had been so much, and so easily married that she was full of these misleading references to gentlemen."

With his usual oblique solemnity James assures us that "Nancy Headway" was notorious, and to tell us why she was notorious, he refers vaguely to her many marriages, though in a day when women with her social obscurity were the regular fodder for the American "divorce mills," they would not have been remarkable. He said "she's not respectable"; she had "done things"; and Victoria fills the gaps.

The story is told from the viewpoint of a pair of omniscient bystanders, and to one of them Nancy Headway says, as Victoria Woodhull might have said: "I'm burying my past. . . . You can't be delicate when you're trying to save your life. . . . You think me a bad woman—you don't respect me. . . . I have done things I don't understand myself, today. . . . But I've completely changed, and I want to change everything. . . . I hate everything that has happened to me before this; I loathe it; I despise it. I went on that way trying—one thing and another. But now I've got what I want. Do you expect me to go down on my knees to you? I believe I will, I'm so anxious. . . ."

Nancy Headway was anxious for "Littlemore" to convince "Sir Arthur Demesne" that she was respectable.

John Biddulph Martin read a speech called "The Future of the United States" before the American Association for the Advancement of Science at Philadelphia, that was a sturdy, stodgy digest of politics and economics, stuffed with minute statistics. Sir Arthur Demesne "sent regularly to his bookseller for all the new publications on economical subjects, for he was determined that his political attitude should have a firm statistical basis." And Demesne, who "thought himself indispensable in the scheme of things, not as an individual but as an institution" had "never seen anything like Mrs. Headway; he hardly knew by what standard to measure her . . . as he was very much under the charm he compromised matters by saying to himself that she was only foreign. . . . The unfortunate young man was fascinated. . . . He asked her a good many questions but her answers were so startling that, like sudden luminous points, they seemed to intensify the darkness around their edges."

Victoria's protestations to the press were tastefully transferred to Littlemore, the omniscient by-stander on whom, "She had worked a certain spell; she had succeeded in making him feel responsible," but he kept her from his sister as if her past had been infectious. His sister, married to an Englishman, knew as much about English society "as if she had invented it."

And she said, as so many Anglo-American women must have said of the Woodhull-Martin affair, "The English are very romantic. . . . They do the strangest things from the force of passion—even those from whom you would least expect it. . . . They marry their cooks—they marry their coachmen. . . . What I see is a fine old race . . . and a dreadful disreputable, vulgar, little woman, who hasn't an idea of what such things are, trying to force her way into it. . . ."

Whereupon Littlemore said what so many American men must have said, "But he's a nonentity, and she at least is somebody. She's a person, and a very clever one. . . ." Which was as untrue of the Nancy Headway of fiction as it was true of Victoria Woodhull in fact.

Nancy Headway told Littlemore she had "explained things fifty times over. But some things are rather complicated . . . and he keeps coming back to them. . . . He won't come to you himself, but his mother will . . . I guess she'll send the lawyer—the family solicitor, they call him. She wanted to send him out to America to make inquiries, only she didn't know where to send."

Then with Woodhullian audacity Mrs. Headway arranged for Littlemore to meet Sir Arthur at her house, and asked Littlemore to "speak for me. . . . He will tell you whether he . . . knows anything against me," and she swept out of the room.

" 'I am placed in an impossible situation,' Littlemore said at last, 'and I don't imagine that you accept it any more than I do. . . . Have you any questions to ask me?' "

"Sir Arthur's hesitation was . . . brief. . . . 'Certainly I have no questions to ask,' the young man said in a voice of cool, almost insolent surprise."

The next day Nancy Headway wrote Littlemore that she was engaged to Sir Arthur. " 'He won't tell me what passed between you—he requested me never to allude to the subject. I don't care; I was bound you should speak.' "

For neither Nancy Headway nor Victoria Woodhull was capable of imagining a crisis in which so much chivalry was enacted with such reticence.

There is no record of a similar crisis or its equivalent in the annals of Victoria Woodhull; but few drawing-room crises leave records in anybody's annals. And if Victoria filled the gaps in Nancy Headway's story, by all the laws of probability, couldn't Nancy Headway's story fill the gaps in hers? We only know for a fact that Victoria Woodhull married John Biddulph Martin on the thirty-first of October, 1883.

In the England of the 'eighties there still were elderly aristocrats who wouldn't dine with doctors or bankers, as neither were considered gentlemen; society was so neatly arranged to spare the effort of appraising personalities. There was another caste of hereditary opulence whose members wouldn't dine with the new industrialists (for dining was the social touchstone), and to this caste the Martins belonged.

Martin's bank at 68 Lombard Street was of ancient origin. According to the tradition, Matthew Shore was a goldsmith there in the fifteenth century and handed on the business. Its origin also is associated with Sir Thomas Gresham, who died in 1579 and whose family crest, the grasshopper, displayed outside the building, is the emblem of the bank. Sir Richard Martin, the first Martin known among the goldsmiths of London was called to the livery of the Goldsmiths' Company in 1558; and then, after a blank in the records of the firm, the name Martin reappeared in 1703 and has been represented among the partners ever since.

As soon as Victoria Woodhull breathed that atmosphere of ancestor worship she produced some of her own. She was marvellously adaptive, but she still told the public what she wanted them to know.

She issued a little folder to tell them that the

"MEMO:
beneath
The WASHINGTON PEDIGREE
as on the Chart, reads as follows:
JOHN DANDRIDGE HAD TWO DAUGHTERS

King Robert III of Scotland,	George Washington married
King James of England	Martha Dandridge.
from whom are descended	Penelope Dandridge married
The Dukes of Hamilton,	Michael Biddulph,
to whom was related	who died in 1800.
Alexander Hamilton	Their son
the friend of Washington.	John Biddulph married
Thomas Hamilton married	Augusta Roberts.
Anna Underwood	Their daughter
Their grandson was	Mary Ann Biddulph married
Rubin Buckman Claflin (born	Robert Martin.
in 1796 at Sanderfield,	Their son
Mass., U. S. A.), the father	John Biddulph Martin
of	Married
VICTORIA CLAFLIN	VICTORIA
WOODHULL and	WOODHULL."
TENNESSEE CLAFLIN.	

To avoid any misunderstanding, she said this showed "that Victoria Claflin Woodhull-Martin and Tennessee Claflin, who are descended on their father's side from the kings of Scotland and England and on their mother's side, from the Hummels and Moyers of Germany, who also were of royal blood, are related to the famous American legislator Lieut.-Colonel Alexander Hamilton (whose statue adorns the Central Park, New York City); and they are connected by marriage with the family of Washington himself."

Whereupon George Blood wondered whether "H.R.H. the Prince of Wales would find his claim to the throne disputed on the demise of Victoria Rex." But others must have wondered why Victoria chose such a missing link as Alexander Hamilton to connect her with the kings of Scotland and England. For his legitimacy has been gravely doubted, and apparently she had a free choice, unhampered by any facts whatever. In none of twelve competent tomes on the Hamilton family, is there any record of a Thomas Hamilton's marriage to an Anna Underwood. The Underwood genealogy, which is equally competent, records an Anna Underwood who married a William Claflin in 1794, and a Silence Underwood Pond whose second husband was John Claflin. The Claflin genealogy, a sketchy affair in which supposition is more apparent than research, was published after Victoria's marriage to Martin, and Margaret Ann Miles furnished the material for their branch of the family. It states that Reuben Buckman Claflin's mother, instead of his grandmother, was Anna Underwood, and that his father was Robert Claflin, a statement which is not verified by the Underwood genealogy.

In the England of the 'eighties, the thinking class writhed in a white light of perplexity between the dawn of science and the dusk of their old beliefs. But the ruling class basked in dim serenity, unaware of mental revolutions, as unmoved as tin soldiers in a toy village; and to this class, the Martins and the industrialists belonged. They were aware of an "industrial revolution," because it had let them into the ruling class.

But in their private lives they repeated the stock of observations their parents had learned from their grandparents, resting comfortably on the authority of

MRS. JOHN BIDDULPH MARTIN OF NUMBER 17, HYDE PARK GATE

dignified experience, avoiding an original opinion as earnestly as an original costume. And yet, as if to prove the futility of generalizations, one of them married Victoria Woodhull.

She must have outraged them as she had outraged the Woodhulls in her lustier 'teens when a lifted eyebrow was food for rage instead of fear. Now there were more inducements to conform. She wanted to be an accepted member of an honorable family; she wanted respectability and a social position. Apparently she longed for the opportunity to be magnificently bored, and she had to wait some time for it.

She went to live at number 17 Hyde Park Gate, a somber house on a somber London street, which was as ugly as it was exclusive. But number 17 only presented its shoulder to the street; it seemed to dodge at a crazy angle, to face a small garden with a high ivy-covered wall. Its dun-colored door opened into a hall like a Pompeian villa, adorned with marble busts of Aphrodite and Hermes, and the blue and gold domed ceiling was after Mrs. Martin's own design. A winding stair led to the drawing-room, where you could slip with white bear skin rugs on the parquetry floor. The chandelier was made of Venetian wood, carved into little cupids. The largest inlaid table exhibited a spider's web in mosaic, and around the edge were mosaic medallions of the great musicians. And in a recess, against a background of purple velvet, stood a large silver statue of the Greek goddess Nike, and a copy of "The Fortuna." In another corner strips of silk were caught into a loop and fastened to a silver ring on the ceiling, to surround a pillowed nook with just room for two. The background was leafy green, and the pillows harmonized. Elsewhere were ivories and bric-a-brac and flowers, and Herbert Spencer's "Synthetic Philosophy."

And yet few people called to see all this. On Sunday evenings young American students went there, (most of them had no other place to go.) But the talk was often brilliant, though Victoria led it somewhat oratorically.

She had one of the best cooks in London, where food was considered more of a necessity than a pleasure; and after a supper such as few Englishmen enjoyed, John Biddulph Martin sat there, listening to her, the picture of a proud and happy man.

No doubt she knew how to make a man happy; she had had so much practise. And when Arthurian chivalry was most admired, it must have been exhilarating to be a heroic as well as a comfortable example of it.

Then Tennie C. changed her name back to Tennessee, and captured the affections of Francis Cook, an elderly widower who had made a fortune importing India shawls. She told him that his wife had sent a message from the spirit world advising him to marry her. And he married her in October, 1885.

So Tennessee went to live at Doughty House, a magnificent residence noted for its remarkable art gallery which overlooked the Thames. Francis Cook also had a famous collection of antique rings; and he had spent so much money on his estate at Cintra near Lisbon in Portugal, that the King of Portugal gave him the title of Visconde de Montserrate. He was fabulously rich.

RUBIN BUCKMAN CLAFLIN IN HIS LATER YEARS

When this marriage was announced the *New York World* printed some annals of the sensational sisters, and Victoria sent a letter to the *New York Sun:*

"Sir:

"My father, Reuben B. Claflin died of grief caused by the malicious libel published in the *World* of October 25th. Has not our family suffered enough? Please insert this notice for our heart-broken family.

"Victoria Claflin Martin."

And that inspired the *Chicago Herald* to repeat the story. Perhaps some reporter remembered Buckman and was irritated by the preposterous suggestion that he, who never was unduly sensitive, had died of grief. He was eighty-nine.

No doubt Victoria wanted to turn gossip into sympathy. But Buckman's death produced another letter.

"Justice" wrote to the Lord Mayor of London that "a mysterious death occurred on the nineteenth of November . . . of a much respected and honored citizen by the name of Reuben B. Claflin. His papers were spirited away as well as the will that is known to have been made by him, including money and bonds. . . . His death was sudden. His sickness and burial was very mysterious. It would be well to have this matter investigated at once by the proper authorities, as delay may defeat the ends of justice."

Then it was announced that Reuben Claflin had died of old age. He had had a paralytic stroke at 17 Hyde Park Gate.

But Scotland Yard had to investigate the case, and poor John Biddulph Martin's troubles began. They found the letter a matter of malice, and a reward was offered for the detection of the writer, until they suspected that it came from a member of the Claflin family.

Tennessee's husband was richer than Victoria's, but he was a mere industrial; to remove the social barrier between the sisters, Tennessee persuaded him to endow an artist's home in London. The Prince and Princess of Wales attended the opening, which made it an important occasion. Tennessee was acknowledged the prettiest and best dressed woman there; she was animated and imperturbable, "as if she had been a born aristocrat," said one of the papers. Mrs. Martin was elegantly dressed, cold, intellectual and refined, "the mistress of herself and of the situation."

After that Francis Cook was promptly made a baronet, and then the sisters could dine together with propriety.

They went driving with each other in Hyde Park, behind sleek highstepping thoroughbreds, almost every afternoon. Roxanna was living with Tennessee now, and it must have delighted her, that at last her daughters, rid of Colonel Blood, "rode around in their own carriages."

They rode alone, for sedate society scorned women whose questionable past couldn't be forgotten when it constantly blazed in the press. The Claflin tendency to melodrama, which they invariably took into law-courts, lit the fires of more publicity. Through sister Mary Sparr a terrible story came out now, a story that was meat for London's shilling shockers.

It was the story of Mary Sparr's dead daughter, Rosa Burns, and it came out because Mary Sparr contested her will on the grounds that she had been improperly influenced. For Rosa had inherited forty thousand dollars from her father, Ross Burns; and, when she died, she willed it to Francisco de Martin, the Chancellor to the Council-General of Spain in New York City, her "friend and more than father," instead of to her mother, who was devoted to forty thousand dollars.

At fifteen Rosa Burns had married one Charles Farlan; but, when she discovered he had another living wife, he abandoned Rosa and her unborn child. Mary Sparr was a practising "electric and magnetic physician" then, and de Martin testified that she wrote him to call and learn something of importance about his friend Utica Brooker, who had died in 'seventy-three. He did so, and Mrs. Sparr gave him one of Utica's photographs to have copied. He saw Rosa, and she was very beautiful. De Martin testified that Tennessee called at his office on lower Broadway a few months later and said that her niece Rosa had made an unfortunate marriage and was very poor; she wondered if he knew of some man among his friends who would take care of a pretty girl? De Martin told her he knew of no such person, and she invited him to "The Psyche Club," where they were going to discuss free love. De Martin went there, but he refused to head a subscription list with a check for one hundred dollars, and, as he was leaving, he saw Rosa.

"My child," he told her, "this is no place for you. . . . They're discussing things here which you shouldn't listen to. . . ."

De Martin testified that Rosa said her mother had forced her to come. She was hungry, she said, she had

had nothing to eat since morning. De Martin took her to dinner, and visited her often after that. One day he found her in tears because she had given birth to a dead baby. Mrs. Sparr showed it to him and accused him of being the father, which he indignantly denied. She said she had no money for the burial; they were so poor. De Martin paid for it.

Finally, to help them, he went to board at Mrs. Sparr's, with his step-daughter, Rosa Lena.

But Mrs. Sparr began to hate her boarder, and she was not a quiet hater. She went to the Collector of the Port, and accused de Martin of smuggling; a charge that was dismissed as soon as it was investigated. When de Martin returned to the house, he found Mrs. Sparr gone with the furniture, and he took the two Roses to live with him uptown.

He advised Rosa Burns to get in touch with her father, and he wrote the letter to Ross Burns, as the girl was illiterate. Rosa visited her father in Topeka and then came back to the de Martin household, where she died after a long and painful illness. Her body was scarcely in her coffin when Mary Sparr appeared and accused Martin of mal-practise. She said he had led Rosa astray, whereupon the body was exhumed and an inquest was held which proved the charge unfounded.

And then Mary Sparr had to drag Victoria into it. She told a reporter from the *Herald,* who said her face was "of the trial and tribulation kind", that "Mrs. Woodhull was very thick with Blood and Andrews, and of course I would have nothing to do with her. What about the club Mrs. Woodhull started in Twenty-third

Street? She had to foster free love. I don't know anything about free love. I've got the marriage certificates to both my husbands and I was honorably and legally married, let them say what they will. Just because my sisters were public characters, people pitched into their club. Free love and social clubs, indeed. Do you know what is going on in hundreds of brown stone houses in this city? There's where you want to look for free love! . . ." Which was a perfect example of the way the Claflins would smite and then defend one another.

The "Psyche Club," a short-lived activity of Victoria's "Madam Roland" period, was mentioned occasionally in *Woodhull & Claflin's Weekly.*

But John Biddulph Martin wrote a sturdy letter to the *Herald:* "Referring to reports of the case of Sparr vs. de Martin that recently appeared in your columns, it is impossible to remain silent or to refute seriatim the innumerable falsehoods and malignantly libellous statements and insinuations that have been directed in that law suit against my wife, Victoria Woodhull Martin.

"They originated, to our certain knowledge, in personal malice. They have been revived in certain false evidence in the said law suit; and they are now being re-echoed in the more unprincipled portion of the London press. I can only stigmatize them, one and all, as infamous falsehoods.

"While it is necessary I should take time to consider how such libels may best be dealt with, I cannot but thank you for granting me this opportunity of meeting them with an emphatic and public denial."

The fact that the men Victoria married were her most faithful lovers implies that she had the gift of making love survive shock as well as time. For she gave them all shocks, according to their natures, and they gave her an unwavering devotion.

It must have shocked John Biddulph Martin when such stories appeared in the paper about his wife's family, and about his wife, though it is unlikely that he believed any of the latter. Drawing on the noble capacity for self-deception which the mind has when emotions are concerned, he wouldn't let himself believe them.

Moreover, John Biddulph Martin's marriage probably had all the glamour of an Arthurian romance for him (that was its only explanation), and the defense of the lady fair he had snatched from a world of enemies was his brave, but very natural part.

With neither happiness nor comfort at stake, society refused to associate romance with reality. There was too much scandal in print. In 1887 the New York *Sun,* published a signed and very accurate sketch of Victoria. In 1888, Henry Ward Beecher's biography came out with "Victoria Woodhull, blackmailed by" in the index as well as in the text. Victoria summoned a reporter and said, "I don't believe Mr. Beecher ever made or wrote such a charge. . . . Whither has the chivalry of American editors and writers fled since I quitted America, that occurrences of sixteen and twenty years ago should even be referred to, much less falsified to strike at a woman. . . . At any risk of personal annoyance my husband and I are prepared to bring the libellers to book. . . ."

But they didn't. Then Victoria announced that the

publishers had promised to suppress "any objectionable allusions", but they didn't. The allusions to blackmail are in the book now.

Victoria wanted to fight print with print. The uneducated, or the lately educated, have so much faith in it; and, when Victoria remembered too many humiliations, it must have been soothing to see her apotheosis in "black and white",—that magic phrase. But the newspapers apparently tired of printing her protestations of virtue. In time they grew monotonous, and somehow such protestations never are as exciting as their antithesis. So she began to issue biographical pamphlets; she and Tennessee issued them at intervals for the next forty years. It was a quaint habit. Many people have issued pamphlets to defend their ideas, but few have issued them to defend their characters.

"The Talebearer" told how Victoria had taken John Biddulph Martin to The Temperance Hotel in London to see a Mrs. Warner of Elizabeth, New Jersey, who was "poor and ashamed to live in her own country." Mrs. Warner had been saying that Victoria Woodhull ruined her husband and half the men in New York and Brooklyn. She said she had never seen Victoria, but she would "become a demon" if she saw her. "I am Victoria Woodhull Martin," said Victoria in the pamphlet, ". . . I have never known Mr. Warner. . . . You have traded in London on this infamous story to elicit sympathy and get money. It is through just such wretches as you that my name has been blackened in London and America." Whereupon Mrs. Warner, instead of becoming a demon, signed a statement saying, "I deeply regret that I had given credit to any of the stories which have been told to me by persons who envied her pure and marvellously beautiful spirit. . . . After meeting Mrs. Victoria Woodhull Martin I consider her to be infinitely above any such conduct . . . as my husband and friends reported to me." One M. M. Schonberg stated that she had claimed money from Mrs. Martin and Lady Cook. "I was then the tool through circumstances of bad, weak men who had hatched the plot to destroy if possible, the grand destiny of two noble women," confessed M. M. Schonberg.

"One Moral Standard For All" was illustrated, and signed by M. F. Darewin, with a long apostrophe to the sisters. "Women! they have dared more than to go among the jungles to chase lions and tigers, they have dared to go into the human life of the world and still more dangerous has it been. . . . They have vanquished; but they bear yet the horrible scars of the jaws and teeth of ferocious ignorance." Then came their royal pedigree, an exaggerated account of Mrs. Woodhull's nomination for the presidency, and of the terrible persecution they had suffered because they advocated intelligent maternity and an equal standard of morals. "In the lives of these two women we find the history of woman's cause, and we are waiting for the last chapter, the acknowledgment of the endured suffering, the apotheosis." Then "The Beginning of the Battle", by Tennessee Claflin, was reprinted from the scandal issue of *Woodhull & Claflin's Weekly*. And, said M. F. Darewin, "(This) caused the writer . . . and the entire staff of *Woodhull & Claflin's Weekly*, to be arrested for obscenity."

In fact this article about women's wrongs never was mentioned in any of the obscenity trials; but the sisters evidently thought it a plausible pretense, for "The

Beginning of the Battle" was repeated in a separate folder, with a similar legend.

A brochure called, "A Page of American History" was more fraudulent; because, after irrelevant quotations from Lord Macaulay and the Sacred Books of India, came "The Naked Truth," a sonnet by William Cullen Bryant, which had given Victoria the title for her Cooper Union lecture. It was introduced by "The following is taken from William Cullen Bryant's paper, *The Evening Post,* of New York City," and immediately after it, appeared a vivid account of that Cooper Union speech when Victoria Woodhull entered the hall disguised as a Quaker lady, an account which Anthony Higgins had written for *Woodhull & Claflin's Weekly* of December 28, 1873, ending "The much-dreaded 'naked truth' had reached the public ear through the silver-tongued Woodhull, the brave. She is the superior strategist. The terrible syren has defeated you, and charmed your cohorts and battalions to silence and inaction. The night of the ninth of January, 1873, passed into history and the bravest and truest of her sex moves further up Calvary from the rostrum to the prison." This was arranged in "A Page of American History" as if it had been published in *The Evening Post,* whereas *The Evening Post* didn't even mention that Cooper Union speech. And for years, at intervals, Victoria reproduced that impression in other pamphlets and in proof-sheets which she sent to newspapers for reproduction.

It was unfortunate that Victoria spent her energy on such futility. If she hadn't been so eager not to be herself, if she had joined a cause to fit her phase, according to her old custom, she might have become a personage, instead of "only a name," which is the impression she left in the minds of English publicists. The suffrage movement was very active in England during the first years of Victoria's marriage; she played no part in it. The Fabian society was formed in 1884. That same year commissions began to investigate sweated trades and housing, and they continued so respectably that the Prince of Wales often served as chairman to examine the state of the submerged. It was the era of the "settlement" when university graduates went to live among the poor. The first skirmish of the New Unionism succeeded in 1888 with the strike of London girls employed in making lucifer matches, because of the friendly social atmosphere.

Victoria knew the patter of all these movements through *Woodhull & Claflin's Weekly;* with her splendid oratorical gift she might have played such a part in them that those leaders of society who happened to have been leaders in practical sociology would have dismissed her past, as the pasts of really useful people always have been dismissed. Then the lesser folk would have followed their betters.

Unfortunately, Victoria tried to placate the lesser folk, and of course she failed, inasmuch as tin soldiers never take to tigers, not even to fawning tigers.

Apparently respectability dazzles those who have been deprived of it. It was love at first sight with Victoria. She went after it with all her old intensity. Of course it involved John Biddulph Martin, who represented the only safety, the only stability she had ever known. It involved balm for aching scars from Homer

SIR FRANCIS COOK

LADY COOK

and elsewhere, too, and a future for her daughter Zulu Maud.

But Tennessee shifted the responsibility and enjoyed herself; and by way of social irony, or poetic justice, she made more friends than Victoria did, and more important friends. Victoria spent her personality on restraint, when she was with English people. She tried to be dignified and succeeded in being cold. Tennessee gaily advised an old friend to "Give up your work in America, and come to England to live; I'll find you a rich husband." Evidently she found hers worth while. Sir Francis was an agreeable old fellow, tall, and large and slow of speech, given to pleasantry and to calling his wife "that little woman." She had step-children, instead of powerful in-laws. She dressed exquisitely, and gay Londoners who adored Americanisms roared at her "last."

She gave a garden party at Richmond and invited all the drapers, and dukes, and bankers and bakers she could think of; and everybody came. She had neglected to count them, and there was a terrible crush until she cheerfully summoned an army of workmen to tear down the fences and let the crowd into the meadows, the most assorted crowd that London ever saw. But they were amused. This was the sort of diversion they expected from Americans.

Sir Francis took her to Lisbon, where he had been a great benefactor, and the natives nearly smothered his wife with flowers as the carriage drove slowly through the village. Music played to welcome her, and rockets pierced the air. Flags of every nation floated from the turrets of the Cook castle at Montserrate, and a real marble castle it was, with turrets and everything, like the ones in fairy tales.

There was a famous garden, where plants flourished from over the globe, and Tennessee opened it to tourists and allowed them to wander about alone. But on their way out, they always were stopped at the lodge, and the gardener would ask what language they spoke before presenting a pamphlet called "The Primrose Path," which Lady Cook had had printed in every tongue. After wandering at will among exotic palms and shrubs and flowering trees, they could read "The Primrose Path" and see the dangers of prostitution, set forth in their own language.

Then in London the Athletic Club gave a dinner, and John Biddulph Martin, who was its president, invited his wife and Lady Cook. But a Mrs. Taylor, the wife of an army officer, declared the sisters were not "proper persons to be associated with;" and under her leadership the other women refused to sit at the table with them. And so Victoria and Tennessee actually were left alone in the banquet room, mute victims of woman's inhumanity to woman, in a era when chastity was the only virtue society required.

The society press related this episode with gusto; and it is a harsh comment on the spirit of the time that none declared that the women who were capable of such a public exhibition of organized cruelty were not proper associates for anybody.

Chapter Sixteen

THE LEOPARD'S SPOTS

THERE is nothing more futile nor more irresistible than to wonder what might have been. And yet we can't help wondering whether if the sisters had said, "Yes, most of the scandal is true, but what of it?" they wouldn't have won the best of liberal England (and there was a sturdy liberal England in the early 'nineties), as well as those robust aristocrats who live in every age, aloof from the taboos of the crowd, and responsive to any show of gallantry, the trait they always cherish. But such a gallant gesture might have lost John Biddulph Martin and Sir Francis Cook, which would have been a calamity for Victoria and Tennessee.

So they talked about libel suits, and sent out an eight-column proof sheet to every newspaper in England and America, offering a reward of one thousand pounds for the names of those "concerned in the conspiracy to defame" them. To indicate that Victoria C. Woodhull and Tennessee Claflin had "suffered a martyrdom for a good and just cause," they printed authentic excerpts from papers that did name and denounce their persecution in 1873; they rehashed the accusation that Colonel Blood had inspired the Treat pamphlet from *Woodhull & Claflin's Journal* of 1881. To prove the recklessness of rumor, a tale that Victoria Woodhull and Tennessee Claflin had crossed on the Gallia in men's clothes was traced to a judge's wife, who unwittingly told Victoria herself, whom she never had seen before, that she knew the Claflin sisters and

VICTORIA C. WOODHULL and TENNESSEE CLAFLIN.

REVIVAL OF A PAGE OF AMERICAN HISTORY

[From The Times (*London, England*), January 22nd, 1890]

£1000 REWARD.

"Mr. John Biddulph Martin and Sir Francis Cook will pay the sum of ONE THOUSAND POUNDS STERLING to anyone who shall reveal the names of the person or persons concerned in the conspiracy to defame their wives, Victoria C. Woodhull, now Mrs. John B. Martin, and Miss Tennie Claflin, now Lady Cook, a who shall give such evidence as shall secu a conviction.

"TWENTY POUNDS will be paid the above named gentlemen for the nan of the author and printer of an obsc and libellous leaflet entitled "The Sex Problem," that has recently been circula in England.

"All communications to be addressed to 17, Hyde Park Gate, London, England."

"Any person who has been interested in the case of Mrs. C. B. Warner, of Elizabeth, N.J., recently an in-patient at the Temperance Hospital, Hampstead Road, is requested to communicate with Charles W. Stevens, Esq., 14, Queen Victoria Street, London, E.C."

[TWENTY POUNDS will also be paid by the above named gentlemen for the name of any paper, issued in England, that has published a recent libel against their wives.]

[Or to 142, West-70th Street, New York City.]

on the previous day, executed bonds in $16,000 each for the release of Mrs Woodhull and Miss Claflin they were there awaiting the decision of the District Attorney as to their capability to become sureties. In a short time the bondsmen were informed that they had been accepted.

"While the women-brokers were in the District Attorney's office, a gentleman stepped up to Mrs. Woodhull and told her that it was his duty to tell her that there was a conspiracy against her. He said that it was understood between certain officials and prosecuting parties that Mrs. Woodhull and Miss Claflin should be forced into Jefferson Market Prison, and, while there, the prison would be fired and they left to perish in the flames. He added that the parties referred to were determined to be rid of them at any cost. Mrs. Woodhull and Miss Claflin could barely credit the story, but the earnestness of the man, and the promise that, at an early day, he would tell all he know of the plot, forced them to place credence in his story

"The women-brokers then entered their coach, and an officer of the Jefferson Market Police Court stepped up to the door, and placing his hand on Miss Claflin's shoulder, said in a kind tone, 'Stop' A gentleman hastened to the rescue, and pushing the officer aside, said, 'No you don't. Mrs. Woodhull and Miss Claflin are still United States prisoners, and you cannot arrest them again, as they have been warned of your infamous plot.

"The officer wilted. The women-brokers were then taken back to their old quarters in Ludlow Street Jail. To-morrow they will probably take their departure from that jail and procure bail in the other suits.

"The authorities seem determined to do their utmost, by placing every obstacle in their way, to prevent them from obtaining their freedom."

Herald, December 1st, 1872. New York City.

"Mesdames Woodhull and Claflin were taken again to-day from the County Jail to the Federal Building, preparatory to giving bail They were accompanied by their counsel Soon after their arrival they were conducted to the office of Commissioner Shields, where the bail-bonds were prepared. When the case was called,

"The counsel said they were prepared to give unexceptionable bail, but it would be useless for them to do so, as an officer of the Jefferson Market Court was outside in the hall, waiting to re-arrest them. He thought it would be better that his clients remain in the County Jail than to go to a cell in the Jefferson Market Prison. He had heard that the judge had been spirited away for the purpose of preventing the prisoners from being bailed

Pioneer, January 18th, 1873. Houston (Mo.).

"These women, among the most intellectual, pure and true of our country, have been driven from pillar to post, and refused a place to rest their overtasked bodies and brains, and at last, to add to their great sorrow and misfortune, and the further disgrace of the United States authorities, were cast into prison. And for what? for exposing the baseness of the pretenders of righteousness."

Republican, January 26th, 1873. Waverley (Iowa)

"Mrs Woodhull is again incarcerated. We can only look upon her incarceration as persecution by those who are afraid of this fearless woman. 'Truth crushed to earth will rise again;' and yet, though at present plunged into a New York prison, she will yet triumph over her enemies. Unable to defend their position like men, they seek to cover up their characters by casting their accuser into prison

"This is but a resurrection of the persecution that attended the advancement of ideas by fearless men when they were bound at the stake for their opinions. Shame upon such manhood."

Independent Thinker, February, 1873. Greenville (Ala.).

"Social revolution is a thing that takes place not once in a century, for social ideas of all others are the most difficult to change yet nothing less than a social revolution in the United States has been inaugurated, and from the zeal with which it is being urged and the persecution that is heaped upon Mrs Woodhull and Miss Claflin, if it does not ultimately prove triumphant neither its friends or its enemies will be to blame.

"Mrs. Victoria C. Woodhull is the most perfectly intellectual woman in all probability that now lives Her intellect is vigorous, powerful, comprehensive, voluble, accomplished, and refined Her motives have been rather misunderstood, misconstrued, or wilfully perverted. She is directing the splendid powers of a great mind and, perhaps, a greater amount of energy and individual effort than ever before proceeded from such a source Demanding intellectual elevation of her sex, she asks for equality for woman with men before the law, and the same treatment at the hands of public opinion, that the male libertines and debauchees shall be degraded as well as female prostitutes She demands nothing but justice at the hands of society and the Government.

"She had to be crushed at all hazards, and the paper that was being circulated, broadcast over the country must be suppressed She was indicted in eight different cases and required to give bail in $8000 dollars each Friends were intimidated by threats from going upon her bonds, and those more intimately connected with her were also arrested on hatched-up charges

and which the press, after having misstated them, has refused upon proper occasion to state them correctly? Does the *Sun* mean the deeds which it has been insinuated by the press that she has committed, spread broadcast over the land to poison the people against her, or those which constitute her real life? Are they the imaginary figments of envenomed brains, pumped up into the public mind to help on the very persecution that the *Sun* criticises, or the actual experiences of the woman's life? What opinions? I repeat. My own opinions, set forth by myself before the two hundred or more audiences whom I have addressed in the last eight months, have been universally endorsed Is it these opinions that, in the estimation of the *Sun*, entitle me to public contempt, or are they not rather those which the press has endeavoured to foist upon the public as mine, but which I utterly repudiate and reject, and which the *Sun* should know that I repudiate and reject, because it has had the opportunity to know? Let my opinions be properly and fairly presented to any audience that can be gathered from the most conservative circles of any society, and they will be endorsed. Why, then, should the *Sun* present them to the public as something to merit contempt?

And the same for her deeds. I repeat: What deeds? We have been traced from our cradles through every place in which we have ever resided, to our prisons, by detectives paid without stint by friends of Mr Beecher, to fasten some single deed upon us that might be brought into court to be put in evidence against us, and they failed to find a blemish even. All the vile insinuations of dark deeds and darker lives, when traced vanished into thin air in the mouths of their inventors. After passing such a crucial ordeal as this, is it not time that we should cease to be pursued by the press, after the fashion of the *Sun's* article? It seems so to me But if it do not to the press, why do they not rummage the mass of filth, and from its vile depth exhume some one fact to substantiate the insinuation of deeds that merit contempt.

But again · "Had the victim been other than what she was;" "to crush some person who is not a Woodhull." Worse and worse, and wherefore? The muddle into which the *Sun* has fallen about her opinions and deeds has caused it to reverse the facts in this case. It was because the victim was a Woodhull, was a Claflin, who possessed the sympathy and had the assistance of some of the best and noblest people in the world, who knew us, and who extended their sympathy and assistance because they knew us to be just what we were, that we were not convicted and railroaded to Sing Sing in ten days, according to the original programme. It was the strong hands and the

ONE OF THE PROOF SHEETS THAT WERE SENT TO ALL THE IMPORTANT NEWSPAPERS IN ENGLAND AND AMERICA had seen them dressed so. Victoria visited another detractor who told her that Victoria Woodhull had been driven out of London; and when Victoria revealed herself, she begged for mercy and said she was "controlled by the evil one to talk so about a person she had never seen and really knew nothing about." Here, too, William Cullen Bryant's sonnet, "The Naked Truth" was printed above Mr. Higgins' "Terrible Syren" story with no line between, as if both were Bryant's tributes to Victoria!

In fact rumors were started recklessly in those days when pure fiction forced the imaginative to draw on real life for the smut which seems to be one of their necessities, and a dog with a bad name was called every name. John Biddulph Martin came home from the City with his pockets full of attacks on his wife; anonymous letters and blackmailers beset them. Which must have made it easier for Martin to believe in persecution.

Then the Taylor faction published a leaflet made of choice quotations from *Woodhull & Claflin's Weekly*, and called it "The Sexual Problem." They sent two detectives to Chicago to get proofs that Victoria and Tennessee "had not conducted themselves properly in America." And such relentless activity sprang not only from the energy with which the chaste pursued their erring sisters in those days; it was the reasonable result of the Martin-Cook threats of a libel action, for a libel action is not a joke in England.

The sisters issued a long galley-proof which they claimed was a reprint from the New York *Sun* of June, 1876. And that was only one false statement, for not a word of it appeared in the New York *Sun* on any day in June, 1876. It described Buckman as a retired lawyer who "commanded universal respect . . . because of the honorable manner in which he carried himself through his professional career." He was "an affectionate and exemplary father," too. Roxanna, "a strictly religious woman . . . states that during her married life she never had an unpleasant word with her husband." The family were all in "perfect accord." And that Victoria and Tennessee revered their mother "is evidenced by the fact that they take her along wherever they go." Of course they only wanted women to receive the same compensation as men for the same labor; and men to receive the same ostracism as women for the same immorality. And for this heroic vindication of their sex they were assailed and imprisoned; they survived only because "The royal blood of their ancestors and their fine personal physique" brought "them through the contest."

Unfortunately a more accurate history of the Claflin clan appeared in the *Brooklyn Eagle,* and other papers, in a piece Police Inspector Thomas Byrnes wrote about a number of adventuresses who "made a stir." It was more concise than circumstantial, but it was widely read.

John Biddulph Martin and Sir Francis Cook decided it was time to stop such "foul aspersions" on their wives. They were told that a "designing hand" inspired them all, as it had inspired Mrs. Warner and M. M. Schonberg in "The Talebearer." Victoria and Tennessee announced somewhat ambiguously that it "All comes from unknown enemies, for whenever we face a traducer . . . he or she has without exception retracted their abuse and confessed their charges were without foundation."

According to Victoria, when she saw this last "calumny," she said to herself, "Who is Thomas Byrnes?" She thought it the nom de plume of "some insignificant scribbler, but the subject was serious," and she asked an American newspaper correspondent about him.

"My God!" he exclaimed, staggering back so that he was supported by one of the drawing-room doors —according to Victoria. "Don't, don't have anything to say to that man! He is the czar of New York. . . . He could do anything to you. Don't, don't, do not anger him."

Victoria admitted her alarm, but in spite of being warned of "dreadful things," including assassination, she decided to go to New York. "They may do what they choose with me," said she. "I shall show all my enemies that I have nothing to be afraid for!"

Which was at least a twisted sort of gallantry. She had nerve.

So it was reported in America that John Biddulph Martin had rented a house in New York in order to start suits of criminal libel. He gave out an interview, saying, "I will incur any inconvenience to obtain justice and redress. It is not a question of damages. No damages, however exemplary, would be any satisfaction for injuries that cannot be measured by dollars."

Now that was no way to talk at Thomas Byrnes, a powerful citizen, risen from the ranks through more force than finesse. He was a master of the third degree. He was the founder of the "dead line" for criminals. When he read the Martin ultimatum, he smiled grimly and said a legal contest would develop interesting features.

But Victoria took Zulu Maud, John Biddulph Martin and Tennessee to New York. Fortunately Sir Francis Cook had to visit his estate in Portugal.

She told a reporter at the dock that they had obtained "retractions" in London of "the malicious stories. . . . The press of this country is generous. I have confidence in American manhood, and know that I shall be vindicated." Her figure had grown more matronly, but the gray tinge in her brown hair was becoming; her face glowed with health and dimples played around her fascinating mouth. John Biddulph Martin couldn't keep his eyes away from her; it was obvious that he idolized his wife.

They saw the George Ellerys. Apparently Victoria was afraid of old friends who might be less conventional. She went to see none but Mrs. Severance, and it may not be significant that Mrs. Severance was the one who might have seen Colonel Blood. But Victoria was heavily veiled; and, when Mrs. Severance didn't recognize her immediately, she left murmuring, "If soul doesn't speak to soul—"

Then Margaret Miles' second husband, Denis O'Halloran, arranged an interview with Inspector Byrnes. O'Halloran claimed that Byrnes told him that he merely had furnished a reporter with notes for an article on "brainy women," which naturally would include Victoria and Tennessee, and then a syndicate published them in an exaggerated form, and used Byrnes' name without his consent.

So O'Halloran, and Victoria, and Martin and a portmanteau full of papers drove to police headquar-

MR. AND MRS. JOHN BIDDULPH MARTIN

ters in a smart coach with a pair of jet black horses. They went into the Inspector's private office; the Inspector summoned a witness, asked them to be seated and asked them to state their business.

How Victoria's heart must have fluttered when she felt his hostility! Irrespective of the merits of the case, it is a terrible thing to have so much staked on the words of another.

But she started to tell Byrnes all about those foul plots. After the first fifteen minutes he interrupted her.

"If you have any business with me, please state it," he said coldly.

Whereupon she opened the portmanteau, and took out some pamphlets and began to read the lovely things that had been written about her and Tennessee in England. She wanted him to read some nice letters, too, but he refused.

Then Victoria referred to the *Eagle* article.

"It has done me a great injustice!" she said dramatically.

Byrnes said he had written the article and was ready to meet her in court at any time. He said he understood they had come to America to bring a suit against him.

They denied this; and then Mr. Martin spoke, "Won't you refute this newspaper article in some way, Inspector?"

"No," said Byrnes.

"I think that article does my wife a great injustice." He handed Byrnes a few of their best pamphlets, but Byrnes said he didn't want to read them.

As they started to go, Martin said, "I'm very sorry you will do nothing."

"I am sorry, too," replied Byrnes (and surely that estimable gentleman with those pamphlets in his hand, was enough to make the devil sorry!) "But," said Byrnes, "I am a public official and any statement I make I may be held responsible for. And you have the courts to which you can have recourse at once."

A policeman escorted the Martin party to their coach, and Victoria tried to control her agitation.

This situation was serious; Martin had seen her bluff called. But Victoria held one ace, and our guess is that she played it.

There is no doubt that Victoria was tarred with some of Tennessee's pitch. Couldn't she tell Martin she was tarred with all of it? Of course the pitch was pure, but he must have noticed that Tennessee was careless in her speech. She gave people the wrong impression. . . . And then their enemies . . . and those plots. . . . Victoria had sacrificed herself to protect sister Tennessee. . . .

A few noble words like that would build a sweet image for a sentimentalist, who wanted one.

But when reporters came to the O'Halloran house to hear about the interview with Byrnes, Mr. O'Halloran told them that he was "authorized by the Inspector to tell what occurred. . . . When the Inspector shook hands with Victoria, he said he had never laid eyes on her before and knew nothing prejudicial to her character or to Lady Cook. Mrs. Martin said if he did know anything now was the time to say it, for her husband was present and she wanted him to know the truth. The Inspector then explained how . . . the writer for a syndicate had repeatedly asked for his recollections concerning famous criminals or notorious persons. The Inspector assured us that he gave some facts and then threw himself on a sofa while a subordinate gave details about other people. In short, Inspector Byrnes made an abject apology."

At that moment the folding doors opened. Victoria entered, looking "queenly in her beauty," and said, "Inspector Byrnes assured us solemnly that he never gave out the facts coupled with the names of the Woodhull-Claflin sisters, that he had no evidence." She invited the reporters into the parlor and introduced them to Martin, who "has come all the way across the ocean to help me trace these foul aspersions on my character as a woman."

". . . It is about time that these scandals were silenced forever," said he.

Victoria announced that "The Inspector has made a manly reparation and that is all I can ask at his hands. He confessed that he knows nothing about my past life and that the use of his name has been unwarranted."

Naturally Police-Inspector Byrnes read this with "no little surprise." He gave all the reporters a detailed account of what actually had taken place, and said he had had a witness present. He did not "greet them with handshaking, as they claimed." He was satisfied after reading their story that they had sought the interview in order to cable it to England. He said he was the author of the *Eagle* article; he alone was responsible for it. He made no apology to the Martins. "I didn't expect to see Mrs. Martin here, but I think she was afraid to let her husband come alone. I want it distinctly understood that I am not making a fight against the two women myself, but I am here where they can find me, if they want me."

Whereupon Mr. Martin announced earnestly that "It is most unfortunate that the account of our visit to Mr. Byrnes got into the papers in the shape that it did. It certainly looked as if we had immediately given it to the press, when, as a matter of fact, nothing was further from our intentions. After our interview with the Inspector . . . reporters began to come. We didn't see them all, and to those that we did see I never alluded to Mr. Byrnes' statements as an abject apology." He said the Inspector had not apologized but he had said that he did not write the *Eagle* article and that his official position made it impossible for him to deny it.

Which was puzzling. Byrnes told a straight story and he stuck to it. There was no reason for him to lie. On the other hand, it is unthinkable that John Biddulph Martin participated in what seems to have been a cunning trick to get Byrnes' "apology" printed in England; for it was a sage conclusion that his denials wouldn't get there, since denials never get anywhere. Victoria must have hypnotized Martin. Maybe she made him think that Byrnes had denied the authorship of the article! Indian fakirs have done more, and she had a way with miracles as well as with men. One might suspect the newspapers of inaccuracy, but their reports agreed perfectly, and she kept on making misleading statements.

She summoned more reporters and insisted that Byrnes had made a "manly apology. He also said he was very sorry that it had been published." At her most dramatic she couldn't understand why "he continues to persecute me and my sister. For years I have been exposed to the merciless and devilish malignancy of an enemy. . . . Marked newspapers have been sent to English newspapers, banks, friends and leading scientists to destroy our reputation." Her beautiful eyes moistened. "My little girl said to me this morning, 'Mama, if these men continue to attack you, we will die together in each other's arms, down in the East River.'"

Inspector Byrnes said he had no more time to bother with such people.

Victoria shrugged her shoulders contemptuously. "The mere fact that Mr. Brynes disputes my word is a matter of very little consequence when compared to the long battle I have waged against calumny and attacks on my happiness while I have been in London. . . ."

"Why don't you sue the Inspector?" she was asked.

She shook her head decidedly. "No, no, by no means. I can understand from what I have been told of the power of this man that I could not expect to secure any justice from the courts. Such a case might take years. I might be dead," she went on sadly, "when the case closed. No, I shall appeal to the newspapers for fair treatment and through them to the people. I have received assurances—not from the editors but from the proprietors of our great papers—that when I get ready to make a statement I shall be given a full opportunity. No, my court shall be in the public press and its readers shall judge of the attacks which have been made upon my reputation these many years." Then she told the truth, "My friends in England shall see that I am not afraid to confront my accusers here."

Two days later the papers announced that those old indictments against Tennessee Claflin for manslaughter and fraud had been revived in Ottawa, Illinois. They must have been discovered by the detectives the Taylor faction sent to Chicago.

The Martins made statements to the press, as Lady Cook was prostrated, but she saw two of the reporters. Tennessee looked pale and thin, and very beautiful in her fragility. "My God!" she said, "so they are to fulfill their threats. Well, let them do it. Now that they have begun their attacks anew, I will insist on going to the bottom of all the foul charges. But why have they not brought this up before! Manslaughter —and after twenty-six years. It is all persecution. All the old filth throwing, all devilish malignancy, and hate and envy because now we are rich and up in the world."

Victoria was calm. (She wasn't mentioned in the indictments; they were Tennessee's pitch). She tried to soothe Tennie, and perhaps to warn her, "Now dear, don't let your feelings carry you away," she said.

"I never heard of this case, absolutely never heard of it, sir," Tennie cried, "until a few years ago in London when a paper from Ottawa was mailed to my husband demanding one hundred thousand dollars as hush money to prevent the revival of that indictment. The whole truth needs to be told and shall. Victoria, you need not try to stop me."

She stopped for a moment, almost exhausted by emotion, and then went on, "You know we have clairvoyant power. We are Spiritualists, and I especially have the power of laying on hands." She gave her version of the story of Rebecca Howe. "Afterwards she died of course. Her case was hopeless. . . . And I was such a young girl."

Victoria said it was "devilish malignancy that can hound two women so."

Of course the Ottawa cases never were brought to trial, but their sordidness was brought to light, and the Martin-Cook libel suit against the Taylor faction was heard of no more.

No wonder Victoria and Tennessee sailed for England in a state of nervous prostration. Victoria's daughter stayed in America, and said Victoria's health "had been injured . . . by the way she was received in America. No one would believe what my mother has been compelled to endure." Western newspapers were vindictive but "fear does not enter my mother's composition. There is not a word of truth in the report that she fled the country to avoid threatened disclosures. My mother is engaged in a great work, and she intends to prosecute it here where she began to labor for social reform."

Zulu Maud was a devoted daughter.

On the way back to England, Victoria and Tennessee kept to their cabins. And John Biddulph Martin made the acquaintance of Charles Loring Brace and his daughter, who were charmed by this cultured Englishman.

He said his wife and sister-in-law were ill, but he didn't say they were Victoria Woodhull and Tennessee

Claflin, or even that they were Americans, a fact he naturally might have mentioned to their compatriots. Which was not necessarily significant, and yet it indicates that the poor man, who had heard enough to be profoundly bewildered, was afraid to hear any more.

On the last day out, Victoria came on deck, and Martin introduced her to his steamer friends as Mrs. Martin. But when Charles Loring Brace mentioned the Children's Aid Society which he had helped to found, Victoria couldn't resist her favorite drama. Without revealing her identity, she said, "Perhaps you would like to hear what Victoria Woodhull thought about it."

"I wouldn't like to hear what Victoria Woodhull thought about anything," said Mr. Brace, sincerely. And he was puzzled when the lady turned on her heel and left him.

Nobody knows what John Biddulph Martin's thoughts were at that moment.

And as for Victoria, she must have known she couldn't call such an eminent philanthropist a party to a plot. Obviously he was neither a "foul" nor a "malignant" enemy, nor was he anybody's tool. His hostility was only another fact piled on her wall of fables. If it cracked, what would become of her? There was a limit even to Martin's credulity. There was a limit to her explanations too; already they were a monotonous refrain.

So she played her last card, the ultimate move in her game of self-preservation. As soon as she arrived in London, she had a physical collapse. She was dangerously ill, genuinely ill; for fear and strain are hardy carriers to that plane between life and death where there is grim release from responsibility as well as the divine unction of anxious sympathy, and enough danger to dispel any lover's doubts.

Of course in time Victoria recovered to be a remarkable example of the survival of the fittest.

The Humanitarian appeared in July, 1892, with "Mrs. Victoria Woodhull Martin," as editor, and Mrs. Zulu Maud Woodhull as associate editor. It was a monthly magazine to advocate Victoria's current notions, as well as her current presidential campaign, and her latest personality, a personality that at fifty-four began to be convincing. And it is a measure of her marvellous vitality that at fifty-four she wanted to convince.

Printed in large type on sixteen pages of fine paper, with an illustrated cover, it was an expensive outlet for a pseudo-scholarly banker's wife. But she said she refused the jewels and rich raiment which "belonged to her station," that she "might help the unfortunate."

In fact she had to publish herself or be unpublished, (and apparently that was psychically and physically impossible) for though she had learned to read and write fluently, her old eloquence had gone with her new restraints. And whether she wrote the stuff, or dictated it or outlined it to staff writers is unimportant. *The Humanitarian* was Victoria Woodhull Martin, and it stopped when she stopped it, just as *Woodhull & Claflin's Weekly* did.

Moreover, though *The Humanitarian* came out twenty years after the *Weekly*, it was ten times as old-fashioned, for with all its faults the *Weekly* crackled with the fire that never dates, while *The Humanitarian* limped in the limits of its time.

It droned on about stirpiculture, the science of breeding human beings, which Stephen Pearl Andrews had introduced to Victoria, and which has since become eugenics, and that was supposed to be "advanced" in the 'nineties. But Victoria was incapable of handling it scientifically, and so she made it as wearisome as any profound subject is, when handled with ignorance and tranquillity.

The first number opened with what Victoria imperially called a "Manifesto." It announced that "The aim of this journal is to discuss all subjects appertaining to the well-being of humanity. We desire to have every hereditary law thoroughly threshed out, so that we may have scientific data to build upon. The children of today are the citizens of the future, and their value as citizens will depend upon the sum of their inherited qualities and the education and training that they have received.

"We recognize that the overworked, the badly bred, and the under-fed will not have their higher faculties sufficiently developed to appreciate real value. We think the physically exhausted should not be allowed to breed in ignorance of the injurious effects that their depleted condition will have on their offspring. We think it right that every effort should be made by those who have the true interests of humanity at heart to teach the consequences of ignorance on those vital subjects. . . ." And so on, until the last issue of December, 1901.

Nobody could disagree with any of it, but others

were doing it better; and no sparks were seen on the Thames. *The Humanitarian* didn't get many followers. Nobody seemed to notice it. It was neither profound nor entertaining; but it supported Victoria's reputation as a solid citizen.

It was obliquely subjective.

In a long article on "The Aristocracy of Blood," she observed that titles often meant mere money and were a false standard of excellence. The aristocracy often was unhealthy. Families should have pedigrees to register their physical inheritance. (Hers was superb.) Now blackmailers were monsters to whom "a murderer who slays outright is as nothing. . . . You can kill a man by the slow torture of mental agony." (She was blackmailed constantly.) And elsewhere she said that it was absurd to claim that "ripe beauty" was less attractive, than "the fresh beauty of sweet sixteen. The fullness of beauty does not reach its zenith under thirty-five and forty." She blamed a hundred social ills on depleted energy. (And what a part it had played in her own life!) State socialism robbed "those who think and work and exercise prudence to give the spoil to those who practise none of these virtues." Which were strange words from one who figured in every history of socialism in America, but very natural sentiments from a banker's wife. So were the reiterated conclusions on the economy of buying the best of things, and on the importance of teaching the poor to judge values. Several references to the scarcity of eugenically eligible young men and to the social isolation of nice young girls in a city sprang from a mother's heart. And that "Those children who are taught to lie, beg and steal for the benefit of their parents, grow up with the idea that evil is good and after attaining manhood or womanhood, they carry into practise the training of their youth and are punished accordingly," may have sprung from a daughter's.

Just twice the old Victoria crept in to plead for the new. She observed that the "charming woman has no age. Helen of Troy was over forty when that famous elopement took place. Cleopatra was past thirty when she made the conquest of Anthony. . . . Madam de Maintenon was forty-three when she married Louis XIV, and Ninon de l'Enclos received a declaration of love on her eightieth birthday. The names of many other ancient society ladies might be added to the list."

And an unsigned poem called "Two Women" was too relevant to have been printed through a mere coincidence:

"I know the one and one is chaste
And cold as the snow on a winter waste;
Stainless ever in act and thought
(As a man born dumb in speech errs not)
But she has malice toward her time
A cruel tongue and a jealous mind
Void of pity and full of greed—
She judges the world by her narrow creed—
A breeder of quarrels, a breeder of hate
Yet she holds the key to society's gate.

"The other woman with heart of flame
Went mad for a love that marred her name
And out of the grave of her martyred faith
She rose like a soul that had passed through death.
Her aim is noble, her pity so broad

It covers the world like the mercy of God
A healer of discord, a savior of woes
Peace follows her footsteps wherever she goes
The worthier life, too, no doubt,
But society locks her out."

The Martins probably considered spirits "not quite the thing," but Victoria couldn't desert them. They were "Illusions of Great Men," and she printed a column, to show how fifteen of the greatest, ranging from Goethe to Napoleon, had "fondly believed" they saw things from the otherwhere.

And no doubt real doctors had cured Victoria's illnesses; *The Humanitarian* gave much space to medicine. Dr. Charles Steuart Welles who had married one of Margaret Miles' daughters, conducted a "Medical Department," in which such sound observation was combined with so much common sense, that it was like a light in a fog.

But it was only a twinkle on a sea of ineptitude.

With the naieveté of the lately educated, Victoria continually quoted from the great: "Plato represented Socrates as urging on his pupils an analogy . . . between the lower animals and man. . . ." (In regard to "The Multiplication of the Unfit"). Alas, she informed her readers that, "Socrates died for a bold criticism just as this; but his thoughts did not die."

She reprinted the old "Woodhull Memorial," with carefully selected press notices from the 'seventies. Articles by the venerable Archdeacon Farrar, D.D., on "The Curse of Drunkenness," on "Education" by the Reverend Dean of St. Pauls, and on "The Key to the Social Problem" by His Eminence Cardinal Vaughan were reprinted from other sources, "by special permission"; and when the *Holly Weekly News,* of Ellis County, Texas, and the *Home & Mart* of East Boston, and the *Maxwell Mercury* of Calusa County, California, spoke well of *The Humanitarian,* they were quoted in its pages, along with Franklin, Burns, Byron and the Indian Vedas. With scissors and paste-pot, *The Humanitarian* roamed at will.

On "Marriage" Victoria had to pontificate herself, to prove that though people had brutally accused her of preaching its abolition, she only toiled for its reform. Why did she marry three times, if she didn't believe in it, she protested stoutly?

And so we were told that, "The attraction between two individuals becomes more and more psychical as humanity develops along the line of evolution . . . but the instinct which impels the sexes to marry is procreation. . . . Selective choice becomes more conscious as self-control or self-command is developed. . . . It is when self-control is developed that a man or woman will not yield to passion. . . . When passion masters and controls the higher nerve centres, then the being is slave; when the higher nerve centres control passion then the being is free.

". . . What could be more inspiring than the ideal of a Holy Madonna embodying all that is purest and best in Motherhood? The coarser nature of man must needs become ennobled before such an ideal. . . ."

Legal marriage was beneficial to the community, but it too often was destructive to the happiness of the individual, because a woman might legally marry a man for his money, knowing him to be diseased, and have sickly children, and yet be considered virtuous; she might marry without knowing anything about a man's character, family, history, or habits, and curse the community with the fruits of her marriage. If the family, instead of the individual were the unit of society, young people would have a greater range of choice for selection. In order to breed individuals with "the higher controlling centres well-developed," they must not be "over-worked and devitalized, for then they lose the power of self-control," and "The legal tie must carry with it a clearly defined moral obligation."

The Humanitarian treated suffrage rather casually. But when Victoria embarked on her third presidential campaign, she said, ". . . Although the physical disabilities of sex may be very convincing against women taking an active part in politics . . . still continued reflection on this subject has convinced me that under present conditions of social life the enfranchisement of women would be beneficial to them as individuals and to the race. . . . She . . . needs healthy occupation for her mind."

Victoria's presidential campaigns were not only grotesque; they were ingenious. For inasmuch as the scandals which gnawed at her security and blocked her from society, came from America, from there must come an apotheosis in the form of a public tribute, or the impression of one, to dissolve them. And Victoria had learned that as far as the effect was concerned, between an impression and a fact, there was only will and reiteration given time and space. She knew that if the women of England believed the women of America had chosen her as their representative to "get men used to the idea of a woman president," they might believe that Nast cartooned her as Mrs. Satan in 'seventy-two, because she "advocated the principles of purity which are now preached from platforms and pulpits." That was the tale she told in her latest pamphlet. Moreover, presidential campaigns produced publicity.

There might be "eulogies" in black and white; she had had so many public humiliations she needed them, as well as white-wash to ship to England where some were as impressed by print as she was.

So Victoria and Tennessee and John Biddulph Martin went to America in April, 1892, to organize "Victoria Leagues." It was a brave journey and a silly one.

Victoria announced through the press that "I have come back to ask my people to put me in the White House, not to fight for the position. I only care for it so far as it will give me the power to inaugurate a system of education which will waken people to the responsibility of creating a race of gods instead of the inferior human beings who encumber the face of the earth today. It is my destiny to work out the salvation of my country as an individual. . . ."

Mr. Martin said he had come to this country to "stand by my wife."

For awhile she needed no defense. Newspapers were not on guard against paid publicity agents,—theirs was a new profession in the 'nineties, and Victoria's so-called secretaries made the press reek with her views on stirpiculture and "The Aristocracy of Blood." She said money-bags were too highly valued in the marriage mart; the standard of humanity should be a young man's guide. She thanked God that she had lived to read an article headed, "Medical Experts on Criminality," in the *Herald*. For similar opinions she had suffered "everything but martyrdom." She deplored the predominance of aliens in government. Our best citizens were intimidated because their reputations might be jeopardized in political campaigns. She said something almost every day, in some paper, and only once the *New York World* remarked that running for president was an expensive method of advertising and regretted that Mrs. Martin "chooses to make herself the target for shafts of every kind when she might be living a life of perfect ease and luxury in England."

The papers were eagerly supplied with proper versions of the lady's life history. And a new generation of reporters neglected to look her up in their own reference libraries where her bulky envelopes would have puzzled those without a taste for research. For they were crammed with accounts of her free love speeches and with pamphlets denying them. She had sent her pamphlets to every big newspaper on two continents.

Then Victoria, and Tennessee, and Martin went to Chicago.

Victoria probably believed she was the regenerator of the human race. In regard to herself she was as credulous as Martin and for the same reason; both were devoted to Victoria. She certainly believed that a human race which could snub Victoria Woodhull needed regeneration. She wasn't whipped. Like healthy flesh, her ego swelled when it was bruised.

But the world is full of people who are violently irritated at the sight of a successful fraud. Now that Victoria no longer attacked her old friends, her pretenses didn't hurt anybody. In a way they were socially beneficent; they furnished so much conversation in so many homes. But they outraged Chicago. To have Victoria Woodhull flaunting herself as a leader of the Woman's Movement in this country was no less than a "libel on American womanhood." (Which was another magic phrase.) Encouraged by a prominent clergyman and others, the *Chicago Mail* printed some memories of "Tennie and her Vicky," and insinuated more to the initiated than they told to the uninformed. It was not a vicious article.

But it infuriated John Biddulph Martin so that he forgot to realize that few newspapers even in America, printed libels about anybody's private life, without documentary evidence. The next morning before the doors of the Criminal Courts building were opened, he was there with his attorney, seeking a warrant for the arrest of the editor of the *Mail* for criminal libel.

Whereupon the *Mail* announced that they were prepared to produce enough evidence in court "as to the bad character of the two women to make him the laughing stock of everyone who knows anything about the record of the royal and noble family into which he has entered." But Martin thundered and blundered into a suit for the sum of one hundred thousand dollars damages.

Then the *Mail* proceeded to print their evidence in a series of two column articles. "If this notorious adventuress had remained in the obscurity of her London life, certainly the *Mail* would have had no word to say about her; but when she, heralded by cablegrams and enslavered by newspapers . . . has the effrontery to come to Chicago, it is different. This woman, known to be of bad character, remembered in police and detective circles in this city, . . . has the hard gall to talk about regenerating and educating the American people . . . Victoria Woodhull and Tennessee Claflin . . . expose this country to contempt and ridicule by their absurd but offensive impudence; they need but to have their records exhibited to drive them back where they belong. . . ."

Beginning with the story of their trickery in the Byrnes affair, the *Mail* published names, dates and circumstances in the career of the Claflins extending back to Buck's exploits in Homer. It was a remarkable journalistic feat. A retired member of the Cincinnati police force stated that Tennessee Claflin had conducted an assignation house in Cincinnati and that he had made arrests there, and he gave a detailed account of those arrests, together with his own name and address. Nine citizens of Ottawa, Illinois, testified as to the "bad characters" of both sisters. Those old indictments were reproduced in full. The *Mail* admitted that "Some of the annals of the Woodhull's Chicago residence are still to be verified, but it may be said of them that they are of a very pronounced carmine hue, and that they include the interposition of the police and the worry and bother of a very surprising and sensational domiciliary visit. . . ."

So another Martin-Cook libel action was heard of no more. The defendant entered a motion for the dismissal of case number 103173 in the Circuit Court of Cook County, Illinois, and it was dismissed for want of prosecution.

By this time John Biddulph Martin must have decided that there was a conspiracy against his wife.

There are stubborn Englishmen, and no doubt he was one of them. And she probably convinced him that there was no justice in the American courts; it was useless to fight for it. Nobody knows what she told him. But she was a fluent conversationalist, as well as a siren.

It was said that Tennessee was deeply hurt when Victoria made Zulu Maud associate editor of *The Humanitarian*, instead of sharing the enterprise with her. But Tennessee was one of Victoria's real devotees, and they never were rancorous. Maybe they fed on her infectious energy; it would atone for a lot.

And Tennessee had the consolation of being Lady Cook. How she must have enjoyed that title! She, too, issued biographical pamphlets, as well as a series of essays by Lady Cook, on "The Evils of Society and Their Remedies," in pamphlet form, and another bound in nice red cloth, dedicated "To the Memory of my Dear Father and Mother, The Kindest and Best of Parents," which was a singular tribute from one who had sworn out a warrant for their arrest.

But if we can believe the story that Tennessee's first husband, John Bartels, told on his death-bed to a friend, she played a charming little comedy during that stormy visit to Chicago.

John Bartels had not prospered; he was driving a hack in those days. One morning he received a note telling him to go to a certain address. He went there and waited, and nobody appeared. Finally a servant came out and said, "Here's ten dollars for your trouble. Call again tomorrow morning at the same time." The next morning Bartels went there, and the same thing happened, and it kept on happening every morning for three weeks. The servant never failed to give him a ten dollar bill "for his trouble." On the last day he saw a woman watching him through the portières, and he recognized Tennie. He made a dash for the window, but she disappeared and nobody would answer the door. Then he remembered that he had first quarreled with Tennie about a ten dollar bill.

Chapter Seventeen

WHITER THAN SNOW

THEY returned to England; and in spite of the *Chicago Mail* and case number 103173 in the Circuit Court of Cook County, Victoria brought Martin back to America a few months later to pursue her presidential campaign. Victoria Leagues had been formed (in Victoria's imagination, and in a few press notices) on "The Humanitarian Platform," which was a de-sexualized version of Stephen Pearl Andrews' "Institute of Humanity," sometimes called the "Pantarchy." It proposed revenue and tariff reforms, tribunals of health, free courts of justice for the poor, bureaus of anthropology connected with every police station, laboratories for the analysis of impure foods and liquors; woman's suffrage; scientific reorganization of the criminal code; physicians to examine children in schools; improved dwellings for the poor; labor tribunals for arbitration; national encouragement of arts and sciences, and the aristocracy of blood.

Fifty women met in the parlor of the Willard hotel in Washington and nominated Victoria Woodhull Martin for president of the United States, and Mrs. Mary L. Stowe for vice-president, "Whereas, under the Fourteenth Amendment no citizen is deprived of the franchise through law, but by custom and habit;

"Therefore be it resolved, we, the representative women of America, ask the officers in charge of the election precincts through the United States in the coming campaign to give us the opportunity to cast our ballots on the first Tuesday in November, 1892, for our candidates.

"Resolved, that by the united efforts of the women voters of this nation we will drive anarchy, crime, insanity and drunkenness from our midst by our humanitarian efforts, backed by the ballot."

A reporter from the *World* went to the house the Martins had taken at 142 West 70th Street, in New York, and found Victoria looking as "fresh as a daisy." When she dropped her point lace handkerchief, Martin shot across the room to pick it up. His devotion was "too marked for a candidate who must depend on susceptible men for support, but it was edifying."

Victoria didn't suppose she would "carry any of the doubtful states or any other states, but I am going to be aggressive just the same." Her campaign was merely "educational," but, "before many years there will be a woman president." Nominated by the National Woman Suffrage Association, she was composing a letter of acceptance to the president, "that brainy woman" Mrs. Anna M. Parker. "There are no factional differences in our party. We are firmly united," she said for the benefit of her English public.

For apparently this was a repetition of the Byrnes interview trick. Miss Lucy Stone spoke for the National Association, "The statement that Mrs. Biddulph Martin is the candidate for president, of the National Woman Suffrage Association is wholly without foundation. We have no presidential candidate, and we do not even know the persons who are said to have nominated her."

Miss Frances Willard had "nothing to say against Victoria Woodhull. If she wants to be president of the United States that is her business, but it is a mistake to say that she is a candidate of that numerous body of women saints like Susan B. Anthony, who devoted their lives to woman suffrage. Victoria Woodhull has stood more pelting than she deserved. I was right glad when she married an English gentleman and has someone to defend and care for her . . . ," Miss Willard added kindly in the *New York World*.

Victoria "expressed surprise" at these "attacks." She "is not only representing the women's cause and the cause of humanity itself, but she originated the movement, and claims that the Fourteenth and Fifteenth Amendments to the Constitution permit this right to women." She asked if the women of America were to be "dictated to by a few cliques. . . ."

On election day Victoria sat in the library at 142 West 70th Street, sipping tea with her daughter, as she scanned the returns and talked to a reporter. Brother-in-law O'Halloran insisted there was corruption at the polls; not a single vote was reported for Victoria Woodhull Martin, though he had voted the Humanitarian ticket. Then he discovered that his ballot had been thrown out, because he had made no provision for presidential electors.

Victoria was not depressed. ". . . To be perfectly frank, I hardly expected to be elected. The truth is I am too many years ahead of this age, and the exalted views and objects of humanitarianism can scarcely be grasped as yet by the unenlightened mind of the average man. . . ." Somewhat illogically she pattered on about stirpiculture and "The Multiplication of the Unfit" and "The Humanitarian Platform," before she stooped to inform the average man, "The impression prevails that I was a candidate for the Woman Suffrage Party," she said, as if she hadn't started it. Evidently she was one of those fortunate people who believe that when they say anything, they prove it. (And in time, they do!) "Now that is all wrong," she announced, with another sip of tea. "I ran on the Humanitarian Platform. . . . I am an enthusiastic advocate of universal suffrage. But I am no fanatic. I have no sympathy with such radical views as those expressed recently by Miss Couzens of London, who advocated dynamite and other such unpleasant things. . . ."

So do the bomb-throwers of one generation become the tea-drinkers of the next.

But Victoria Woodhull was indomitable. In 1893, at St. James Hall in London and at Carnegie Hall in New York, she delivered her lecture on "The Scientific Propagation of the Human Race," to enormous audiences.

She still was handsome, and as she walked on the platform of Carnegie Hall in a pretty violet dress with violets at her throat, the crowd felt her old magnetism and burst into applause.

But she took a roll of manuscript from a handbag at her belt, adjusted some spectacles and told them that, after seventeen years of silence, she was moved to speak in London and in America to "waken mothers to the crime of propagating children to only live upon their betters and become a curse to the race. . . ." She told them her views on stirpiculture, and that in London, twenty thousand people waited in the streets outside her lecture hall, unable to get in. And her audience was not interested, if it were convinced.

Time had tarnished the silver tongue; cant had warped it.

It is neither necessary nor desirable for most people to tell the truth about their private lives; nor is it necessary for orators who are scholars or humorists. But most of the spell-binder's force springs from an impulse to reveal, an impulse that must at least be momentarily sincere or go to waste on inner conflict. Without it, that tide of emotion which swings between orator and audience (a ground-swell that is the inspiration of such oratory as well as its reward) slacks. Nothing happens. Such an occasion is tragic for the orator and painful for the audience. It is like hunting with a dog whose scent for game has gone.

Victoria read through her manuscript and then nearly fainted. It was announced that the lecture tour she had planned, was abandoned "in compliance with the wishes of her husband."

And she left New York for Chicago, of all places! But John Biddulph Martin was one of the British Commissioners to the World's Fair, and the *Chicago Mail* didn't bother Victoria; it had enough to say about the Fair.

But Victoria sent a long article to the *New York Herald* on the "Humanitarian Movement."

Inasmuch as her exalted views were beyond the unenlightened, Victoria could endure her presidential defeats without depression, but social slights continued to humiliate her. Energy and perseverance had brought her fame; charm had brought her wealth. All three must vindicate her character.

Oddly enough she was obsessed with the idea that it could be vindicated in a court of law. Of course the Claflins always had gone to court as readily as most people go to their baths, but this idea of Victoria's must have been shared by John Biddulph Martin. It was profoundly English. For an English libel action is like a baptism. The one who wins it comes out with a character whiter than snow. A naïve performance enacted with gravity, it is a boon to biographers as well as to barristers.

And so a Mr. Moon, who included Victoria Woodhull Martin in his list of world celebrities, went to the British Museum to study her literary work. He said he did not go at the instigation of Mr. and Mrs. Martin, but he found "The Story of Henry Ward Beecher and Theodore and Mrs. Tilton, with portraits, by the editor of the *Anglo-American Times,*" which could not have been catalogued under Woodhull, as well as "The Beecher-Tilton Scandal, a complete history of the case from November, 1872, to the present time, with Mrs. Woodhull's statement, as published in *Woodhull & Claflin's Weekly,* November 2, 1872," which might have been.

During the Beecher trial all of the evidence, letters and documents remotely connected with it, were published in books and pamphlets. There were dozens of them.

Hence Mr. Moon saw an account of Beecher's refusal to introduce Victoria's social freedom speech, her interview with him, and the alleged blackmail thereof, as well as Tilton's version of his relations with "the

Woodhull," and Victoria's artless admission that any woman who couldn't love Theodore was "dead to all sweeter impulses of nature," from the *Chicago Times*.

Mr. Moon complained of "The Beecher-Tilton Scandal" to Dr. Garnett, the keeper of the printed books, and Dr. Garnett locked it away. But when Mr. Moon told the Martins about those foul aspersions on Victoria's character, her husband complained to the trustees of the British Museum. Whereupon both pamphlets were withdrawn from circulation, and the trustees wrote a letter to the Martins, regretting that the Martins had been annoyed. This was in March, 1893.

On February 24th, 1894, the Martins brought an action against the trustees of the British Museum, to recover damages for libel and for an injunction, "the libel being in permitting two books to remain on the shelves of the British Museum and lending them to the readers thereat."

It was the first libel action ever brought against the British Museum.

The defendants denied the publication of the libel; the books were placed on the shelves under statutory powers; the books were bought without any knowledge that they contained scandalous or libellous matter.

The case was tried before Mr. Baron Pollock and a special jury; Mr. Baron Pollock wearing his wig and cloak, the full regalia of a judge in the high courts of the British Empire.

Sir Richard Webster, Q.C. apeared for the Martins; he said it was a remarkable case. His clients were compelled to come to court to clear the character of Mrs. Martin, who had been accused of the greatest immorality. The wicked imputation was especially cruel as she of all women in the world had labored to insure the emancipation and uphold the purity of her sex.

He drew a touching picture of Victoria, "married at fourteen and one-half to an inebriate, at fifteen years and three months the mother of a child of weak intellect." (He was careful about those dates.) Saddened by this early experience, Victoria had studied marriage from every viewpoint. She thought the contract was sometimes too binding. Marriage should last only as long as the mutual love and affection. But she never advocated free love.

Sir Richard lightly mentioned her divorce from Woodhull, and her subsequent marriage to Blood, whom she divorced for infidelity. She was imprisoned because she "took a strong view of the Beecher-Tilton case," but she was acquitted. She prosecuted Treat for his libellous pamphlet and "compelled him to pay a fine of fifteen thousand dollars, and had him locked up, after which he died in a hospital." One Jones, who attacked her, was shot dead before the trial, "by a man who made himself the instrument of her vengeance." (Was this a subtle warning for the Archbishop of Canterbury and other trustees of the British Museum?) But Sir Richard said she did not seek damages; she only wanted an apology and an expression of regret.

Sir Charles Russell, Q.C. the defendant's counsel, was himself a trustee of the British Museum, as well as the Attorney-General. Lord Coleridge called him "The biggest advocate of the century." It was said of him that "ordinarily the judge dominates the jury, the counsel, the public—he is the central figure of the piece. But when Russell is there the judge isn't in it. Russell dominates everyone."

This must have been said before he was in a piece with Victoria.

He cross-examined her severely, but the spectacle of a gentleman questioning a lady about her past, however questionable that past might have been, was not sympathetic to the Victorian public, especially when the lady happened to be the wife of an eminent banker.

Moreover, he might as well have tried to cross-examine an eave-swallow. She skimmed and fluttered and soared elaborately. She was fluent, but she was vague. Which was the only way she could have disconcerted a logician like Sir Charles Russell.

The *London Times* said she branched off into such a variety of subjects with such long explanations that it was impossible to report her replies in full. She insisted that she neither had had the interview as stated with Theodore Tilton nor had she misconducted herself with him. The incriminated articles were written "by a man named Andrews, employed without her knowledge and consent as she was often hundreds of miles away when they appeared." When asked if she ever had been guilty of immorality, she said she was daily before the American public from 1870 to 1877 and that no charges had been made against her character.

Whereupon Ananias gave up his ghost.

She said she was an educated doctor, too, but "I do not remember if I was ever on the stage. It may be I acted in San Francisco if you say so. . . . I never knew that love was anything but free." She was prosecuted shortly after the Beecher article appeared, ostensibly by the District Attorney. She denied that her paper was without the statute as not being a book or pamphlet. "The opinion of the whole press of America forced them to abandon their 'obscene literature prosecution.' "

Sir Charles asked if it were true that the Reverend Henry Ward Beecher dropped on his knees and begged her to let him off. Mrs. Martin said that required a great deal of explanation, but "if we are going to try the Beecher-Tilton case over again, I must have time to get the facts leading up to my article. I had been persecuted for advocating these things and refused admission to hotels and my daughter refused at school."

And before Sir Charles could remind her that she said Andrews wrote what she now called "my article," and before he could ask her what things she had advocated she was off on how the men were her persecutors, but she did not think Mr. Beecher was one of them. "They all acted in a cowardly way."

Sir Charles asked her about Demosthenes, and she said she would not say her spirit adviser was not Demosthenes. "There is an apparition appearing to me now." Whereupon there was laughter in court. She didn't remember whether her Greek guardian came to her in a deep sleep and dictated on a scroll the contents of her memorial, as Tilton related in her biography. She did "not feel disposed to tell you now" how she wrote her memorial. She was "a woman battling against the world." She aired all her latest theories about love and marriage, and Sir Charles said he wouldn't argue with her. She denied that she had given "the first voice in the public press to the charge against Mr. Beecher. I wrote a letter to the *World* on May 22, 1871, or something to that effect. The charge against him was publicly known and talked about before the *exposé* of November 2, 1872. I have a dim recollection of writing to Beecher for an interview; I do not know if I had such an interview. I did not ask him to take the chair at the meeting at Steinway Hall and back me up and act in the way I desired him to do. Some one else may have sent it in my name to him. S. P. Andrews had a motive of secret animosity against me."

This mummery actually stirred people who saw a woman in the witness box, defending her reputation. And when Victoria was excited, she could make the alphabet exciting.

Sir Charles was in the unfortunate position of a bulldog baiting a Pekinese. The British Museum was not involved enough to warrant a thorough investigation of the case. But Sir Charles hoped to demonstrate to the jury that "This action was not brought by the plaintiffs with any hope of damages . . . or of a verdict against the Trustees, but to allow this lady to make a statement in the box to contradict a number of publications offensive to her. . . . The Trustees had withdrawn the incriminated pamphlets . . . the doctrine was strange and alarming that by allowing a man to take down a book from the shelves, the Trustees were . . . publishing a libel. . . ."

Mr. Baron Pollock suggested that it was a pure question of law, but Sir Richard Webster said he was "entitled to a verdict on the issues that must go to the jury. There has been no expression of public regret."

Sir Charles reminded him that the Trustees had written a letter of regret. "Does my friend want the Archbishop of Canterbury or myself to stand forth in a penitential sheet?"

The British Museum acquired three hundred and fifteen thousand publications in one year. It would take at least a hundred and ten libel experts to read through them. "Fancy a hundred and ten legal experts let loose in the British Museum to scrutinize the books, and seeking for a needle of libel in a bundle of literary hay!" exclaimed Sir Charles.

The trial went on for five days.

John Biddulph Martin testified that he had followed Victoria's career before she came to England. "There was nothing in her speeches to endorse those disgusting passages," he said. He "heard of the books in 1890, but could not obtain a copy. I could not find them in New York, either at the Astor Library or the Cooper Institute."

They must have been at the binder's, for those books or similar ones have been in all the New York libraries for years. The Attorney-General said he had no questions to ask Mr. Martin. No doubt he considered it bad sportsmanship to question a man so obviously bewitched.

Sir Charles criticized the books in question, "with much regret, as the matters must be painful to the lady, Mrs. Woodhull-Martin. . . ." As far as they could find out, very few people had seen the books in question. The "Beecher case in New York had lasted one hundred and fifteen days, exciting the greatest interest . . . (it) threw a flood of light on the interior life of American citizens and the doctrines and conduct which prevailed therein . . . (it) possessed a historical interest to the student of manners or morals. The pamphlet, as far as it referred to the plaintiff, only contained a reprint from the plaintiff's own weekly paper, for which she was legally responsible, however much it might have been altered by other people. How could she come here and complain after she had signed the article in the paper?"

He cited numerous libel cases to show that there was no precedent for this one, inasmuch as the trustees were the statutory depositors for every published work. He neglected to cite the case of Alice vs. Wonderland.

But Sir Richard argued for the plaintiff that the evidence showed that no care was taken to guard against publishing libels calculated to give pain to individuals. The publication in question was "a direct attack on the plaintiff, who stood before them a pure woman." "Her article had been perverted and garbled by the wretched man Pearl Andrews. . . . My client has been forced to face this ordeal and disclose the piteous story of her life . . . his clients are responsible for the putting of these questions, and I hope that whatever the effect of this trial may be, or the result on any technical grounds, the result of your verdict will be that Mrs. Martin may go forth to the world as the pure woman she has always been, and pronounced by you as a fit associate for the brightest and best in all the land."

Mr. Baron Pollock summed up to the jury. He, too, said it was a remarkable case, important to the plaintiff because "nothing could be graver than anything affecting her character," important to the British Museum because it "has a high duty imposed upon it to guard over the interests of the public . . . there is no more personal relation between the plaintiff and the Trustees than there is with any foreign potentate. The defendants have no possible object to malign the character of the plaintiff. . . ." The jury must decide whether the books were libels. The defendants "set up a privilege" for the copyrighted book. That was a matter of law. He reminded the jury that, in case they brought a verdict for the plaintiff, no heavy damages were asked for, "Mrs. Martin did not desire to put the price of her reputation into her husband's pocket. . . . It is open to you to give a farthing or any other larger tangible sum, say five pounds. . . . You must not forget that many questions of a very uncomfortable character were put to Mrs. Martin. . . . Has her reputation been even clouded by what the defendants have done either in or out of Court? The plaintiffs say that their advisers told them this was the only course left open to them to vindicate Mrs. Martin's character. . . ."

The jury found the documents complained of libels on the plaintiff; but the defendants or their servants in buying, cataloguing, producing the books in question, did so in the belief that they were acting in discharge of their statutory powers and duties. The defendants didn't know that the books contained libels, they were not guilty of negligence; but they did not discharge their duties with proper care, caution or judgment. The jury assessed the damages at twenty shillings, to be paid by the defendants in case they were held liable in law for a publication.

The *London Times* remarked that whatever the result of the legal effect of the jury's findings, no time should be lost in making another such action as that of Mrs. John Biddulph Martin's impossible.

When the case was brought before Mr. Baron Pollock for further consideration on March fifth, 1894, counsel for the plaintiff contended that the last finding of the jury "showed a want of care. If the defendants bought books, which they were only allowed and not compelled to do, they must exercise due care not to purchase libellous or obscene publications. . . . The defendant's servants might have discovered this fact from the title of these works," said Mr. R. M. Bray, with Sir Richard Webster.

The judge intimated to the Attorney-General that he need not argue; he proceeded to give judgment in favor of the defendants. No evidence had gone to the jury in the matter of negligence. The plaintiffs had failed to prove their case against a public body. There would be a verdict for the defendants and with costs.

Mr. Bray was granted a stay of execution pending an appeal.

On the twentieth of April the case of Martin and wife against the trustees of the British Museum was appealed to the Supreme Court of Judicature.

Sir Richard Webster said the plaintiffs, being satisfied that the character of Mrs. Martin had been thoroughly vindicated during the trial, did not desire to dispute the legal decision which had been arrived at. And understanding that the defendants were ready to express regret for the annoyance which had been caused to them, they did not propose to press the matter further and were willing that the appeal should be dismissed.

The Attorney-General said the defendants had obtained judgment in their favor and they relied on that judgment, nor would he in any way be a party to a course which might throw any doubt on a decision which had relieved them from all responsibility. As the plaintiff did not intend to prosecute the appeal, he asked that the appeal might be dismissed with costs. . . . He desired to express the defendants' regret for the annoyance which had been caused to the plaintiffs in the terms of a letter which had been written as far back as March, 1893.

The court thereupon ordered that the appeal should be dismissed with costs.

The counsels for the plaintiffs may have changed their tone between March fifth and April twentieth because a Mrs. Holland sued Sir Francis Cook for breach of promise and seduction. At first she had lived with him in his house at Richmond, before the death of his first wife; then he moved her to Blackfriars Road where they were known as Mr. and Mrs. Cook. She claimed that he compelled her to undergo an operation from which she never recovered and that he had promised to marry her when his wife died, and then married Tennessee Claflin. Mrs. Holland was an elderly woman, who wore a long maroon colored cloak in court, with a black bonnet, heavily decorated with violets, and posies and primroses at her waist.

Sir Francis admitted the intimacy and denied the promises. She had accepted money for her favors, and the jury returned a verdict for the defendant with costs.

Of course this was not Victoria's affair, but she was

brought into it, because she had bought some letters from Mrs. Holland for thirty pounds. Most Victorian ladies didn't know, or were not supposed to know, that you could buy such letters for thirty pounds.

So it was wise of Sir Richard Webster to be satisfied with a "thorough vindication" of Victoria's character. The Archbishop of Canterbury might have refused to wear a penitential sheet for a lady who had played any part in such a sordid drama; archbishops were very particular.

Meanwhile John Biddulph Martin attained the presidency of the Royal Statistical Society. The question of the wear and tear of gold coinage interested him also. (Colonel Blood might have converted him to Greenbackism!) And he studied the traditions and history of the ancient emblem of Martin's bank, and wrote a book on "The Grasshopper of Lombard Street."

Victoria issued the first chapter of her autobiography in 1895 in pamphlet form. It began thus: "Sitting here today in this north room of 17 Hyde Park Gate, London—dreary, smoky, foggy, insulated as you are in the customs and prejudices of centuries—I am thinking with all the bitterness of my woman's nature how my life has been warped and twisted out of shape by this environment, until, as I catch a glimpse of my haggard face in the mirror opposite, I wonder whether I shall be able to pen the history of this stormy existence."

She wasn't. No other chapter followed, but she said her life and works, as well as Tennessee's, had been "one chain of spiritual phenomena." Her loyalty to her spirits never wavered. They were part of herself.

She quoted accounts of the arrests and trials in 1873.

"When I recall those scenes of enthusiasm, the fires of enthusiasm kindle in every vein and nerve and a voice of thanks to heaven arises from my soul that I have been accounted worthy to be the chosen instrument of such prescient wisdom and such political power."

This sounded as if her present depressed her more than her past. Maybe she was associating with some of the "best in all the land" after the vindication of her character. In the 'nineties the worthies of the upper middle class had developed their characters at the expense of their personalities until they were lofty but dull. Devoid of that spontaneity which was one of Victoria's greatest charms, they discouraged it in others. The men gravely discussed the merits of this wine and that, or deplored the wheat-blight, or solemnly agreed with what the *Observer* had said about the latest measure of Lord Salisbury; the women gravely discussed the merits of hydrangeas and strawberries, or deplored the present presumption of servants, or solemnly agreed with what their husbands had said about what the *Observer* had said about the latest measure of Lord Salisbury. It would depress anybody to reach a heart's desire, and find it undesirable.

The Martins went to America frequently. And once Victoria drove into Homer, Ohio, from a neighboring town, in a fine carriage with a team of horses. She was "quietly but richly" dressed, and the Homerites were pleased, and proud of her prosperity. If this were another dream coming true, it may have been another disappointment, since it is no fun to strut for the pleased. And Homer must have seemed so small!

But after awhile a Claflin feud burst into the newspapers.

Victoria wanted *The Humanitarian* published simultaneously in New York and London. So Zulu Maud Woodhull took a house with Dr. Welles and his wife, (who was a daughter of Margaret Miles O'Halloran) at 302 West 72nd Street, not only to conduct *The Humanitarian* but to establish a literary salon in connection with a boarding house. The three were to share powers, privileges and profits, but the lease was in Miss Woodhull's name. On the ninth of April, 1895, she served notice on the Welles to surrender the house within thirty days. At the expiration of that period she instituted dispossess proceedings against them in the Eleventh Judicial District Court. Whereupon Dr. Welles said she owed him two thousand seven hundred and fifty dollars arrears of salary and to prevent her returning to England with her mother, he attached their furniture and personal effects.

Mrs. O'Halloran told a reporter from the *World* that Victoria had asked Dr. Welles to write her if any young men were attentive to Zulu Maud, as she didn't want her daughter to marry. When Dr. Welles reported that Miss Woodhull had an admirer, Mrs. O'Halloran thought Miss Woodhull must have denied his statement and persuaded her mother to turn him out. Mrs. O'Halloran said Victoria induced Dr. Welles to give up his practise and devote himself to *The Humanitarian,* and then didn't pay him the salary she promised. Moreover, Victoria declared the Welles furniture wasn't good enough for the literary salon and gave it to the servants. She said everything belonging to Mrs. Welles was cursed, and burned some furniture in the furnace, as well as Mrs. Welles' dresses and the children's toys.

Mrs. Welles told a reporter from the *Herald* that Victoria promised to pay for the things she burned, but when she spied a trunk in a corner, Mrs. Welles protested. It contained photographs that couldn't be replaced, but Mrs. Martin broke it open, and found a photograph of Colonel Blood, and burned no more. Mrs. Welles said that was her object; the story of the curse was her excuse.

Victoria announced through the press that the statement about her burning furniture was absurd. She had burned a few "valueless rags." She didn't mention the photograph of Colonel Blood. She said it was "entirely a case of ingratitude." They had helped the Welles until the burden became intolerable. Mr. Martin said, "Frankly this family disturbance is caused by money. We became tired of being played."

A reporter from the *Herald* saw Mrs. O'Halloran in her pretty little house at 142 West 94th Street. She said, "I believe that Mr. Martin is under the impression that he does support the whole family . . . he gives his wife enough money to do it, and is under the impression that it all comes to us. My sister . . . would come to me with a check drawn to my order and ask me to let her deposit it in my bank and let her draw it as she wanted it, because she didn't want to let Johnnie, meaning her husband, know how much money she had. . . . Lady Cook has done everything for the family that has been done. . . . (Victoria) abused different members of the family, until outraged by her, they have written her letters by which she tries to prove that her relatives are persecuting her. . . ." Mrs.

O'Halloran declared that her sister Victoria, "loves notoriety, and in three months has spent ten thousand dollars to gain it."

When the Martins started to sail for England, Victoria was arrested on complaint of her niece Mrs. Welles, in connection with a suit for the value of the goods she had burned.

It was a regular Claflin squabble, the sort they thrived on. It must have been a tonic for Victoria after too many discussions of what the *London Observer* had said about the latest measure of Lord Salisbury.

She strategically surrendered the lease on the house at 302 West 72nd Street to its owner, and the Welles had to get out. The Martins gave bond for a thousand dollars and caught their steamship, Victoria declaring that she was the victim of a persecution.

But Mr. Martin was upset, as any lamb would be, in a tiger's lair. He said the technicalities of American law were more than he could understand. (Indeed they must have seemed rather adult to him.) Mr. Martin announced that he had had enough of America; he was going back to his London banking house to stay.

Two years later, John Biddulph Martin died of pneumonia at Las Palmas in the Canary Islands. He had had a dangerous illness in November; and, as soon as he could travel, the doctors sent him there to convalesce.

According to his obituary in *The Humanitarian,* his last conscious act was to send a blanket to the doctor who was sleeping near an open window in his room. He was shy and reserved. His "sensitive nature shrank from publicity," but he was "in sympathy with his wife's views." He was a martyr. "The last few months of his life were embittered by a fresh outbreak of the cruel persecution which he and his wife had faced together for years. In consequence of failing health his wife's enemies thought he was no longer able to defend her in the same way as formerly. In this they were mistaken for his vigilance never halted, but the mental wear told on him severely." In consequence of her own "ill health and shattered nerves," she was unable to go with him to Las Palmas. They were parted "for the first time in eighteen years of married life . . . for more than three weeks. . . . Theirs was a perfect union, marred only by persecution. . . ."

Like Dr. Woodhull's obituary in the *Weekly,* it was full of Victoria's persecution.

But John Biddulph Martin left an estate amounting to one hundred and seventy-one thousand, seven hundred and seventy-nine pounds sterling to his wife. His will directed that no invitations to the funeral be issued. He wanted to be cremated, his ashes to be "scattered, or otherwise dealt with as my dear wife sees fit."

In the meantime the papers had reported an estrangement between the celebrated sisters. From Portugal Tennie cabled, "Darling sister: Can you wait until I return? If not, may God bless you is the prayer of your devoted sister Tennie." This was forwarded to Victoria in America in 1893, and she gave it to the *New York World,* saying, "After all the trials we two have passed through, hand in hand, suffered every hardship, how could we be separated now? . . ."

Tennie was in delicate health then, but she had become the Lady Bountiful of Cintra. She established seven schools for children there, and sent twelve little girls to Catholic convents in London. She clothed the poor and cared for the sick.

Her philanthropies were lavish and sudden, like the dispensations of a fairy godmother, and they might be just as suddenly withdrawn. She was extremely generous to all the Claflins, until an unfortunate word or a significant look snapped the golden wand and their fine horses would turn into mice again.

She announced that she was going to build a home for unmarried mothers in Richmond. Committees waited upon her. "Dear Lady Cook, you will simply ruin our lovely town. And besides your plan will encourage vice, and it is all so dreadful." So she gave up the idea. But she announced that she wouldn't give another penny to any church or charity in Richmond and that she was going to start a banking house to make enough money to build such homes everywhere.

In fact the banking house called "Lady Cook and Company," only made money for reporters on space rates.

Sir Francis was in his dotage, and yet when he died in 1901, he bequeathed only twenty-five thousand pounds to his wife, and an income of fifty thousand pounds, as well as the use of his house at Richmond. He made no further provision for his wife, as he had amply provided for her in his lifetime. She certainly was amply provided for, but he was wise enough to know she could squander any fortune, if she had it outright.

A few weeks after the death of Sir Francis, Tennessee applied to the Home Secretary for an order to exhume his body, and made an extraordinary statement to the press: "I am determined to bear no longer the suspicions cast upon me by certain persons concerning my poor husband's death. These people, embittered by not being provided for under his will, have been making demands on me. One of them, a girl, was, I think, entitled to something from my husband. I complied up to a point with the financial demands she and the others made, but these demands increased and I refused to concede anything more. Now they are circulating infamous stories and threatening me with revelations about how he came by his death. . . ."

Her husband's family hurried to London, and made her abandon the exhumation. Government officials said the stories she spoke of were without any foundation and they "could not think of letting a sorrowing widow open a husband's grave to prove something that needed no proof."

Of course the Claflins had the autopsy habit. (No wonder poor Mr. Martin wanted cremation.) But apparently this was a macabre move in Tennessee's devious scheme, to get a nice legal vindication of her character, like sister Victoria's. Unlike Victoria, however, Tennessee was not adaptable by nature. She never understood her new environment. She didn't know that homes for unmarried mothers were not as respectable as stirpiculture. She couldn't distinguish between a genteel comedy played with an honored institution, and a melodrama in which an old employee was the villain.

And so she said enough to make John Henry Wallace, who had been her husband's secretary as well as the manager of "Lady Cook and Company," sue her for slander.

"I am anxious to have this case come to trial," she told reporters naïvely. "It will be more sensational than this . . . divorce suit that all London is talking about now. But I propose to have my character vindicated. Everybody knows how I loved and cared for Sir Francis. I will spare no money nor pains to have those horrible charges against me fully ventilated."

Wallace gave some interesting testimony. He said Tennessee had employed him to shadow her husband and find out whether a certain Mrs. G. was "carrying on with Sir Francis." (This was a tribute to Sir Francis, who was then in his eighties.) Wallace said the man who met Mrs. G. was not Sir Francis, but he was not paid for his services. Then Lady Cook procured some gypsies from Epping Forest to watch the old man. Wallace said a Mr. Higgins wrote all her pamphlets. Her past and Victoria's were lugged into court. Referring to Tennessee's charge, Wallace's counsel said: "That is a very serious statement from a lady . . . who cannot for one moment say she didn't know what it is to be a blackmailer herself. . . . She could not possibly have read what was said by the American papers about her without knowing what it means. . . . I notice in the certificate of her marriage that she was married twice to Sir Francis, on October first at Kensington, when she described herself as spinster, and later in June, 1899, when she described herself as a divorced wife."

Sir Edward Clarke, K.C., appeared for Tennessee and admitted the slander, but he said Lady Cook was

GETTING OLDER

VICTORIA WOODHULL MARTIN

in a state of "nervous agonized excitement." He refused to put her in the witness box.

She had been sitting in one of the usher's seats, and, when the verdict of fifty pounds for the plaintiff for work rendered and five hundred pounds damages was announced, she arose and dashed to the clerk's table, excitedly flourishing a paper.

She almost shrieked at the Lord Chief Justice:

"Lord Alverstone, I am an American, and I appeal to you to listen to me. I want this case reopened. It has cost me thousands of pounds, and I entrusted myself in the hands of an English judge and jury ——"

"Leave the court, madam, please," said the Lord Chief Justice.

"Will you allow me to have the case reopened and go into the witness box, Lord Alverstone? I have been had by my counsel and the jury. This is all I ask. It has cost me thousands of pounds."

"The case is over," said the Lord Chief Justice. "Usher, remove the lady."

"I have been had by my counsel and the jury," she began. The usher took her arm. "Don't pull me about, I will walk out." And as she walked out she said, "I have done more for England and America than anybody else, and my reputation is ruined. I am a sorrowful woman. Oh, cruel, cruel, cruel— After thousands of pounds. I brought it to go into the witness box, and I gave those instructions, but they did not want me to go into the box."

In fact Tennie still was a child at fifty-eight, a gifted child, who happened to act the fantasies which other children sometimes dream of. She was such a pretty child, too, with a pink and white face framed in snow-white hair, like a piece of Dresden china or a picture by Joshua Reynolds.

Sir Edward Clarke had the Wallace action retried in the Appeal Court. The Master of the Rolls decided the Wallace suit savored of blackmail; the verdict could not stand.

Perhaps it was only a coincidence that not long afterward Wallace's wife was found lifeless in their flat; Wallace, still alive, was beside her on the floor, with his throat cut. He was charged with attempted suicide.

Then Victoria and Tennessee came to the parting of their ways. They no longer drove in Hyde Park together every afternoon. They no longer worked together.

Victoria discontinued *The Humanitarian* at the end of 1901, gave up her house at 17 Hyde Park Gate, and went to the Martin estate at Bredon's Norton in Worcestershire.

Tennessee stayed in the limelight on two continents, while Victoria stayed in the twilight of an English village, for the rest of her long life.

Chapter Eighteen

APOTHEOSIS

VICTORIA renounced the world for nothing less than a crown, in fact, if not in name; it was no longer necessary for her to attain the illusion of importance through running for the presidency of the United States. At Bredon's Norton, she was an absolute autocrat over an army of servants on the estate; she was a landlord with a monopoly and most of the villagers were beholden to her for patches on their roofs; she was the tradesmen's only substantial customer, they had to curry favor; she gave the vicar his home as well as help for the needy. And when one incumbent didn't please her, he was sacked.

Those English villages remote from industrial centres were remnants of the feudal system, and Bredon's Norton was one of them. It was a small kingdom, but it was compact, and its subjects touched at least a figurative fore-lock to the Lady of the Manor. Victoria, who had been the scum of Homer, became the queen of Bredon's Norton, and she reigned in peace, with pamphlets, for nearly thirty years.

Pamphlets streamed from Norton Park, not only to tell the world about Victoria's royal blood, her fight for righteousness, and the persecutions thereof, but to describe the rural charm and historic background in which she triumphed.

Near Tewskbury, in Worcestershire, Bredon's Norton nestles at the foot of Bredon Hill, overlooking the fertile valley of the Severn. Rose gardens twine around black and white thatched cottages, and sunny orchards rustle near an old stone church, with leafy murmurs as soothing as the toll of its old bells, said to "contain much silver."

Below is the Avon River; and up a gentle slope rises a winding road to Norton Park. Then through gravelled roadways, past a large orchard and an evergreen park, beyond the Manor House, and across a bridge that spans a charming noisy, thread-like stream, stands Norton Park, the main dwelling on the estate. Its gabled façades are overrun with ivy and overgrown with roses. And there Victoria's sanctum was known to be the library, whose light filtered in through leaded glass on walls lined with books, whose bindings were known to be exquisite.

The Martin family seat was in the neighboring village of Overbury; and Norton Park, built by the Misses Ann and Penelope Martin, was a dower estate for the maiden ladies of the family until Sir Robert gave it to his younger son, John Biddulph, before his death. And so it came to Victoria.

She usually received callers at the Manor House, a part of the estate built before Shakespeare's time. It was approached through an arch with 1585 chiseled in the stone. Antiquarians claimed the door was eleventh or twelfth century. Thomas Copley, who went with Sir Walter Raleigh to found the state of Virginia, lived there. Indeed, it was a rare old place, with mullioned windows and a newel stair-case, with hidden cupboards in the oak panelling; and it even is supposed to have a secret passage.

The village of Bredon's Norton is of such antiquity that the history of England might be studied there.

NORTON PARK

THE MANOR HOUSE

THE OLD TITHE BARN

It is believed that Queen Boadicea built the village road. In the eighth century a monastery was founded at Bredon. King Edgar mentioned Bredon in a charter granted in 964. During the civil wars, throngs bent on upholding the Parliamentarian cause gathered on Bredon Hill to hinder Prince Rupert from crossing the Cotswolds. "Today Bredon Hill, with all its historic associations is owned by one who has shown herself more dauntless than Boadicea, and who has fought against the hosts of wickedness and corruption in high places and prevailed," vowed a pamphlet in the series called "The Manor House Causeries."

At first the villagers fought shy of Victoria. They were horrified at the thought of Mr. Martin's marrying a divorceé, when divorce was almost unknown. Few ever knew she had been twice divorced. An early motorist and a speedy one, she dashed around in a great white car to tell the farmers about agriculture and to teach the gardeners about horticulture. She wanted to "win them back to the land." She divided one of the farms on her estate into small holdings to let to women only, and called it "Bredon's Norton College"; and there the women were taught to farm. The villagers thought her another "mad American," while in fact, she simply was herself again, once more the preacher and the reformer, the domineering centre of a very lovely stage.

There was an old tithe barn with slits in its creepered wall that dated back to the time when bows and arrows were used for defense. It was built with a high porch to admit wagons laden with the produce contributed by the people when thc lands of each parish were taxed for church support and one-tenth of their produce was paid in kind. Victoria turned it into a village hall for lectures and entertainments and Christmas festivities. Then a good tea with mince pies and all sorts of cake were served; carols were sung by the village choir, and boots, as well as toys and sweets, were distributed to the children by the shepherdess disguised as Father Christmas.

Victoria established a flower show at Bredon's Norton, which later was moved to Bredon, nearer Tewksbury, and finally became an annual agricultural show at Tewksbury, of inestimable value in the opinion of the farming community. Bredon's Norton always was picturesque and beautiful, but it was dreary and neglected, its people unhealthy and uncomfortable, until Victoria repaired the cottages and installed conveniences. She repaired the roads and kept them in repair and eventually she even provided lighting arrangements. She made the place a model for the district.

The villagers decided she was "a good sort where she took." She was "a good customer, to whom money was no object," but she was an energetic one.

"Mr. Williams," she would say peremptorily to the draper at Tewksbury, "Mr. Williams, I need some linoleum. What have you, Mr. Williams?"

When a piece pleased her, "I think that will do," she said snappily, "how much in that roll?"

He told her.

"Well, send it over. Must have it at two o'clock this afternoon."

"But, madam, I can't——"

"Then you should hire it done. Send the bill to me."

After this was arranged, she asked, "Who will come over with it?"

"I'll come myself, madam."

"All right. You shall have lunch. Tell them to give you your lunch."

Later, she had to inspect the newly-laid linoleum.

"Did you have a good lunch, Mr. Williams?"

Mr. Williams hadn't taken lunch. Mrs. Martin insisted that he should have.

"How are you going home, Mr. Williams?"

"Oh, I'll walk, madam."

"You shall have my car."

"But I'd like to walk, madam."

"No, Mr. Williams, you shall have my car."

Draper Williams had her car.

At Christmas she gave her favorites "five quid." The Reverend Webb said, "She gave everything for which I asked." She was extremely generous, and she looked after the poor in ways known only to those who have been poor themselves, and in whose veins there flows that rare virtue, the milk of human kindness.

The villagers learned to adore their benefactress, and to become good listeners. While Victoria's low sweet voice was clear, she talked so fast that she was hard to understand, but they were glad for her to do thc talking. Nobody could tell just how she might take, or mistake, any chance word. She would become angry suddenly and without apparent reason, and then, "I won't have it!" she'd say with an imperious wave of her hand, or "No! I want it that way."

They knew she was a bitter enemy, "a hard woman —like steel." She dismissed a servant girl summarily for returning after hours; and, when another servant gave her shelter for the night, she, too, was dismissed.

She decided one frosty day to take a motor trip.

"But we cannot, on these roads," said her chauffeur.

"You drive," said Victoria.

And when the car skidded and crashed, the chauffeur lost his job.

Sometimes her generosity was domineering too. She discovered that a man was in financial difficulties, and though he did not belong to the class that accepts philanthropy, she asked him to make purchases for himself and his family and send the accounts to Norton Park, to his profound embarrassment, which deepened when she complained, after some time, that she had not received any of his bills.

As of old, she obeyed all her impulses.

In 1908 Victoria built a village school on her estate to reform the English educational methods. And when the county authorities persisted in running it in the old-fashioned way, she offered to pay the extra expenses of installing the Froebel kindergarten system. Though Victoria explained that it was adopted by educators everywhere, the educational committee refused to be responsible for a system they knew nothing about; they withdrew the public grant for teachers' salaries, and threw the school back on Mrs. Martin's hands. Whereupon she installed trained kindergarten teachers, and a motor-bus to collect children from the five villages that adjoined Bredon's Norton, and according to an announcement in the *New York World,* the schools under control of the educational committee were deserted. Mrs. Martin was seeking the co-operation of wealthy residents in the surrounding counties, and "arrangements have been made to have the question of the withdrawal of grant from the Bredon's Norton School raised in Parliament at the coming session."

Victoria was herself again. How she loved to start a fight and take it to court! The end never seemed to interest her.

As she grew older, she retained much of her old charm and all her old vitality. In Bredon's Norton she expanded in an atmosphere of adulation, and in time she found food for her cosmic urge.

The humanitarian movement wouldn't do; the world wasn't enlightened enough. Aviation appealed to her soaring spirit; and in 1912, through the "Women's Aerial League of Great Britain," she offered to present a "sculptured centre piece, one of the heirlooms of her historic mansion, and five thousand dollars to the first man or woman to fly across the Atlantic." But that only meant one newspaper article, and she still adored publicity, though she had learned to seek it with care and get it with dignity.

When Victoria first arrived in Bredon's Norton, before Edward VII was king of England, he happened to pass through the district, and lunched at Norton Park. To the dismay of the neighborhood, Victoria intertwined the Stars and Stripes with Union Jack in the dining room. But the Prince of Wales complimented her on such a "happy" arrangement and sent her some grouse the next day. He knew a charming woman when he saw one, and then Victoria still could turn on the Woodhull witchery when she wanted to.

It is possible that this episode led her to adopt the "Anglo-American relationship" later. She was superstitious; she seemed to think one success led to another. She announced that the English and American peoples were one nation, who happened to live in different countries, and she and her daughter Zulu Maud organized an operatic and dramatic company in Bredon's Norton to produce Anglo-American tableaux in the old tithe barn.

Then in 1913 a committee was formed to celebrate the Anglo-American Peace Centenary in 1914 and to purchase Sulgrave Manor, the home of George Washington's family in England.

Victoria appeared dramatically, as if from nowhere, at a meeting when many prominent people were present, and had it announced that she would give one thousand pounds to the cause. And she gave it. But it was not the last or the first thousand pounds nor did it determine the purchase of Sulgrave Manor, as she afterwards claimed.

However, the Sulgrave Manor Board thought they had found a great benefactress; they didn't know that Victoria had found a pass-key to celebrities and a gate to more newspaper fame. She used the Sulgrave Manor Board for years.

She declared six times in as many publications that she had given the Manor House at Bredon's Norton to the Sulgrave Board to become another "American Shrine in England," a hostel for visiting Americans, but some vaguely theatrical reason always prevented her from signing any deed of gift. Sometimes, she merely said, "It is not in my stars." Ambassador Page, Ambassador Davis, the Marquis of Crewe and other notables interested in the cause were persuaded to visit at the Manor House. Their names were signed in the visitor's book, and their visits were proclaimed in England and America, as well as in the pamphlets now called "The Manor House Causeries." Her nephew, Dr. Steuart Welles, evidently her friend again, had to represent her on the platform on state occasions, though he had no connection with the institution beyond that of a paying member. The Sulgrave officials wrote her long chatty letters. She sent them pamphlets and occasionally she gave them more pounds.

But the Manor House continued to be Victoria's idea of an "International County Salon" and became a harbor for the authors of her pamphlets who could get lovely words about her greatness in magazines of no importance, and for the latest astrologer or palmist and for a few Spiritualists who were not charlatans. Sycophants predominated. They lived on Victoria and spent her money freely, but they fawned on her too. They were jealous of one another, and fought for her favor. It was like any other court circle, in miniature, and no doubt it was worth the price to Victoria. She had a gift for getting what she wanted.

She stuffed the low ceiled rooms of the Manor House with first-rate antiques. Here was a great Chinese vase, and there a mellow-toned tapestry and a piece of rare old fabric. Bottles, urns and inlaid cases stood on tables and taborets, everywhere. Two large tables in the main hall were entirely devoted to pamphlets. One was so arranged that it looked like an enormous mahogany wheel with white spokes. A combination of an astrological chart and a palmist's device immortalized the Woodhull-Martin hand, over a shelf full of books on astrology, a subject that interested Victoria. A charming picture of her was placed near a photograph of an American Ambassador; and the walls were covered with bright woolen tapestries, portraying such events as the "Signing of the Declaration of Independence."

Painted in black or red on the plaster walls, were those quotations Victoria loved, or more modern legends. "IS YOUR EFFICIENCY UP TO YOUR OPPORTUNITY?"

The upstairs chambers were named Nirvana, Asteros, Ohio, and so on, and there the staying guests were housed, subject to Victoria's displeasure. She might turn on one at any time. Surely those hangers-on earned their bread and board.

They had to talk about Victoria's wonderful success when she stood for the presidency, they had to bemoan the fact that she hadn't received enough recognition, they even had to give in when there was an argument over the pronunciation of a word, which must have been a hardship for small minds whose mental integrity is often bounded on one side by a broad A and on the other by a penultimate accent.

Now Victoria spent her old fury on words. "Beautiful doesn't express it—it's impressive!" she'd insist as if life were at stake. "The Manor House Causeries" were filled with familiar quotations. It must have delighted her to see "Kismet" chiseled over the doorway to Norton Park and in a semi-circle over the entrance to the village school was inscribed, "As the twig is bent the tree inclines." On New Year's day, she liked to say:

"What have years to bring,
But larger floods of love and light
And sweeter songs to sing.
Holmes"

She reeked with the best sentiments.

All this was activity, and it kept her young. She always had an enthusiastic interest in something. And when she was ailing, she willed herself well. "I will not be ill," she'd say, and she wasn't. She never lost her infectious energy; she radiated a sort of power that spurred people on. The Spiritualists called this her psychic gift. She had a way of saying, "I see your mother coming into the room behind you," and of describing that mother, long since dead. Spiritualism was her consistent interest; and in connection with it, she found her most desirable friends. Without them and her parasites, she would have been lonely. The potentates of the neighboring estates appeared when some notable appeared, through the Sulgrave Institution, or when the most pretentious affairs took place at "The Manor House Club," but they were not intimate.

There was more than the Atlantic Ocean between them. The eccentricities which they would have forgiven in their own people, they could not forget in her. They were only mildly aware of the old scandals, and she benefited by the changing times which made some of her exploits respectable. But she talked about the virtues they took for granted, which probably made them uncomfortable. She had no regard for the ordinary conventions of the church, but she preached about how only those with pure hearts could see God. She orated about the purity of the body;

which could have interested none but a psychologist or a historian. She pronounced shaking hands "too intimate," a delicious irony from one who used to sleep with any man she really liked. Shaking hands was "a barbaric custom" now. With her old faith in print, she distributed a leaflet on "How Shaking Hands Originated," from an editorial in the *Philadelphia Inquirer,* with "I do not shake hands from a sanitary standpoint, Victoria C. Woodhull" printed beneath it.

A reformed sinner, who was a diverting study, might have been a boresome companion.

Once when Zulu Maud offered her hand to a caller, her mother snapped, "Zulu, what do you do that for!"

Victoria cultivated none of the amenities of gentility, then. She went to a man's house and sent word for him to come out to her car. She wanted to see him on business immediately. And immediately he came.

"I see you don't stop to dress yourself all up before you come out," said Victoria.

"No," said the man who knew her. "I thought you wanted to see the man and not his clothing."

"That's right. I was once kept waiting ten minutes while a man brushed his hair."

And yet she was a priestess of propriety; as all women who want to suppress a past or a possibility, must be.

When young Jackson was the clown and cut-up of the neighborhood, because he had "that kind of a face," he was asked to perform at one of the Manor House entertainments. He had heard Sir Harry Lauder sing "Stop that Tickling, Jock" at one of the

London Music Halls, so he started to sing "Stop that ticklin' icklin' ticklin', Jock" with expression.

Mrs. Martin sat near the stage with the vicar, and Jackson saw them put their heads together. He sang the second verse of his song, and then the vicar came forward and quietly said they would hear no more of it.

A few days later Lauder sang that song for His Majesty, the King. Jackson mailed the news item to Mrs. Martin, but nobody knows how it affected her.

Victoria's unfortunate son Byron was the tragedy of her life, and because she didn't want to leave him with strangers, she and Zulu Maud stayed in Bredon's Norton more and more. Apparently Zulu Maud lived only for her mother, with that extraordinary devotion that Victoria inspired in those who knew her longest and best; a devotion felt by Mrs. Roberts, too, the shepherdess on the estate.

Mrs. Roberts was a power there as well as the factotum; the wiser pamphleteers immortalized the way she tended the little lambs, no matter how bitter the wind, nor how snowy the weather.

Victoria did not return to America, which did not appreciate her.

But Tennessee dashed back and forth as if she had embarked on the noble mission of making reform movements ridiculous.

Lady Cook was going to build club-houses for women all over the United States, with much publicity. She presented the cause of woman's suffrage to President Roosevelt, looking like a "little gray ghost in a gray felt hat, silvery hair and veil and even gray garters," according to the press. She tried to buy a tract of land at Wheatley Hills on Long Island to start a "school for fathers," which brought out all the old free love stories as well as protests from the town of Westbury. She fussed about her American citizenship, and revisited Ludlow Street jail with photographers and sob sisters. She rode around in a motor-car decorated with "votes for women" banners, and said she wanted to die on the platform lecturing for woman's rights. She lectured in Pittsburgh, and distressed a large audience with an incoherent speech delivered with difficulty. She announced that she was going to spend four hundred thousand dollars on an art salon, whereupon eminent representatives from different fields of art met in her apartment at the Marie Antoinette Hotel and were amazed when Tennie talked about eugenics, suggesting that a committee of women be sterilized to take care of the men. She gave out interviews to recommend the registration of visitors to disorderly houses, and consistently and sensibly advocated the legitimacy of illegitimate children.

She was past the age for sexuality, but she didn't react from it, as Victoria did. She was more trivial than Victoria; her reform was a circumstance, instead of a revolution. And instead of power, she only wanted publicity, though, unlike Victoria, she didn't care about its import.

She gave up her big house at Richmond because servants made her nervous. Sometimes she took an apartment with one of her nieces or nephews. Victoria had done more than her filial duty, and now she kept in touch only with the members of the family whom she could view with pride.

Tennessee gave a dinner to some Boer generals in London, immediately after the Boer war, and advertised it, which caused unfavorable comment. She played with the Women's Freedom League and gave money to the militants. She tried to promote a marital mass meeting for unmarried salaried people, object matrimony.

For years she flared in the papers in ways that were extremely distasteful to the Sultana of Sulgrave.

As of old she adored Victoria, but she wouldn't curb her impulses, though it hurt her that they no longer worked together or played together. The sisters were vaguely estranged, without a quarrel. And yet, like a little dog with a bone, whenever Tennessee attracted a celebrity, she took it down to Bredon's Norton, where celebrities were appreciated.

Tennessee's erraticism was amusing, and she still was attractive. She was slender now, and very small. Dressed exquisitely in blues, and pinks and grays, with pretty hats adorned with rosebuds, she was pleasing for a time. Mr. Carl Van Vechten interviewed her in Paris when he was a young reporter. And it is a testimony to the brevity of newspaper fame, that he never had heard of her past. She entertained him with a vivid account of "Soup for Three," her favorite story; the dainty old charmer enchanted him.

When Miss Alice Ives went to London after the enormous success of her play, "The Brooklyn Handicap," she met Tennessee and visited Bredon's Norton with her. Miss Ives was fascinated by the lovely old place. She loved the winding woodland paths that led to a low hooded thatched tea-house set on a crag with a view over groves and hills to the valley of the Avon. She was spell-bound by the Woodhull witchery which Victoria had on tap. After too much Tennessee, Victoria seemed intelligent. She could talk brilliantly when she refrained from preaching, and Tennessee never had her ease or elegance. Victoria dashed off on long walks and came back with crimson cheeks and eyes like sapphires, lithe as she used to be and just as alert, a cameo dressed in tweed; while Tennessee curled up on a couch against a pile of pillows, in a blue tea-gown trimmed with tiny roses, and devoured the penny dreadfuls. Victoria scolded her good-humoredly for missing the fresh air, and the sisters strolled together in the garden after tea. They seemed so friendly that Miss Ives was surprised a few days later, when Tennessee said, "We're going tomorrow. She doesn't want us."

Victoria surprised her too. One evening while she was browsing over the wonderful books in the fine old library, Victoria came in and put her arms around her. "I want you to know that I never advocated free love!" she said intensely.

Miss Ives was simply bewildered. She belonged to a generation that was more interested in manners and morals than in mankind, a generation that read fiction instead of biography, because it was easier to find the good rewarded and the bad punished in a novel then. Her generation ignored the minor characters in American history and gilded the major ones.

Naturally she had not read current newspaper stories

about people who were prominent in her infancy. So free love was only a name to her; Victoria Woodhull was only her hostess.

In fact, some New York newspapers that were cramped for space began to destroy the older envelopes in their reference libraries, and with them the sisters' past. When a young reporter named Richard Silver noticed one of the exploits of Lady Cook, he decided to write an article about her for a Sunday paper, and the only material he could find in the *Journal* office were her own pamphlets. His story pleased her. She happened to be in New York at the time, and she looked him up and asked him to write her biography. She offered such financial inducements that he went to England with her.

He and his family were established in a hotel in London, Lady Cook paying the bills. But he wasn't allowed to be alone with her. Lady Cook's nieces and nephews shadowed them. Whenever he tried to ask her any questions they interrupted. It was an impossible situation, and his livelihood was at stake and so was his family's.

Mr. Silver soon learned that Mrs. Martin was the influential member of her family, and he decided to appeal to her. But when he telephoned to Bredon's Norton she refused to see him or to speak to him. Mr. Silver was a determined young man, and he took the train to Bredon's Norton.

At Norton Park, the butler said Mrs. Martin was not at home. After he was tipped, he said he would see if Mrs. Martin were at home. Eventually Mrs. Martin appeared, but she didn't ask him to come in, which was an unusual proceeding in an English home. She sat down with him on a bench in the big hall, and told him she did not want Lady Cook's biography to come out now. It would bring undesirable publicity.

Mr. Silver was an attractive young man, and Victoria liked to have visitors at Bredon's Norton. She unbent and asked him to stay for dinner; she insisted upon his staying the night. Finally, she asked him to write her biography instead of Tennessee's! But it should not appear until after her death.

Mr. Silver said she was one of the most powerful creatures he had ever seen. He found her "sinister," and he did not write her biography.

He went back to London to find his hotel bills unpaid, and returned to America with his family. One of Lady Cook's nephews finally paid his expenses, but nobody paid for the job he had lost. He brought an action in the Supreme Court of New York State against Lady Cook for alleged breach of contract, and the next time she came to America she was examined in court. She "did not remember" anything. When asked why she paid Mr. Silver's expenses to London, she said, "Why I paid for other persons besides, and I am paying the expenses of about six persons now. I take lots of people over and that is why they think I am dotty. I have no children of my own. I also pay the expenses of lots of people over and give them money to support themselves in London."

A few weeks later the papers announced that "Lady Cook was deeply interested in the casting of her horoscope," at the bazaar held by the Professional Women's League at the Waldorf.

Victoria was seventy-six in 1914, when war was declared. It was such a nice war for women who liked to organize things; and, while it didn't make the world safe for democracy, it did affect county society. At seventy-six Victoria not only had the desire to lead the activities in her district, she had the energy and the equipment, as well as the opportunity. The notables of the neighborhood had to join those activities, which they thought so important to their country.

While unfortunate young men rotted in the trenches, the whole world began to play with words and flags and projects in tune with Victoria and her childish dreams and hates at last.

So she arranged pastoral and patriotic tableaux at the "Manor House Club" for the benefit of the Red Cross, in which "Peace" was represented by Lady Deerhurst's daughter. The women sewed for the Red Cross at the "Manor House Club," and brought their husbands to hear lantern lectures on the war and concerts in the old Tithe Barn. They heard recruiting speeches there, too, that sent them out to die. But when a fête for the Women's Land Army was held on the estate, the Earl of Coventry, the Lord-Lieutenant of Worcestershire, opened it with a tribute to Mrs. Woodhull-Martin's efforts to recognize and encourage the work of women on the land. He hoped the good send-off which she "is so kindly giving to the movement, by the holding of a Land Fête will attract attention to it in other parts of the country."

Four hundred visitors saw a milking competition with cords of red, white and blue, decorating the cows. The Manor House shepherdess, crook in hand, wore a costume displaying the Stars and Stripes draped with the Union Jack. Children trained in the social service rooms maintained by Mrs. Woodhull-Martin in Bredon, exhibited the fruit they had dried and bottled, and heard a lecture on herb collecting. Tea was served to wounded soldiers from the Red Cross Hospital, and the agricultural machinery supplied by Mrs. Woodhull-Martin was shown to all.

Victoria gave smart Holland hats to the Village Land Army, and furnished cottages for Belgian refugees. She organized another fête in 1915 for Red Cross funds, at which works of the great authors were exhibited with examples of butter making, and Lord and Lady Coventry attended it. The Archbishop of Beyrut pleaded in the Manor House for oppressed Armenians. Talks were given there on the Hindu cults. One Christmas Eve a tableau represented the "Signing of the Treaty of Ghent." Another time they showed the "Landing of the Mayflower."

She was "fretful" until America entered the war. She sent what her followers called a "memorable" cable to Washington, "Why is Old Glory absent from shop windows in England today when other flags are flying? United we stand; divided we fall together. Quis separabit." Deliciously consistent, she still wanted others to think as she thought. Moreover, she was so symbolical, maybe she felt that inter-twined flags might inter-twine her American failures with her English triumph, which was local but loud. She talked bitterly about her "lack of recognition" in America. But when it joined the Allied cause the stars and stripes waved over Bredon's Norton and she had a hedge of golden rod, the national flower, planted beside the old gray walls of the Manor House grounds.

It is a curious fact that Victoria rarely appeared in person at any of these fêtes and pageants. She planned them and superintended the arrangements, with her daughter, and then she only wanted her name mentioned on the platform and in print. Some of her circle got occasional articles about her war activities in English magazines; but they wrote pamphlets steadily, to carry the news to all the newspaper offices in England and America, where they were filed, and forgotten, until they were brought out for her obituaries many years later.

Meanwhile Lady Cook's press agents announced that "an amazon army" was Lady Cook's idea, dressed in "khaki uniforms like men, with possibly an addition of knee length skirts. I expect a hundred and fifty thousand women to be armed, drilled and organized into armies in three months," said she. In 1915, she arrived in America to "see President Wilson," and to lecture on conditions in Belgium; but she didn't.

It was said that she was "still pretty in her oldish way, and exquisitely dressed."

She died in 1923.

The Claflins all lived to be over seventy. Mary Sparr devoted herself to the activities of the Eastern Star, the women's branch of the Masons, until she became an invalid, in her old age. Brother Hebern Claflin made the front page of the Chicago papers with a complicated romance in his seventy-seventh year. He was going to marry a lady named Laura from Syracuse, but he got a spirit message from his deceased wife advising him to wed a twenty-year old girl from

California. Then Mabel, a medium, the head of the Church of Scientific Christianity, entered the scene and the press. She was "the Shepherd of Paradise," her followers claimed, as well as Dr. Claflin's last fiancée. But the wedding was delayed because Lady Cook cabled she wanted to attend it, and she couldn't get there because of the submarine warfare; and Mabel unfortunately had to wait for a divorce from her last husband. Hebern died before it took place. He was described as a pioneer physician of great wealth, but his fiancée was "vexed," in huge headlines, when she found a large watch, some sentimental letters and a bank book with a balance of only one thousand thirty-four dollars and thirty-nine cents in his safety deposit box. Mabel said, "The disappointment is overwhelming, but my philosophy sustains me."

When both were over eighty, Victoria was photographed with the Earl of Coventry, "the father of the House of Lords," at Bredon's Norton. No doubt the war made this possible. Victoria figured in the photograph, which was widely reproduced as "The United States Mother of Woman's Suffrage." Neither Mrs. Stanton nor Miss Anthony could protest; they were dead.

In life itself there is victory, and Victoria still seethed with life; like an old cameo outlined in radium, she sent out eternal sparks. This made her a useful companion for other ancients who often needed stimulation. The Earl of Coventry must have found her delightful. She had learned the art of conversation from Stephen Pearl Andrews, and now that she dwelt less on purity and more on affairs, she practised it.

OLD AGE: VICTORIA WOODHULL MARTIN IN THE SIDE CAR IN FRONT OF THE MANOR HOUSE

VICTORIA WITH THE EARL OF COVENTRY

She occasionally was absurd, but she always was spirited. Moreover, admiration is a comfortable background for companionship, and most English earls would have admired Victoria because she managed her estate so well. Estates are as important to English earls as factories are to American millionaires.

On her eighty-seventh birthday, the Reverend Webb presented an illuminated album, in which every person in the village had written his name, to the Lady of the Manor. "She was extremely jealous of it, and would not even allow Miss Woodhull to touch it," said the Reverend Webb. And one inevitably recalls how her more exalted namesake murmured "How kind they are! How kind they are!" with tears in royal eyes, when her subjects showed their adoration at the Jubilee of 1897.

But age did not change the habits of America's Victoria, nor dim her imagination. Her pamphleteers announced that she gave the one thousand pounds to the Lincoln Memorial Fund that made the statue near Westminster possible, and that she was publicly commended by the Duke of Connaught when it was unveiled. But the most minute newspaper accounts of that occasion failed to mention Mrs. Martin. There was an indoor meeting because it rained that day, and Mrs. Martin's gift was presented somewhat dramatically; but the association was not in need and the Duke of Connaught was not there. He did attend the unveiling in the rain, but nobody saw him felicitate Victoria. Nobody saw her at all.

Periodically she announced that she had presented the Manor House to the Sulgrave Institution, and each time newspapers in England and America described her historic mansion, her war activities, her friendship with the Earl of Coventry, and her pioneering past. Her pamphlets prevailed, and combined with the fact that times had changed, to portray her as a left-wing Suffragist, who had been reviled in an age of innocence for views that would be acceptable to anybody now. Thus she appeared in Sunday feature articles, whose writers had read the chronicles of a restricted group which made the 'seventies seem an age of innocence instead of an age of vigor.

But those articles pleased Victoria, and it is a refreshing reflection that she often got what she wanted. Few people do. Desirable publicity seemed to hearten her as religion, or compliments or beefsteak heartens others. And her trickeries were less harmful than the honest tyrannies of the futile or the righteous demands of the weak.

Now that the war was over she said, "The world is my home," and celebrated world amity with national anthems in the old tithe barn, in which the flags of all nations waved. Sometimes the shepherdess sang a lullaby, and it seemed to please the old lady. For at last Victoria, in her late eighties, was an old lady. Her heart began to fail.

She took an apartment at Brighton to get more sun and the sea air. And a reporter went there, when she was eighty-five, to interview her about the "flapper franchise," which would have made twenty-five the voting age for English women.

"I want women to have the vote as soon as they are

fit to use it," said she, "but I do not believe in forced maturity. Twenty-five is young enough for persons of both sexes to exercise the franchise."

The reporter found that time had "not dimmed the eyes of this spirited woman." She added that she "was making history at twenty-one, but I was a wife when little more than a child. My son was born when I was very young, and I had an unusually advanced education at home. My case was exceptional."

She still told her friends she "liked the sound of Victoria Woodhull-Martin." She never doubted that she was a great woman.

But there were bitter times when she realized that she was forgotten in America and unknown in England, outside of Bredon's Norton, and at such a time Mr. William Andrews called on her.

Mr. Andrews had heard her vivid legends from old labor leaders in America when he was collecting material for "The Documentary History of the American Labor Party." He admired her ability to dramatise a cause, and he had seen her loveliest photographs. Moreover, he belonged to the generation that followed Miss Ives', a generation with a zest for striking personalities, and a taste for diagnosis instead of damnation.

Now he saw a thin, fragile, taut old creature at the end of a long room.

"Come closer," she said imperiously.

When he was fifteen feet away from her, she told him to stop.

"Not any closer!" she added emphatically.

He expressed his admiration for her work in America.

"In England, too," she said; and then she murmured, "if more people knew about it, I'd get out of this."

Which might have been a significant utterance, or a manifestation of senility, though people said her mind was clear to the end. Recognition always had been the breath of life to her; maybe she thought it would restore her old vigor, if she had it. Maybe she knew she would have had it, if she hadn't been an apostate to the cause of social freedom, for she had lived to see a generation grasp at the views she used to preach and practise, a generation that would have acclaimed their pioneer, a generation to whom the stuff she claimed she preached was merely quaint. This would have been a hard realization for a self-righteous mind with such a hungry ego!

On the other hand, her apostasy could have been so profound that she believed free love was a "pestilential mire of sensual grossness" and that only the pure could see God. She had said so for fifty years, and those who convince others, often convince themselves. Then, unless she persuaded herself that she never had practised it, she was exposed to all the fears of hell-fire, bred in her youth. Those who had the revival spirit etched into their past could hardly have forgotten how damned ghosts groaned in their torment. Unless Victoria still thought anything was right because she did it, she must have suffered agonies of apprehension. Which is guess-work. We only know that she was desperately afraid of death. Maybe she was in love with life, and didn't want to leave it; that was one force she never feared.

She said she wouldn't let anyone come near her because she was "afraid," afraid they might harm her or give her some infection. When she was half-dead, she spent her days lying back in her automobile, and, when one chauffeur wouldn't go fast enough, she got another. She sped madly around the countryside, as if she were trying to flee from death. For four years the indomitable old creature spent her nights upright in a chair for fear she'd die if she went to bed. This was her last defiance, her last fight, and it was a mighty one.

Finally in her ninetieth year, on the morning of June tenth, 1927, they found her dead. Her last enemy had conquered her quietly, while she was asleep. And according to her wish, she was cremated and her ashes were cast into the sea.

Even then, she wasn't through with life. Her fortune was willed to Zulu Maud Woodhull, but, in case her daughter did not survive her, the bulk of it was bequeathed to the Society for Psychical Research, for a "Victoria Woodhull Trust Fund," to be given in annual prizes for original psychical research. She had been a member of the society for years, but she had done nothing for it beyond paying her dues and receiving the bulletins. Perhaps she wanted to insure her return!

Those pamphlets white-washed her in her obituaries. The English newspapers called her "The United States Mother of Woman Suffrage, the Benefactress of Bredon, and a Promoter of Anglo-American Friendship." In America, she was a pioneer suffragist, a fearless muckraker in Wall Street, and a social reformer who suffered for views now generally accepted;

on an inside page, for Lindbergh's flight across the Atlantic came first.

A few weeks later a Sunday editor refused to print a feature story about Victoria Woodhull-Martin. "Nobody is interested in the old suffragists now," he said. For those pamphlets had white-washed all her color away, a consummation which must have horrified that priestess of publicity, if she knew about it from the otherwhere.

But the Reverend W. H. B. Yerborough, M. A., the Rector of Bredon, preached a long and eloquent sermon, in which he said she did not wish a memorial service, but he knew she would not object to a "tribute." After describing her good works (according to the pamphleteers), as well as her material benefactions in Bredon, he said, "Frail and weak though she was, she could communicate to others something of that indomitable energy and spirit that alone kept her alive during these last few years. . . . Professor William James speaks of people who 'start life with a bottle or two of champagne' and speaks of them as 'the twice born.' She was one of those 'twice born,' the people of genius, not always understood or appreciated as they should be by the more dull 'once born' . . . she was in advance of her time, and accordingly suffered persecution. . . ."

He hoped his congregation not only would realise that "we have been privileged to have one of the world's greatest personalities among us," but that they would espouse causes as she did, "and she would say: 'Have the courage of your convictions; don't mind what the world says; don't try to be popular—do your duty. Come out from the ruck of grumblers, who do nothing, who criticise only, and try to do something to help onward your fellow men.' "

A soiled young mother leaned wearily against the rickety door of a smelly little cottage near Long Green, and said, "I wish we had a lady like her now. We have no gentry now, to look after the poor."

BIBLIOGRAPHY

Papers of Ohio Church Society, Vol. VI. Oberlin, 1895.

The Kentucky Revival and Its Influence on the Miami Valley, by J. P. MacLean.

History of American Revivals, by Rev. C. L. Thompson. Rockford, Ill., 1878.

Psychology of Methodist Revivals, by Sydney Dimond. London, 1926.

On Two Continents, by H. Brake. 1858.

Autobiography of Clarissa Emily Hobbs.

The Pioneers of Morgan County. Indiana, 1856.

Forty Years a Gambler.

Historical View of Clinton County, Pennsylvania, by D. S. Maynard, Lock Haven, Pa., 1875.

Newark (Ohio) *Advocate.*

The *Mail.* Chicago, Illinois.

The Golden Age Tracts No. 3, *Victoria C. Woodhull.* A biographical sketch by Theodore Tilton. New York, 1871.

A Psychic Autobiography.

The Deathblow to Spiritualism, by Reuben B. Davenport.

Spiritual Wives, by W. H. Dixon. London, Hurst & Blackett, 1868.

Mediums and Their Dupes, by Bradley Shaw.

Free Love and Its Votaries, by Dr. John B. Ellis. 1870.

Mediums Unmasked, by Mrs. Garrett. 1892.

On the Witness Stand, by Hugo Münsterberg. New York, 1925.

The *Interocean.* Chicago, Illinois.

The Rise of American Civilization, by Charles and Mary Beard. New York, 1927.

The Americans at Home, by David Macrae. Edinburgh, Edmonston & Douglas, 1870.

The Emergence of Modern America. 1865-1878, by Allan Nevins. New York, The Macmillan Co., 1927.

The Selinsgrove *Times*. Selinsgrove, Pennsylvania.

The *Brooklyn Eagle*. Brooklyn, N. Y.

Commodore Vanderbilt, by Arthur D. H. Smith. New York, 1927.

The Vanderbilt Will Case. Scrapbook at the Public Library, New York City.

Sunshine and Shadow in New York, by Matthew Hale Smith. 1868.

Bulls and Bears of New York, by Matthew Hale Smith.

Fifty Years in Wall Street, by Henry Clews.

Inside Life in Wall Street, by Wm. Worthington Fowler. 1873.

The Great Metropolis, by Junius H. Browne. Hartford, 1869.

The *New York Herald*. New York City.

"Boss" Tweed, by D. T. Lynch. New York, Boni & Liveright, 1927.

The Principles of Government, by Victoria C. Woodhull. New York, Woodhull, Claflin & Co., 1871.

Constitutional Equality, by Tennie C. Claflin. New York, Woodhull, Claflin & Co., 1871.

Socialism in the United States, by Morris Hillquit.

History of Labour in the United States, by Commons and Associates. New York, The Macmillan Co., 1926.

Butler's Book, by Benjamin F. Butler. Boston, 1892.

Damaged Souls, by Gamaliel Bradford. Houghton Mifflin, 1923.

A History of the United States Since the Civil War, by Ellis Paxson Oberholtzer. New York, The Macmillan Co., 1926.

The "Also Rans," by Don C. Seitz. New York, Crowell, 1928.

Journalism in America, by Frederic Hudson. 1873.

The Life and Work of Susan B. Anthony, by Ida Husted Harper. Indianapolis, Bobbs-Merrill, 1899.

Elizabeth Cady Stanton, as Revealed in Her Letters, Diary

and Reminiscences, edited by Theodore Stanton and Harriot Stanton Blatch. New York, Harper & Brothers, 1922.

Eighty Years and More, by Elizabeth Cady Stanton.

The History of Woman Suffrage, prepared by Mrs. Stanton, Miss Anthony, and Matilda Joslyn Gage.

History of National Woman's Rights Movement for Twenty Years, by Paulina Wright Davis.

The Revolution, edited by Laura Curtis Bullard.

The Dreadful Decade, by Don C. Seitz. Indianapolis, Bobbs-Merrill, 1926.

Horace Greeley, by Don C. Seitz. Indianapolis, Bobbs-Merrill, 1926.

Charles Bradlaugh, a Record of His Life and Work, by Hypatia Bradlaugh Bonner. London, Unwin, 1894.

Notes and Anecdotes of Many Years, by J. B. Bishop.

Woodhull & Claflin's Weekly, New York City.

The *Tribune.* New York City.

The *Times.* New York City.

The *World.* New York City.

The *Daily Graphic.* New York City.

The *Sun.* New York City.

The *Evening Post.* New York City.

The *Nation.* New York City.

Harper's Weekly. New York City.

Frank Leslie's Illustrated Weekly. New York City.

The *Christian Union.* New York City.

Pomeroy's Democrat. New York City.

The *Times.* Chicago, Illinois.

A Biography of Henry Ward Beecher, by William C. Beecher, Rev. Samuel Scoville, assisted by Mrs. Henry Ward Beecher. New York, Charles L. Webster & Company, 1888.

Henry Ward Beecher, An American Portrait, by Paxton Hibben. New York, Doran, 1927.

History of the Beecher-Tilton Case. American News Co., 1874.

Theodore Tilton *vs.* Henry Ward Beecher, Verbatim Report, action for Criminal Conduct, tried in City Court, Brooklyn, Chief-Justice Neilson presiding. 1875.

The Romance of Plymouth Church, by J. E. P. Doyle. Hartford, 1874.

Official Report of the Trial of Henry Ward Beecher by Austin Abbott. New York, George W. Smith & Company, 1875.

The Great Brooklyn Romance, All the Documents in the Famous Beecher-Tilton Case, Unabridged. New York, 1874.

The Great Scandal, History of the Famous Beecher-Tilton Case. New York, 1874.

The Beecher-Tilton Controversy. Chicago, 1874.

The Beecher-Tilton Scandal. A Complete History of the Case, with Mrs. Woodhull's Original Statement. Brooklyn, 1874.

The Beecher-Tilton War. New York, 1874.

The Beecher-Tilton Investigation. The Scandal of the Age. Philadelphia, 1874.

Brooklyn Argus.

Sunday Press.

Tempest Tossed, by Theodore Tilton. New York, Sheldon & Company, 1874.

Henry C. Bowen's Scrapbook compiled in the office of the *Independent.* At the New York Public Library.

Anthony Comstock's Scrapbook at the office of the Society for the Suppression of Vice.

Anthony Comstock, by Heywood Broun and Margaret Leech. New York, Albert and Charles Boni, 1927.

The *Thunderbolt.* Troy, New York.

The *Crucible,* edited by Moses Hull. Boston.

My Life in Many States and Foreign Lands, by George Francis Train. New York, 1902.

Beecher, Tilton, Woodhull, the Creations of Society, by Joseph Treat. New York, 1874.

The Drama of Deceit, a Satire in Verse. Published by the Independent Tract Society, Worcester, Mass., 1875.

San Francisco *Alta.* California.

The Hartford *Times.* Hartford, Conn.

The *Daily Courant.* Hartford, Conn.

The *Vineland Historical Magazine.* Vineland, N. J.

Unpublished letters from Colonel James H. Blood.

Individual Liberty, by Benjamin R. Tucker, selected by C. L. S. New York, Vanguard Press, 1926.

Unpublished letters from Benjamin R. Tucker.

Liberty. Boston, Mass.

The Cuckoo. London, England.

The *London Court Journal.* London, England.

The Siege of London, by Henry James.

Queen Victoria, by Lytton Strachey. New York, Harcourt, Brace & Co., 1921.

British History in the Nineteenth Century, by G. M. Trevelyan. New York, Longman's, 1922.

My Apprenticeship, by Beatrice Webb. New York, Longmans, 1926.

Biographical Studies, by Walter Bagehot. New York, Dutton.

The London *Times.* London, England.

The Life of Lord Russell of Killowen, by R. Barry O'Brien. New York, Longmans, 1901.

The Seven Lamps of Advocacy, by Judge Edward A. Parry. London, T. Fisher Unwin, 1923.

The *Humanitarian.* New York and London.

Record of Public Work Done in America, by Victoria C. Woodhull.

Synopsis of the Lives of Victoria C. Woodhull and Tennessee Claflin, by G. S. Darewin. London, 1891.

The Life and History of T. C. Claflin, now Lady Cook. London, England, 1892.

Two Noble Women, Nobly Planned, by Legge.

Lady Cook's Essays. London, England, The Roxburghe Press.

The Woodhull Genealogy, the Claflin Genealogy, and Twelve Genealogies of the Hamilton Family. The Underwood Genealogy.

Campaign Document, No. 2, of the Equal Rights Party, consisting of the Address of the Central National Committee to the People of the United States, The Plan of Organization for the Victoria Leagues, and the Permanent Organization of the Party. New York, Woodhull, Claflin & Co., 1872.

Lady Cook (Tennessee C. Claflin) on the Evils of Society and Their Remedies. Published by The University Publishing Company, 110 and 111 Strand, London, W. C., 1895.

"Some Reminiscences of a Happy Three Years' Residence at Bredon's Norton," by Rev. G. W. Webb.

"Two American Shrines: Sulgrave Manor and Bredon's Norton."

"A Great Reformer: Victoria Claflin Woodhull-Martin. History in Biography: A Study by Henry E. Branch."

"A History and a Prophecy. Victoria C. Woodhull (1876)." From the Reference Department, *Daily Chronicle,* Salisbury Square, London, E. C. 4.

"A Page of American History, 1870-1876."

The Story of Bredon's Norton, with Notes on Bredon Hill, by Rosa M. Barrett and F. C. Champion.

Mrs. Victoria C. Woodhull and Her Social Freedom, by Austin Kent.

Some Miscellaneous Articles Reprinted from "Woodhull & Claflin's Weekly," Etc. London, 1892.

Memo: beneath The "Washington Pedigree," as on the Chart. Reprinted from the 13th edition of *Men and Women of the Time.* 1891.

Beginning of the Battle, by Tennessee Claflin, now Lady Cook.

The Women's Land Fête in Our Village, by Sarah A. Tooley, Cheltenham, Norman, Sawyer & Co., Ltd., Printers, St. George's Hall.

"Manor House Club Causeries. Mrs. Victoria Woodhull-Martin."

The *Future of the United States,* by John Biddulph Martin, F.S.S. Read before the American Association for the Advancement of Science, Philadelphia, September 5, 1884. London, Blades, East & Blades, Printers, 23, Abschurch Lane, E. C.

Our Village in War Time, by Sarah A. Tooley.

NOTE

It would be impossible, in this limited space, to enumerate all the people who have helped to make this book possible. I am deeply grateful to the newspaper librarians and editors; to the public librarians; to the state historians; to the writers who have studied Victoria Woodhull's period; to her contemporaries and the children of her contemporaries; to the district attorneys and others, who gave me access to court records; to so many who have given me the most liberal assistance.

E. S.

NEW YORK
Publishers of BOOKS and of
HARPER'S MAGAZINE

Established 1817